Comparative Empirical Analysis of Cultural Values and Perceptions of Political Economy Issues

Comparative Empirical Analysis of Cultural Values and Perceptions of Political Economy Issues

Dan Voich, Jr.

With the assistance of the members of the International Consortium for Management Studies

Foreword by George Macesich

Westport, Connecticut
London

Library of Congress Cataloging-in-Publication Data

Voich, Dan.
    Comparative empirical analysis of cultural values and perceptions
of political economy issues / Dan Voich, Jr., with the assistance of the
members of the International Consortium for Management Studies; foreword
by George Macesich.
      p.   cm.
    Includes bibliographical references and index.
    ISBN 0–275–95169–3 (alk. paper)
    1. Economics—Cross-cultural studies. 2. Social values—Cross-
cultural studies. I. International Consortium for Management
Studies. II. Title.
HB199.V58   1995
330—dc20   95–2212

British Library Cataloguing in Publication Data is available.

Library of Congress Catalog Card Number: 95–2212
ISBN: 0–275–95169–3

First published in 1995

Praeger Publishers, 88 Post Road West, Westport, CT 06881
An imprint of Greenwood Publishing Group, Inc.

Printed in the United States of America

The paper used in this book complies with the
Permanent Paper Standard issued by the National
Information Standards Organization (Z39.48–1984).

10 9 8 7 6 5 4 3 2 1

Contents

Figures and Tables

Foreword

This is an important companion book to the initial volume developed by the International Consortium for Management Studies, *Cross-Cultural Analysis of Values and Political Economy Issues* (Voich and Stepina, eds., Praeger, 1994). The essays developed in the first book by members of the Consortium provide important theoretical ideas for analyzing values and issues from the perspective of a diverse set of cultures and a multidisciplinary mix of disciplines of Consortium members. While these essays describe and analyze important literature and research results that exist in different countries, this volume provides a comparative empirical picture of differences in people's values and perceptions of issues that are based on different socioeconomic and political systems. Together, the two books provide useful and important insights into the economic, political, and cultural processes in a number of diverse countries throughout the world.

This empirical analysis contrasts people's cultural, workplace, and family values, and their perceptions of political economy issues at the organizational, national, and international levels. Particularly useful is the manner in which Consortium conducted this study. It is truly multinational and multicultural, and it draws on diverse disciplines to examine the important issues before the world. This type of empirical analysis is especially noteworthy in that it involves a large amount of empirical data pertaining to diverse socioeconomic and political systems. Moreover, the nature and structure of the data facilitate extensive comparative analyses of values and issue perceptions to identify significant differences between cultures.

The extensive amount of empirical data analyzed by the author is important in view of recent and emerging developments in diverse cultures throughout the world. The comprehensive breadth of data analyzed in search of significant differences in values and issue perceptions provides important insights about different socioeconomic and political systems. Moreover, this comparative analysis explores the relationships between values and issue perceptions. The overall analysis of empirical data provides a much needed foundation and structure for comparing different socioeconomic and political systems in the future.

This empirical study, when combined with the first study of cultural values, provides a sound resource base for those concerned with the future of global society. These studies are timely and relevant to the socioeconomic and political processes underway in various societies. They do, indeed, provide an excellent, informative, and thoughtful source.

George Macesich

Preface

The differences in people's values and their perceptions of political economy issues that may occur because of their differences in socioeconomic and political systems provide the general focus of this book. These differences are analyzed using empirical data compiled from eight countries reflecting different socioeconomic and political systems. Three of these countries are considered more market-oriented, namely, Germany, Japan, and the United States. These three countries are also very industrialized with highly developed economic systems. Three other countries are considered to have a more collectivist orientation, and they include the former Soviet Union (with an emphasis on Russia), the People's Republic of China, and Yugoslavia (with an emphasis on Serbia). The first two of these countries are very large and somewhat developed, while the latter was a smaller, developing economic system at the time of the survey. The remaining two countries are Venezuela and Chile, two Latin American nations with evolving socioeconomic and political systems.

This book is the second volume involving cross-cultural collaborative research by members of the International Consortium for Management Studies. The first volume, *Cross-Cultural Analysis of Values and Political Economy Issues* (Voich and Stepina, eds., Praeger, 1994), presents a group of essays written by various members of the Consortium. These essays reflect the current literature and research that exist in each country, and they provide insights on the nature and importance of values and how these values generally impact people's perceptions of management and society. The members of the International Consortium for Management Studies not only bring a variety of perceptions based on their different socioeconomic and political systems to this collaborative research, they also reflect an array of multidisciplinary perspectives. These disciplines include economics, human resource management, law, management strategy, multinational business, political science, risk management, marketing, psychology, and sociology.

While the first book provided some of the theoretical foundations for analyzing values and issues, this volume provides empirical insights using data compiled through an extensive survey research project conducted by the Consortium members in each of the countries named. This empirical analysis looks at three types of values: cultural, workplace, and family, as reflected in the previous research initially developed by Hofstede (1980) and Buchholz (1976), as well as research found in current sociological literature. The focus of this part of the analysis is on the significant differences that exist in people's values according to their respective socioeconomic and political systems.

In addition to analyzing differences in people's values, this book analyzes the differences in people's perceptions of political economy issues at the organizational, national, and international levels from the perspective of each of their own socioeconomic and political systems. Moreover, the empirical data dealing with values and perceptions of issues provide an opportunity to analyze how values are related to perceptions of political economy issues according to the country of the respondents, in other words, according to each respective socioeconomic and political system.

This book contains four groups of chapters. The first group discusses the general nature, importance, and selected classifications of values within an organizational and societal framework. Moreover, a survey of selected values, beliefs, and attitudes and their historical development follows (Chapter 1). The first group of chapters concludes with a discussion of the procedures and the general approach used to develop, implement, and complete the empirical research conducted by members of the International Consortium for Management Studies. This includes the design of the project variables and the survey instrument, the organization of the project team, the data collection and processing methodology used, the demographic profiles of the eight countries and of the respondents from these countries, and other related methodology and data issues (Chapter 2).

The second group of chapters analyzes the values of people as reflected by responses to the survey instrument. The focus of this analysis is on the significant differences in people's values according to the country of respondents (e.g., their respective socioeconomic and political system). The initial analysis deals with those values that tend to reflect a tendency toward individualism as a general value, within the framework of workplace, cultural, and family values (Chapter 3). Next, an analysis is presented for those values that reflect a general tendency toward collectivism as a general value using a framework similar to that used for individualism, such as workplace, cultural, and family values (Chapter 4). Finally, the congruency of people's values is analyzed as they relate to individualism versus collectivism. This is followed by an analysis of differences in the value priorities of people as reflected in a rank of 10 values pertaining to individualism and collectivism according to the country of the respondents (Chapter 5).

The third group of chapters analyzes people's perceptions of political economy issues at three levels, organizational, national, and international. The general focus of this analyses is similar to that relating to values (i.e., a search for significant differences in people's perceptions of issues according to each respective socioeconomic and political system). This analysis begins with organizational level issues that deal with important factors such as participation, communication, standard of living, paternalism, motivation, and productivity (Chapter 6). Next, national issues relating to factors dealing with the favorableness of the national economic climate, the adequacy of the national standard of living, and the sociopolitical climate are analyzed (Chapter 7). This is followed by a similar analysis of international issues relating to the favorableness of the international economic climate, the need to develop resources, the effectiveness of world governance, and the overall emphasis on nationalism (Chapter 8). Similar to the rank of values, an analysis of the rank of 15 political economy issues perceived by respondents is presented within the context of economic, sociopolitical stability, and world governance factors (Chapter 9). Finally, this group of chapters concludes with an analysis of differences in views concerning a number of propositions relating to capitalism, socialism, the need to change political ideologies, and the requisites for effective government (Chapter 10).

The final group of chapters begins with a search for relationships between people's values and their perceptions of political economy issues. This analysis focuses on how the two broad values, individualism versus collectivism, are related to people's perceptions of organizational, national, and international issues, and their views about several basic socioeconomic and political tenets (Chapter 11). Finally, an overall summary and conclusion of the major significant differences in people's values and their perceived issues are presented, with some observations about future research guidelines and directions (Chapter 12).

In conclusion, this book represents a major cross-cultural comparative analysis of the differences in people's values and their perceptions of political economy issues at three levels, organizational, national, and international. As an empirical study it involves a large sample of data compiled through a 250-item survey instrument over about a two-year period. The eight socioeconomic and political systems surveyed are varied, ranging from highly developed market-oriented countries to collectivist countries at different stages of economic development. Moreover, two of the countries tend to be more evolving in nature in terms of their economic and sociopolitical systems. Superimposing the wide mix of disciplines of the members of the International Consortium for Management studies makes this empirical research project truly cross-cultural and multidisciplinary.

I wish to acknowledge all members of the International Consortium for Management Studies for their vision, dedication, and cooperation relating to this project. Special recognition is given to Ljiljana Baćević and Mijat Damjanović (Yugoslavia), Fengzeng Yan (People's Republic of China), and Lee Stepina, Joel Nicholson, and Urban Ozanne (United States of America) for their contributions relating to the initial development of the research topic and survey instrument. Moreover, as the study progressed, the following individuals provided valuable liaison and coordination relating to the data collection effort for the following participating countries: Nina V. Andreenkova (the former Soviet Union); Mijat Damjanović (Yugoslavia); Rosalind Greaves de Pulido (Venezuela); Robert King (Japan); Heike Simmet (Germany); Luis Werner Wildner (Chile); Fengzeng Yan (People's Republic of China); and Lee Stepina and Joel Nicholson (United States).

Special acknowledgments and thanks are given to the following persons, who, in addition to their active involvement, were instrumental in obtaining funds for the project and for the three annual meetings of the Consortium members: Mijat Damjanović, Professor, Center for Law Investigation, University of Belgrade (Yugoslavia): Ljiljana Baćević, Director, Center for Political Studies and Public Opinion Research, Institute of Social Sciences, University of Belgrade (Yugoslavia); Hans Günther Meissner, Chair of Marketing, University of Dortmund (Germany); and E. Ray Solomon, Professor of Insurance and former Dean, College of Business, Florida State University (United States). These funds were critical for completing the study, and for providing opportunities for face-to-face discussions among members of the Consortium.

Finally, I wish to acknowledge and thank Professor E. Joe Nosari for providing insightful comments and help relating to some of the analytical processes used in this research and concerning the overall structure of analysis. Thanks also to Kelly Shrode for her outstanding assistance in developing the manuscript for publication.

In closing, it is important to note that the analyses, observations, and generalizations presented in this book are solely those of the author, based on his personal frame of reference and preference for data analyses and presentation of results. While more sophisticated analytical procedures could be used, the preference was to present the analysis of the empirical data in a more complete format using descriptive statistics to highlight differences in values and perceptions among the respondents from the eight participating countries. Moreover, as is the case in all large empirical studies, there are numerous specific research questions that can be analyzed, but because of manuscript limitations, these need to be relegated to future publications.

1

Overview of Cultural Values

INTRODUCTION

This book is the second volume on the impact of culture-based values on political economy issues. The first volume, *Cross Cultural Analysis of Values and Political Economy Issues* (Voich and Stepina, eds., Praeger, 1994), provided some introductory material and a general overview of the research issues for this chapter. While the first book primarily dealt with reviews of relevant literature and historical surveys of values and political economy issues, this book focuses on the analysis of empirical data. These empirical data were compiled in eight countries throughout the world through a lengthy survey questionnaire administered by faculty peers in each respective country. These faculty collaborated as members of the International Consortium for Management Studies that was organized in 1989. The eight countries represented in this empirical research are Chile, the Federal Republic of Germany, the former Soviet Union, Japan, the People's Republic of China, the United States, Venezuela, and Yugoslavia.

Defining culture has proved to be a difficult exercise. Volumes have been produced by anthropologists attempting to pin down the concept of culture. One area of general agreement is that individuals in the same culture tend to share common values. Values are deeply held assumptions about how things should be and about how these ends should be achieved. Values, in turn, lead to a set of specific ideas or personalities in the form of attitudes. Finally, attitudes are the precursors to behavior.

While there is general theoretical agreement concerning the relationships among the variables described, there has been little empirical research on how values, beliefs, and attitudes vary cross-culturally. Beyond G. Hofstede's (1980) groundbreaking research on values, and other polls on attitudes, few researchers have gone beyond simple two-country comparisons. Further, there has been very little research on how specific values and beliefs lead to important variations in attitudes toward national and international issues.

This chapter provides an introduction to the nature and importance of values, a review of selected classifications of values, and a look at values within organizational and societal frameworks. Within this framework, values also are discussed in the context of cross-cultural similarities and differences.[1]

GENERAL NATURE AND IMPORTANCE OF VALUES

A simple but useful way to view the nature and importance of values is as follows: values shape attitudes, which in turn influence behavior. In these basic relationships, values reflect the fundamental beliefs and need criteria of people acting individually and within groups, organizations, and societal settings. In this way values reflect a general purpose or philosophy of life, and the absence of values usually results in nondirectional behavior. Thus, values provide the unifying force, in terms of a mission or objective, that shapes attitudes and influences behavior.

Attitudes can be viewed as perceptions about conditions that exist within the environment. These conditions often relate to organizational, national, and international socieoeconomic and political issues, and they are often assessed in terms of how they might affect people's needs as dictated by their values. In other words, environmental conditions are perceived or interpreted on the basis of value-driven attitudes of people. Thus, the analysis of values provides a basis for understanding people's attitudes in terms of how they perceive opportunities and threats in their environment.

The ultimate result of this values-attitudes-behavior cycle is reflected in the behavior of people in terms of their actions to resolve problems or conflicts or to take advantage of opportunities and to make needed changes. This behavior in response to environmental conditions or stimuli is shaped by the value-driven attitudes which people form over time. As such, people's behavior reflects a value-based purpose or objective.

The values-attitudes-behavior cycle reflects a process of motivation as shown in Figure 1.1. Even though we usually view the motivation process as it relates to the individual's behavior, the relationships shown

Figure 1.1
Values-Attitudes-Behavior

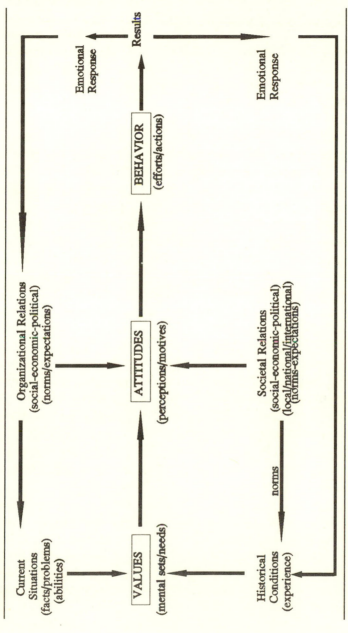

Source: Voich and Stepina (eds.), *Cross-Cultural Analysis of Values and Political Economy Issues* (Westport, CT.: Praeger, 1994), p. 4.

in Figure 1.1 apply in a general way to groups, organizations, and larger societal units. The motivation process includes three major levels of relationships: individual, organizational, and societal. For example, a person's values are directly shaped by current and historical situations, each of which is influenced by socioeconomic and political organizations and societal relations. These values in turn shape the person's attitudes and how various work, family, and societal issues are perceived. Subsequently, values and attitudes combine to produce behavior resulting in specific efforts and actions, ideally producing desirable results.

After this cycle of values-attitudes-behavior is completed, the individual will experience an emotional response or feeling about what has transpired. This response or feeling is shaped by the economic and work related compensation received, as well as the attitudes of others in the organization or community regarding the results achieved. Especially critical to this emotional response is the amount of mental congruency that has been achieved between values and results. In other words, the values-attitudes-behavior cycle embodied in the process of motivation is highly subjective and emotional, even though the efforts and actions may involve highly measurable work activities.

As we know, emotions are often the primary considerations for sustaining high levels of morale and productivity. Moreover, we know that the values that drive attitudes and behavior that create emotional responses are shaped by many things. These include individual personality, group and organizational norms and expectations, and socioeconomic and political issues at the local, national, and international levels. Throughout these relationships family, work, and cultural values are often very critical.

SELECTED CLASSIFICATIONS OF VALUES

There are a wide range of value classifications that have been developed over time in psychology and sociology reflecting individual, group, organizational, and societal values. The following discussion focuses on a selected group of value classifications that reflect a mix of individual, work, societal, and cultural value classifications as shown in Table 1.1.

Table 1.1
Selected Value Classifications

Maslow	Buchholz
Self-Actualization	Work Ethic
Esteem	Organizational Beliefs
Love	Humanistic Beliefs
Safety	Marxist Beliefs
Physiological	Leisure Ethic

Allport	Hofstede
Aesthetic	Individualism vs. Collectivism
Theoretical	Masculinity vs. Femininity
Religious	Power Distance
Political	Uncertainty Avoidance
Social	Paternalism
Economic	Timeliness

Perhaps one of the most widely recognized values classifications is Maslow's needs hierarchy. This hierarchy of basic needs reflects value criteria that influence workers' attitudes toward incentives designed to influence work behavior. These needs range from lower-level physiological and safety needs to higher-level esteem and self-actualization needs. The underlying notion embodied in Maslow's needs hierarchy is to develop work conditions and incentives to motivate people according to the needs that have not been satisfied.

Somewhat related to Maslow's needs hierarchy is the work belief values classification of R. A. Buchholz. This values classification includes two extreme sets of work values: a work ethic versus a leisure ethic. The other values inherent in Buchholz's classifications include several collectivist oriented systems: the organizational, humanistic, and Marxist. Again the underlying notions are to understand workers' work value criteria better and to design better motivational systems to influence behavior.

A third value classification is provided by G. Allport and relates to general societal needs or value criteria. To be viable, each society as a whole must satisfy a number of basic economic, social, political, religious, aesthetic, and theoretical needs of humanity. These combined needs form a set of societal values that reflects the general culture of society. In a healthy and viable society, some minimum mix of each of these needs usually is found.

The cultural value dimensions advanced by Hofstede comprise a fourth values classification that is useful for analyzing culture and society. These value dimensions focus on the emphasis on individualism versus collectivism, masculinity versus femininity, uncertainty avoidance, and power distance that exist in individuals within cultural and societal groups. The initial four-part classification has been expanded in later research to include two other value dimensions, a society's emphasis on paternalism and on timeliness. Using Hofstede's values classification helps to provide an understanding of the stronger inherent values in a culture or society. This understanding provides useful input not only to develop socioeconomic and political initiatives, but also to gain acceptance for the need for changes.

In a very general way the preceding four values classifications reflect several major themes. First, there appears to be a continuum of values that cluster around a tendency toward individualism, on one end, and a tendency toward collectivism on the other. The values inherent in individualism are those associated with a work ethic, economic productivity, personal individualism, power distance, masculinity, and self-actualization. These values reflect the Protestant, market, and liberty ethics derived from the cultural rebirth and provided the foundation for the industrial revolution. The work-related values inherent in the collectivism are those associated with organizational, humanistic, and Marxist belief systems. The cultural values inherent in the tendency toward collectivism include personal collectivism, femininity, and uncertainty avoidance, while societal values include social, political, religious, theoretical, and aesthetic value dimensions.

While the preceding values, which are inherent in the individualism-collectivism continuum, are not mutually exclusive, this classification provides a useful way for analyzing major cultural and societal trends. On one hand, the tendency toward individualism focuses on the individual as the primary unit of analysis, while the tendency toward collectivism emphasizes social relations as the most important focus for analysis. In other words, a basic tenet of individualism is that improving individual productivity for individual gain will result in the greatest benefits and satisfaction for the individual, organization, and society. On the other hand, collectivism contends that the satisfaction of the group will optimize both individual and organizational productivity and, therefore, provide the greatest overall benefits for society.

The central issue relating to values seems to be the priority placed on individual freedoms, private property rights, local and state rights, and the opportunities provided to take individual risks and develop initiatives. The individualism-collectivism continuum of values that are selected directly involves how individuals will be treated in organizational work situations and how they will be affected by socioeconomic and political initiatives at the local, national, and international levels. The next section discusses how values, attitudes, and behavior interact within an organizational and societal framework.

ORGANIZATIONAL AND SOCIETAL FRAMEWORKS

In assessing the values-attitudes-behavior relationship, a fundamental premise, if not an axiom, is that this assessment must include the interaction that takes place among individuals within groups, organizations, and larger societal relationships. The analysis of a single person's values does not provide a full understanding unless it is viewed in relation to the values of others. If a person does not come into contact with other individuals, his or her values are probably of no importance. This section uses this premise to present a framework to discuss the values-attitudes-behavior relationship. The focus of this discussion is that people are both influencers and evaluators of organizational actions.

Perhaps one of the most general models of any organization is the input-output system developed in systems theory. Figure 1.2 provides one example of this model, which reflects two major cycles. One cycle relates to the flow of resources, including technology and knowledge, into a series of transformation or production processes within an organizational setting. These processes consume resources obtained from other organizational transformation processes in order to create value in terms of products and services. The pattern of this flow of resources, in terms of quality, volume, timeliness, technology, and cost into and through organizational value-creating transformation processes, is directly shaped by the values and attitudes of potential users, suppliers, workers, managers, and environmental interest groups (social and political).

The decisions relating to qualitative, quantitative, timeliness, and cost aspects of this organizationally added value (outputs) reflect the assessment of the values (and needs), attitudes (and perceptions), and

Figure 1.2
Input-Output System

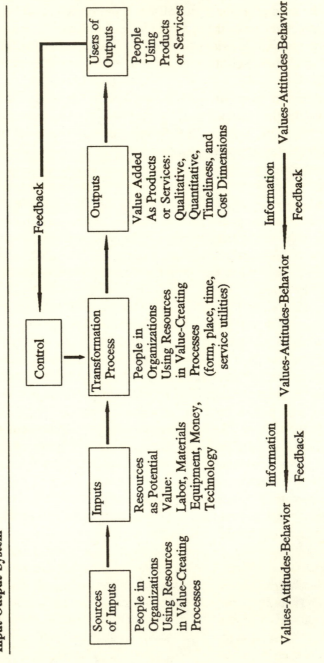

Source: Voich and Stepina (eds.), *Cross-Cultural Analysis of Values and Political Economy Issues* (Westport, CT.: Praeger, 1994), p. 8.

likely behavior (and actions) of potential users (customers). This assessment before the fact, plus feedback relating to these decisions, comprises the second major cycle of this input-output model. In other words, the effectiveness of the organization depends on (1) an assessment of potential users' values-attitudes-behavior relationships and (2) feedback from users as to the level of satisfaction they receive from the products and services.

The organization must also obtain and assess feedback about major current and emerging socioeconomic and political values, attitudes, and behavior. The social system directly influences the political processes and the economic system within a society. The goals and values of the social system influence the decisions made by economic organizations directly, through users of products and services, and indirectly, through political initiatives, laws, and regulations. This socioeconomic and political interaction of goals and values may be further influenced by other goals and values that emerge from the social system. These include some of Allport's religious, theoretical, and aesthetic societal values or needs, as well as environmental, international, and cultural/ethnic considerations.

Modern communications and media play a major role in assessing, conveying, and modifying values-attitudes-behavior in the work organization and in other societal groups. To be most effective, multimedia systems must exist so that greater diversity in communications occurs, and ideally media objectivity will increase. The internal communications and information systems of organizations generally focus on customer and public opinion issues which might affect economic growth and productivity. Sociopolitical communications focus on more macro issues that usually involve socioeconomic and political trade-offs or issues at the local, national, and international levels. These communications attempt to interpret developments for the public objectively, but in reality, they often influence public opinion.

As societies mature, values, attitudes, and behavior evolve, often driven by major economic and social events, international conflicts, technology developments, or cultural issues. In a general way, we can see the differences in values, attitudes, and behavior between nonindustrialized and industrialized societies. R. Inglehart's (1977) model of materialist-postmaterialistic value preferences provides a useful framework with which to assess changes in societal values, attitudes, and behavior that occur in response to economic productivity and growth. This model relates generally to Maslow's needs hierarchy as it pertains to an individual's economic status.

However, in the case of all models which are only general representations of reality, we can see that factors other than the solely economic can and do drive changes in societal values, attitudes, and behavior changes. One such major factor is the need for safety or security in terms of protection from other societal, cultural, or ethnic groups.

GLOBAL VALUES IN TRANSITION

In recent years we have seen major changes in various parts of the world concerning tendencies toward individualism versus collectism. Today, there are a number of major value-oriented trends which seem to be moving in different directions. For example, the movement away from centralized societies and economies in Central and Eastern Europe and the countries formerly making up the former Soviet Union reflects a general shift toward individualism. Yet within each of these new countries, as well as old ones, the patterns and speed of developments are different, depending on each society's previous position, its ethnic and cultural makeup, and the strength of its economic system.

During recent years the driving force or value criterion tends to be economic; this is a natural tendency during recessionary periods. It is difficult to change the attitudes of people to accept (and pay for) initiatives and programs which are sociopolitically oriented and are perceived by people to reduce their economic status. The economic value criterion seems to gain considerable strength as the economic productivity and employment within a country decreased, and has done so especially during recent years when these factors have been low worldwide. Thus, the tendency toward individualism seems to be driven in several ways by Allport's economic value criterion. On one hand, you might expect that Buchholz's work ethic, Hofstede's individualism, and Maslow's higher-level needs would be reinforced by the greater emphasis on the economic value criteria and the need for increasing economic productivity. However, what appears to be the case is that when unmet economic needs within a society occur in a recessionary period and reach a critically low level, there is greater support for values which support economic and social protectionist, and even welfare, programs. These values also encourage organizational and humanist values, and are often accompanied by more pronounced ethnic divisions.

In the process of changing societal and cultural values, the economic value criterion seems to be the major determinant of change, especially when economic conditions are poor. In periods of prosperity, a society usually can absorb and even support hybrid values, such as those inherent in both the individualism and collectivism value tendencies. The question that remains is which value tendency produces the best economic conditions for society? In other words, do the benefits derived from individual innovation, risk taking, private property, and political pluralism outweigh the possible inequality of income to people, thereby increasing the need for social welfare and health care programs? Put another way, do the benefits derived from social and human rights equity, and from more centralized socioeconomic policies and initiatives, outweigh the possible dilution of the work ethic and encouragement for risk taking and innovation? The answer to these questions can only be analyzed in terms of people's basic values relating to work, family, culture, and society within the context of international developments.

However, the careful assessment of people's values is difficult because people's basic underlying values are not easy to identify or to measure in terms of their relative strength. Their strength only seems to appear when a crisis occurs, and then they often become very personal, emotional, and often selfish. When major changes occur in socioeconomic and political systems, such as those in the former Soviet Union and in Eastern and Central Europe, people tend to cooperate more easily within common social or ethnic groups, rather than in more diverse sociopolitical systems. The extent of this cooperation is, in part, related to the seriousness of economic conditions (i.e., the more serious the conditions, the greater clustering of social and ethnic groups).

While it is difficult to discern the basic underlying values of people, it is essential for us to attempt to do so. This is necessary so that we can develop organizational and societal initiatives which address the needs embodied in these values and result in the implementation of meaningul programs over time.

From the preceding discussion of selected major changes occurring throughout the world, we can see that the general scarcity of resources and hostility in our environment are fundamental forces that influence people's values. These values shape the specific economic, social, and political needs of people, and these needs create various forms of organizations. Thus, people in organizations are used as major mechanisms for producing economic and noneconomic goods and services to satisfy peoples' needs. Figure 1.3 summarizes these relationships among environment, values, needs, organizations, and

Figure 1.3
Resource Scarcity and Environmental Hostility

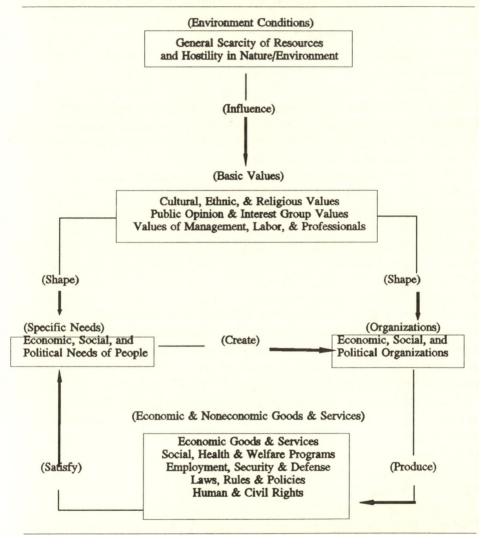

(Environment Conditions)

General Scarcity of Resources
and Hostility in Nature/Environment

(Influence)

(Basic Values)

Cultural, Ethnic, & Religious Values
Public Opinion & Interest Group Values
Values of Management, Labor, & Professionals

(Shape)   (Shape)

(Specific Needs)   (Organizations)
Economic, Social, and   (Create)   Economic, Social, and
Political Needs of People   Political Organizations

(Economic & Noneconomic Goods & Services)

Economic Goods & Services
Social, Health & Welfare Programs
(Satisfy)   Employment, Security & Defense   (Produce)
Laws, Rules & Policies
Human & Civil Rights

Source: Voich and Stepina (eds.), *Cross-Cultural Analysis of Values and
Political Economy Issues* (Westport, CT.: Praeger), p. 14.

goods and services. To analyze how values change we must look at two major segments in these relationships. These two segments in a general way are differentiated by time as well as their impact on basic values.

The first segment is the relationship between the environment and basic values. Changes in values which occur because of scarcity and hostility in the environment tend to be less frequent in the short run; however, when changes do occur, they often are of major importance. One important example is the recent shift from a socialist to a market-system economy throughout Central and Eastern Europe and the former Soviet Union. Another important example is the elimination of apartheid in South Africa. Moreover, the large shift from conservatism to liberalism during the last presidential election in the United States in 1992 reflects significant changes in people's basic values because of increasing scarcity and rising hostility in their environments.

Because these changes in basic values are driven by scarcity and hostility issues that have worldwide impacts as well as origins, these changes in basic values tend to spread throughout different regions or nations of the world. Consider as prime examples the large scale formal movement toward economic protectionism which is reflected in the recent formation of the European Community (EC), and the development of the North American Free Trade Agreement (NAFTA) of the United States, Mexico and Canada. Two sets of basic values are embodied in these developments: free trade between members and preference to the countries in the EC or the NAFTA relative to nonmembers. It must be noted that these types of values consensus were influenced by scarcity and hostility conditions perceived in each respective environment, in this instance, world competitive markets.

It is also interesting to note that in each of these two trading blocs there are some signs of internal dissatisfaction among some members concerning the possible loss of income and jobs in certain industries and the potential dilution of national socioeconomic and political independence. Thus, on one hand the formation of a trading bloc occurs to improve economic conditions and reduce hostility, yet individual countries (especially the more productive ones) lobby for exceptions. When you superimpose the nationalistic tendencies on these issues and agreements, the search for consensus becomes more difficult and emotional.

Building a new consensus of values takes a long time simply because a large number of people are involved. This consensus occurs when scarcity of resources and hostility in the environment are perceived to be so severe that people unite to correct these conditions. This is often accompanied by changes in basic values which usually result in new types of socioeconomic and political organizations or initiatives. Subsequently, there also may be different priorities for economic and noneconomic goods and services produced. It should be noted that in periods when scarcity and hostility conditions in the environment are improving, and becoming less severe, it is more difficult to change people's basic values, even though sporadic issues arise.

The second segment shown in Figure 1.3 depicts the relationships among needs, organizations, and goods and services. These relationships tend to be more involved in the ongoing production, delivery, and consumption of economic and noneconomic goods and services within a society or nation. These socioeconomic and political processes continue to function to satisfy the needs of people reflected in a general level of values consensus. This does not mean that no changes occur in the short run; however, these changes tend to take the form of selected sociopolitical initiatives which have less centralized impacts on segments of society.

The basic societal and cultural tenets, capitalism, socialism, private property rights, pluralism, and so forth, are not overturned by these periodic initiatives which occur. Thus, the fundamental values may be questioned, but a consensus for change usually is not achieved in the short run. Often it is not until new generations of people in society emerge that major changes occur. For example, as we proceed to the end of this century, there appears to be a great potential for change in the basic values of individual societies throughout the world. A major impetus for change seems to be coming from younger generations, somewhat similar to the antiestablishment movement in the 1960s, but perhaps with a more specific thrust. Certainly, the basic values inherent in Mexico's very young population will soon provide a major influence on socioeconomic and political initiatives in that country. In the United States, the new generation of political leaders who are relatively young in terms of established (and some feel outdated) politicians are making major inroads in influencing socioeconomic initiatives. Racial tensions (if not hatred) in the United States are accelerating, especially between young people. In Germany, there is a serious antiforeigner sentiment that also can be observed in many countries throughout the world.

The changes which are emerging embody hostility, protectionism, and competition for scarce resources and markets fueled by racial, ethnic, and national priorities. While these features are not necessarily new, the points of conflict when they occur seem more emotional because of the recent recessionary influences that have occurred, and because of greater levels of socioeconomic and political hostility in the environment. The following are several of the more important areas of disagreement or conflicts which are evident and which are likely to continue:

1. Individualism and capitalism versus collectivism and socialism
2. Free trade versus economic protectionism
3. Decentralized versus centralized social welfare and health programs
4. Materialistic versus postmaterialistic goals
5. Income and employment versus environmental protection
6. National versus world governance and multinational priorities
7. Tax incentives for the rich versus for the poor
8. Individual human and civil rights versus governmental bureaucracy
9. Local and states rights versus federal bureaucracy
10. Conflicting values according to age, sex, race, religion, ethnicism, economic status, and education

The preceding ten areas of disagreement or conflict will likely continue to be sensitive throughout the remainder of this century. With the advances in communications and the expansion of the media, regional, national, and world events and issues will be debated within the context of each society's environmental conditions and people's basic values. Challenges to existing values, needs, organizations, and products and services will be easier to develop and promote. Perhaps the cycle of change relating to basic values will also be shortened.

NOTE

1.   The discussion, figures, and tables in this chapter are taken from the introduction of the first volume in this series, *Cross-Cultural Analysis of Values and Political Economy Issues* (Voich and Stepina, eds., Praeger, 1994).

2

Research Purpose, Procedures, and Demographics

INTRODUCTION

This research project analyzes people's cultural, family, and workplace values and their perceptions of various political economy issues in eight countries with different socioeconomic and political systems. In addition, the demographics of respondents and of participating countries are analyzed as they relate to people's values and attitudes. This extensive multicultural information provides important insights about significant differences in people's values and their perceptions of major socioeconomic and political issues at the local, national, and international levels. The research data are analyzed from multidisciplinary perspectives in that the research group consists of scholars from a number of disciplines. Moreover, these scholars represent different socioeconomic and political systems.

The sample data primarily include values and perceptions of issues of university students representing multiple disciplines, although in selected countries, a smaller sample of data, relating to industry and government personnel, is included. A profile of respondents is analyzed for possible relationships between values and demographic attributes. Also, possible relationships between people's values and their perceptions of issues are explored.

The group of faculty scholars from each participating country analyzed all of the responses and developed preliminary observations about the data relating to their own country's respondents, as well as respondents from each of the other countries. These separate observations were discussed at several meetings of the total research group, and the general results of these discussions are reflected in this book.

This research is important for two major reasons. One, a large amount of empirical data is compiled and analyzed about people's values and their perceptions of issues in different socioeconomic and political systems. This analysis is both multidisciplinary and cross-cultural. Traditionally, past research has developed theories based on a single type of socioeconomic and political system and, therefore, has been incomplete. This research looks for systematic differences that can be explained in terms of culture, stage of economic development, and political ideology.

A second important benefit of this research is the establishment of the International Consortium for Management Studies. This Consortium has opened communications and enhanced cooperation for future scholarly research, study, and exchange. This type of communication and cooperation is necessary for enhancing the quality of, and providing more relevant directions for, future research.

This chapter discusses the research purpose and the procedures used in this study, including a summary of the data involved, and it is divided into three parts. The first part discusses the conceptual framework relating to the overall purpose of the research, and its relationship to previous research in this area. Also, several general research questions are outlined as they relate to cultural values and political economy issues. Part two discusses the general research procedures used to accomplish the research project. These procedures relate to (1) overall coordination and management of the research project, (2) development of the survey instrument and the categorization of questions into sets of values and issues, (3) data collection and processing, and (4) data analysis. Finally, part three presents a demographic profile of the eight countries included in this research project and a demographic profile of the individual respondents in each of these countries.

PURPOSE OF RESEARCH

This research empirically analyzes various cultural, family, and workplace values in selected countries with different socioeconomic and political systems. Additionally, people's perceptions of major organizational, national, and international political economy issues are analyzed. Finally, the relationships between selected values and perceptions of issues, and between selected values and personal and national attributes are analyzed. Figure 2.1 summarizes the conceptual focus of this research project in terms of the survey variables.

In more specific terms, this research project provides empirical in-

Figure 2.1
Political Economy Issues, Values, and Attributes

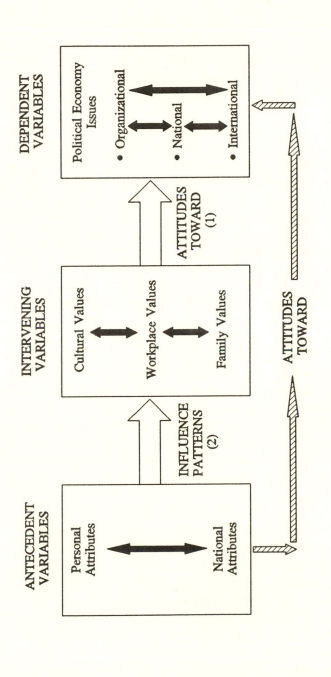

sights about the following three general research questions:

1. Are there systematic differences in people's cultural, family, and workplace values based on their respective socioeconomic and political systems? These values are further analyzed in terms of their tendency toward individualism or collectivism.
2. Are there systematic differences in people's perceptions of, or attitudes toward, political economy issues based on their respective socioeconomic and political systems?
3. Are there systematic differences between people's perceptions of political economy issues based on their values and on their respective socioeconomic and political systems?

The overall research purpose relates to previous research of Hofstede (1980), Buchholz (1976), and Gomez-Mejia and McCann (1986a). The research on values utilizes Hofstede's cultural values framework, which he used to research national cultures spanning 50 different countries. From this research, Hofstede defined four major cultural value dimensions which are incorporated in this research project. The four dimensions are personal individualism versus collectivism, power distance, uncertainty avoidance, and masculinity versus femininity. A fifth value dimension developed by Dorfman and Howell (1988), paternalism, has also been included in this research project.

This project incorporates Buchholz's dimensions relating to beliefs individuals hold about the nature of work. Buchholz developed five major work belief dimensions which are used in this research project. These dimensions are work ethic, organizational belief systems, Marxist belief systems, humanistic belief systems, and leisure ethic.

A major study of perceptions of socioeconomic and political issues was accomplished by Gomez-Mejia and McCann. Their research surveyed about 100 issues in 100 organizations in 20 Caribbean Basin countries. The issues research framework used in their study of the Caribbean Basin provides the basis for the research framework in this project, and similar types of issues they identified have been included.

In summary, the purpose of this research extends Hofstede's, Buchholz's, and Gomez-Mejia's and McCann's research. Their ideas and research thrusts have been integrated into a comprehensive research project to provide empirical insights about the three general research questions presented earlier. Additional value dimensions and political economy issues have been added in this project to expand the breadth of research further. Thus, this research project has a much broader purpose than the three individual research thrusts described. It represents the first major attempt to analyze empirically cultural, family, and workplace values and perceptions of political economy issues cross-culturally and on a worldwide scale, using multidisciplinary faculty as the research team.

RESEARCH PROCEDURES

This section discusses the research organization and procedures, including the design of the survey instrument and the methodology used in acquiring and analyzing the empirical data.

Research Project Team

In 1986 and 1987, several Florida State University faculty members collaborated with faculty from Yugoslavia and the People's Republic of China to develop the initial research project. The conceptual framework of the research was developed along the lines of Figure 2.1. Using this framework, this group of researchers developed an extensive preliminary survey instrument. After numerous discussions and revisions, faculty were added to the research team from the following countries: Chile, Federal Republic of Germany, the former Soviet Union, Japan, and Venezuela. The preliminary questionnaire was again extensively reviewed by the faculty from each of the countries participating in the project. Translations of the questionnaire were also extensively reviewed and modified as needed for each applicable country.

In the early part of 1989, these faculty participants formally organized the International Consortium for Management Studies. This Consortium includes faculty in a number of disciplines such as multinational business, management policy and organizations, international affairs, political science, economics, law, industrial relations/human resource management, marketing, sociology, social sciences, and business. This multidisciplinary group of scholars represent countries throughout the world with different socioeconomic and political characteristics. In 1989, this Consortium began two major interrelated concurrent projects. One project dealt with the empirical research of people's values and their perceptions of political economy issues which is the topic of this book. As the extensive and time consuming data collection process proceeded, the Consortium members began a concurrent project that involved the development of a book of essays and values on political economy issues based on theoretical and conceptual ideas from research in each country. This book provides an important research foundation for the empirical research presented in this book.

As these two research projects progressed, Professor Voich began to serve as the Director of the Consortium and the overall project director for research projects. A primary person served as the Project Coordinator for each participating country: Nina V. Andreenkova (former Soviet Union), Mijat Damjanović (Yugoslavia), Rosalind Greaves de Pulido (Venezuela), Robert King (Japan), Heike Simmet (Germany), Luis Werner Wildner (Chile), and Fengzeng Yan (People's Republic of China). The completion of the book of essays on the empirical research project were coordinated by this group of faculty through Professor Voich, who served as the central communications link among Consortium members. In addition to ongoing telephone and mail communications, the Consortium convened a series of annual conferences dealing with the two parts of the research project: 1990 in Yugoslavia, 1991 in the United States, and 1992 in Germany. These annual conferences were attended by the members of the Consortium, and they were extremely useful for moving the projects forward and for resolving issues or questions that arose. They also helped to standardize in a general way the overall structure of research and provided an excellent forum for discussing research findings.

Florida State University assumed the responsibility for distributing the final survey instrument to each country's faculty representative. Generally, these faculty peers arranged for duplicating the survey instrument, administering it to respondents, and mailing the completed answer sheets to Florida State University. Upon their receipt at Florida State University, the entry of questionnaire responses into a single standardized computer data base was completed. Faculty from Yugoslavia and the former Soviet Union furnished computer disks containing the response data, and these data were integrated into the single data base at Florida State University.

Upon completion of the survey and the computer data input process, Florida State University furnished faculty peers in each of the eight countries a computer disk containing all of the data for all of the countries. Also, two computer printouts containing frequency distributions of responses to questions on the survey instrument, one for the total sample for all countries and one for each of the eight countries, were furnished to members of the Consortium in each country. These faculty then began to develop their individual analyses of the data from the perspective of their own country. These analyses and the essays on values and issues were discussed at the annual meetings, and these inputs have been incorporated into this book.

Survey Instrument

To accomplish the general research purpose and to provide insights on the three research questions, the survey instrument provided data about two major groups of variables. One group of variables focuses on cultural, family, and workplace values patterned after Hofstede's and Buchholz's research, and the other group with perceptions of political economy issues patterned after Gomez-Mejia's and McCann's research. Some additional statements were added about family and organizational values, as well as perceptions of issues, based on input from Consortium members.

Initially, data relating to these two groups of variables are analyzed separately to provide insights about the similarities and differences in values, and the similarities and differences in perceptions of issues based on different socioeconomic and political systems (refer to general research questions 1 and 2). Second, the impact of groups of values (as independent variables) on perceptions of issues (as dependent variables) are analyzed to provide insights about the relationships between values and perceptions of issues (refer to general research question 3).

The survey instrument contains 225 statements pertaining to people's values or their perceptions of political economy issues, or socioeconomic and political tenets, using a five-point Likert scale ranging from 1 (strongly disagree) to 5 (strongly agree). These statements are in the form of value propositions, issue propositions, or propositions about socioeocomic and political tenets. In addition, the survey instrument asked respondents to rank 10 given values in order of importance from 1 (highest) to 10 (lowest), and 15 issues from 1 (highest) to 15 (lowest). With these 25 rank order values and issues, a total of 250 items were included in the survey, plus a number of questions relating to the demographics of each respondent.

Table 2.1 summarizes the variables on the survey instrument according to (1) values grouped into two categories, a tendency toward individualism or a tendency toward collectivism, and (2) perceptions relating to organizational, national, and international issues plus socio-

Table 2.1
Categories of Survey Variables

VALUES	PERCEPTIONS
(94 Value Propositions)	(156 Issue/Tenet Propositions)

VALUES
(94 Value Propositions)

**1: Tendency Toward
    Individualism**
Work Ethic
Leisure Ethic
Individualism
Uncertainty Avoidance
Power Distance
Individualism In Family
Family Economic Orientation
Masculinity
Individualism Rank
Family and Leisure Rank

**2: Tendency Toward
    Collectivism**
Organizational Belief Systems
Marxist Belief Systems
Humanistic Belief Systems
Paternalism
Family Social Cohesion/Status
Family Social Satisfaction

PERCEPTIONS
(156 Issue/Tenet Propositions)

1: Organizational Issues
Participation
Communications
Motivation
Job Security/Standard of Living
Productivity

2: National Issues
Economic Climate
Standard of Living
Government Effectiveness
Economic/Resource Development
Sociopolitical
Nationalism

3: International Issues
Nationalism
World Governance/Cooperation
Resource Development
Economic Development

**4: Socioeconomic and
    Political Tenets**
Capitalism
Socialism
Need for Political Change
Government Effectiveness

economic and political tenets. The 16 values shown in Table 2.1 relating to individualism and collectivism reflect 94 value propositions and ranks included on the survey instrument. Similarly, the perceptions shown in Table 2.1 include 15 organizational, national, and international issues that reflect 144 issue propositions and ranks, plus one group of socioeconomic and political tenets that reflects 12 propositions about these tenets.

Data Collection and Processing

The faculty in each respective country personally administered and coordinated the completion of the survey instrument, rather than mailing them to individual respondents. Therefore, faculty (or their representatives) were personally available to explain the general research purpose and the content of the questions on the survey instrument. In this way, they were available to clarify problems concerning the wording or intent of questions as they occurred.

As answer sheets to the survey instrument were completed, they were mailed to Florida State University for processing into a standardized computer data base. The structure and format of the computer data base were designed at Florida State University. Faculty representatives from the former Soviet Union and Yugoslavia submitted their data on computer disks that were standardized into a single data base at Florida State University.

Data Analysis Procedures

The analysis of the differences in people's values (general research question 1) and differences in people's perceptions of political economy issues or tenets (general research question 2) involves the following general procedure. The response frequencies to the value propositions for each of the 16 values shown on Table 2.1 are analyzed to determine whether significant differences in values occur according to the country of the respondents. This analysis is presented in Chapters 3 through 5. Similarly, the response frequencies to the propositions for each of the 19 perceptions of issues and tenets shown on Table 2.1 are analyzed to determine whether significant differences in perceptions occur according to the country of the respondents. This analysis is presented in Chapters 6 through 10.

The differences in values and perceptions of issues/tenets were analyzed using chi square and analysis of variance (ANOVA) procedures to determine significant differences in values and in perceptions of issues according to the country of the respondents. Subsequently, the ANOVA Scheffe test procedure provided general insights as to whether a significantly greater difference occurred for each possible pair of countries. Moreover, the procedures described were used to analyze differences in the rank order of values, the rank order of issues perceptions, and the perceptions regarding socioeconomic and political tenets. Given the results of the analyses, the demographic profiles of each country helped to provide insights, and perhaps some rationale, for the significant differences found using the chi square and ANOVA procedures.

For the analysis of the relationships between values and perceptions of issues (general research question 3), regression analysis is used to search for differences in the general relationships between the responses to various sets of values and responses to various sets of issues perceptions according to respondents from each country. These relationships are analyzed to ascertain in a general way the different perceptions people may have about organizational, national, and international political economy issues, as well as socioeconomic and political tenets, based on their cultural, family, and workplace values. The data regarding country and individual demographics are also used to discern any patterns which may provide insights to the relationships found. This analysis is presented in Chapter 11.

DEMOGRAPHIC PROFILES

This section provides a summary of the characteristics of each country and of each respondent to the survey.

Profile of Countries

Survey responses were collected from respondents in eight countries. There are three countries traditionally referred to as market-oriented-Germany, Japan, and the United States; three countries traditionally referred to as collectivist-the former Soviet Union, the People's Republic of China, and Yugoslavia; and two countries from Latin or South America. Tables 2.2 and 2.3 present, to the extent available, demographic profiles of each country. This profile includes data for 1987

Table 2.2
Selected National Demographics

	Germany 1987	Germany 1990	United States 1987	United States 1990	Japan 1987	Japan 1990	Venezuela 1987	Venezuela 1990
Population (millions)	62	80[a]	244	250	122	124	18	20
% Urban Population	86	84[a]	74	75	77	77	83	84
Per Capita GNP ($)	14,440	22,320	18,530	21,790	15,760	25,430	3,230	2,560
% GDP Government Consumption	20	18	21	18	10	9	10	9
% GDP Private Consumption	55	54	66	67	57	57	65	62
% GDP Domestic Savings	25	28	13	15	34	34	25	29
Gross Manufacturing Output Per Employee: 1980 = 100	105	115	113	115	120[b]	137	111[b]	107

	People's Republic of China 1987	People's Republic of China 1990	Former Soviet Union 1987	Former Soviet Union 1990	Yugoslavia 1987	Yugoslavia 1990	Chile 1987	Chile 1990
Population (millions)	1069	1134	276	289	23	24	12	13
% Urban Population	38	56	65	66	48	56	85	86
Per Capita GNP ($)	290	370	1,128	931	2,480	3,060	1,310	1,940
% GDP Government Consumption	13	8	76	79	14	7	11	10
% GDP Private Consumption	49	49			46	72	68	67
% GDP Domestic Savings	38	43	24	21	40	21	21	23
Gross Manufacturing Output Per Employee: 1980 = 100	244[b]	251[c]	123	144	98	75[c]	n/a	n/a

GNP = Gross National Product   GDP = Gross Domestic Product   a = Unified Germany   b = 1988   c = 1989

Table 2.3
Selected Annual Percentage Rates of Change

	Germany		United States		Japan		Venezuela	
	1965 - 80	1980 - 90	1965 - 80	1980 - 90	1965 - 80	1980 - 90	1965 - 80	1980 - 90
Population Growth	0.2	0.1	1.0	0.9	1.2	0.6	3.5	2.7
Urban Population Growth	0.6	0.5	1.2	1.1	2.1	0.7	4.8	2.8
Inflation Rate	5.2	2.7	6.5	3.7	7.7	1.5	10.4	19.3
Growth of Exports	7.2	4.2	6.4	3.3	11.4	4.2	(9.5)	1.8
Growth of Imports	5.3	3.9	5.5	7.6	4.9	5.6	8.1	(4.6)
Total GDP Growth	3.3	2.1	2.7	3.4	6.4	4.1	3.7	1.0
Per Capita GNP Growth: 1965 - 90	2.4		1.7		4.1		1.0	

	People's Republic of China		Former Soviet Union		Yugoslavia		Chile	
	1965 - 80	1980 - 90	1965 - 80	1980 - 90	1965 - 80	1980 - 90	1965 - 80	1980 - 90
Population Growth	2.2	1.4	8.0	8.6	0.9	0.7	1.7	1.7
Urban Population Growth	2.3	n/a	7.8	7.1	3.5	2.8	2.6	2.3
Inflation Rate	(0.3)	5.8	n/a	n/a	15.2	122.9	129.9	20.5
Growth of Exports	4.8	11.0	6.6	6.7	5.6	0.1	8.0	4.8
Growth of Imports	7.4	9.8	10.0	10.0	6.6	0.6	1.4	0.6
Total GDP Growth	6.8	9.5	5.9	3.1	6.1	0.8	6.3	3.0
Per Capita GNP Growth: 1965 - 90	5.8		3.4		2.9		0.4	

GNP = Gross National Product

GDP = Gross Domestic Product

(a period immediately prior to the survey) and 1990 (a period near the completion of the survey). Also, the growth or longitudinal data are provided for two periods: 1965 - 1980, and 1980 - 1990. The data in Tables 2.2 and 2.3 summarize the demographic data; and they indicate large differences in the demographics of the sample of countries selected for this research project, especially among the three groups of countries. The data in Tables 2.2 and 2.3 were obtained from various government publications and from faculty peers from participating countries.

Profile of Respondents

The research team collected 7,271 responses to the survey questionnaire during 1989 through the first part of 1991. The response frequencies per country are as follows:

Germany	907
United States	1,773
Japan	304
Yugoslavia	764
People's Republic of China	990
Soviet Union (Russia)	1,251
Venezuela	964
Chile	<u>318</u>
	7,271

Table 2.4 presents demographic profiles of the individual respondents. Overall, the profile of respondents has these characteristics:

- Young
- Well educated, in multiple disciplines
- Not married
- About equal number of males and females
- Diverse work experience

CONCLUDING REMARKS

In determining the sample of respondents, several important constraints were considered. Besides the perennial problems relating to obtaining language translation equivalences, the long distances and com-

Table 2.4
Demographic Profile of Respondents

RESPONSE FREQUENCIES (%)

	GER.	U.S.	JAPAN	YUG.	P.R.C.	F.S.U.	VEN.	CHILE	TOTAL
Age Level:									
20 years or less	7.0	8.4	50.5	54.3	24.3	21.3	12.7	17.9	20.1
21 - 30 years	85.7	55.9	34.6	45.0	42.0	46.3	56.9	39.4	53.5
31 - 40 years	5.1	19.5	6.6	0.3	14.1	16.4	19.6	21.8	14.0
Over 40 years	2.2	16.3	8.3	0.4	19.6	16.0	10.8	20.8	12.4
Married	11.2	36.4	14.8	1.5	39.9	43.9	31.8	45.8	30.3
Children									
None	93.7	68.0	87.5	98.5	62.2	60.3	66.6	50.7	72.1
1 or 2	5.4	24.8	5.1	0.5	26.6	35.8	24.2	26.3	21.2
3 or 4	0.7	5.9	4.7	0.3	10.1	3.2	7.6	18.1	5.5
More than 4	0.2	1.2	2.7	0.7	1.1	0.7	1.6	4.9	1.2

RESPONSE FREQUENCIES (%)

	GER.	U.S.	JAPAN	YUG.	P.R.C.	F.S.U.	VEN.	CHILE	TOTAL
Sex									
Male	64.4	49.0	44.3	36.5	68.5	47.0	49.6	56.7	52.1
Female	35.6	51.0	55.7	63.5	31.5	53.0	50.4	43.3	47.9
Educational Level									
Some/No Secondary	5.3	24.1	–	0.7	17.8	1.5	4.0	7.7	10.9
Completed Secondary	83.4	27.4	66.1	96.1	31.6	43.8	28.7	14.3	46.2
Bachelor's Degree Completed	10.0	34.6	32.3	2.2	46.5	49.4	46.5	62.0	34.0
Graduate Degree Completed	1.4	13.9	1.7	1.1	4.0	5.3	20.8	15.9	8.9
TOTAL (N)	907	1773	304	764	990	1251	964	318	7271

munications time delays between research associates precluded frequent adjustments to the research methodology. In a cross-cultural study, achieving standard classifications of some of the respondent personal attributes and the nature of work organizations is difficult.

Because of these types of factors, the specification of the sample was standardized at the macro rather than the micro level. For example, for this research, the sample was defined simply as the "participating country," rather than subsamples of workers, students, managers, government employees, nongovernment employees, and so forth. This was necessary to get the research started and because of the large number and different types of socioeconomic and political systems involved.

Because the questionnaire was very long, it was inappropriate for mail distribution and response. The research team ideally sought 1,000 survey responses from each country, but realistically expected about 500 responses. Except for two countries (Japan and Chile), the minimum response level was attained, with about 7,200 total responses received for the eight countries.

The results of this first research effort are essentially exploratory, in that they provide preliminary insights on systematic differences in values and in perceptions of issues based on different socioeconomic and political systems. Also, preliminary insights are developed on relationships between people's perceptions of political economy issues and their cultural, family, and workplace values for different socioeconomic and political systems. The analysis procedures and conclusions from this first research effort should be useful for sharpening the research questions and the research procedures, including the sampling of respondents.

3

Profile of Individualism
Values

A person's orientation toward individualism versus collectivism reflects the values that person has developed over time in response to cultural, workplace, and family circumstances. These circumstances, in turn, are conditioned by organizational, national, and international political economy issues that come to bear on a person's existence in the home, at work, and in society. This research analyzes three groups of values: workplace, cultural, and family. The workplace values are those of R. Buchholz (1976), while the cultural values are those of G. Hofstede (1980). The family values included in this research reflect basic concepts developed by members of our research consortium as traditionally found in the sociological literature.

Our research further divides work of these three value groups into two broad sets-those values that reflect a tendency toward individualism versus those values that reflect a tendency toward collectivism. Chapter 4 analyzes the latter while this chapter deals with the individualism values. The specific values that affect individualism consist of the following: relative emphasis on work versus leisure; cultural values relating to personal individualism and masculinity versus uncertainty avoidance and power distance; and values dealing with individualism within the family and the economic orientation of the family.

WORKPLACE VALUES

Buchholz's research provides a methodology that focuses on the comparison of work beliefs across cultures and organizations. Two of these work beliefs, the work ethic and the leisure ethic, are analyzed in the discussion that follows, while the three work beliefs relating to collectivism (organizational, humanistic, and Marxist belief systems) are discussed in Chapter 4.

Work Ethic Value

The work ethic value reflects the extent that individuals believe that work is good in itself and that it will bestow dignity on a person who has a high level of work ethic. Moreover, it implies that everyone should work hard rather than depend on others in order to be a useful member of society. Working hard can overcome all of life's obstacles, thus success is directly linked to a person's individual efforts in performing work. By working hard a person accumulates wealth, and wealth becomes a general measure of the level of work ethic.

The work ethic value consists of the seven value propositions summarized later. The seven value propositions were developed from similar dimensions of the work ethic used by Buchholz (1976). The mean responses of respondents from each country surveyed, and the average mean (A.M.) of the eight means, are also shown for each value proposition. As discussed previously, the mean response is based on a scale of "1 = lowest emphasis" to "5 = highest emphasis." Moreover, it should be noted that the average mean is the average of the eight means, and not the average mean of the total respondents. The median in relation to the average mean can be easily identified since the mean responses are shown in descending order (highest to lowest).

1. Hard work overcomes all of life's obstacles.

VEN.	F.S.U.	YUG.	CHILE	U.S.	A.M.	JAPAN	P.R.C.	GER.
3.49	3.27	3.22	3.11	2.96	**2.93**	2.74	2.42	2.23

2. Work hard until satisfied with results.

P.R.C.	JAPAN	GER.	F.S.U.	A.M.	YUG.	U.S.	CHILE	VEN.
3.77	3.17	2.81	2.69	**2.68**	2.40	2.36	2.14	2.13

3. Avoid dependence on others.

YUG.	F.S.U.	VEN.	P.R.C.	A.M.	CHILE	GER.	JAPAN	U.S.
4.12	3.93	3.84	3.82	**3.61**	3.57	3.52	3.05	3.03

4. Working alone leads to better learning.

P.R.C.	F.S.U.	GER.	A.M.	JAPAN	YUG.	VEN.	CHILE	U.S.
3.87	3.73	3.42	**3.01**	2.98	2.83	2.54	2.40	2.34

5. Only independent people get ahead in life.

F.S.U.	P.R.C.	YUG.	A.M.	GER.	JAPAN	U.S.	VEN.	CHILE
3.54	3.32	3.31	3.00	2.97	2.88	2.69	2.69	2.63

6. Live independent of others.

F.S.U.	P.R.C.	YUG.	A.M.	GER.	VEN.	CHILE	JAPAN	U.S.
3.83	3.70	3.37	3.25	3.07	2.91	2.84	2.82	2.81

7. Work alone to be superior.

P.R.C.	F.S.U.	YUG.	JAPAN	A.M.	CHILE	VEN.	GER.	U.S.
3.18	3.12	2.90	2.64	2.63	2.47	2.32	2.32	2.11

The combined group of seven value propositions reflects the overall emphasis placed on the work ethic value by respondents from each country, and for the combined countries as measured by the average mean. Using the average mean as a general indicator, the respondents from the following countries have mean responses that exceed the average mean for each of the seven propositions: former Soviet Union (7 of 7); People's Republic of China (6 of 7); Yugoslavia (5 of 7); Germany, Japan, and Venezuela (2 of 7 each); the United States and Chile (1 of 7 each). On the basis of these response frequencies, respondents from the former Soviet Union, the People's Republic of China, and Yugoslavia appear to place a greater emphasis on the work ethic value than do the respondents from the other five countries. Moreover, the frequency of mean responses higher than the average mean by respondents from the three collectivist countries is 18 of 21 (86 percent), compared to only 5 of 21 (24 percent) and 3 of 14 (21 percent) for respondents from the three market-oriented and two Latin American countries, respectively.

The first two value propositions pertain to the importance of working hard to overcome life's obstacles, and the need to work hard until satisfied with results. It is interesting to note that the respondents from three countries, Japan, the People's Republic of China, and Germany, place a greater emphasis on working hard until satisfied with the results (proposition 2), but a lower emphasis on the need to work hard as a basis to overcome all of life's obstacles (proposition 1). Moreover, of the respondents from the five countries that place a greater emphasis on the need to work hard to overcome all of life's obstacles (Venezuela, the former Soviet Union, Yugoslavia, Chile, and the United States), all except those from the former Soviet Union place a lower emphasis on working hard until satisfied with results. Thus, respondents from the former Soviet Union are the only ones surveyed that have a consistent emphasis on the importance of working hard as related to the first value propositions.

Value propositions 3 through 7 pertain to a preference for independence as it relates to working with others. This is a dimension of the overall work ethic in that an independent person is assumed to be more goal and performance directed, rather than concerned with group and social work norms. Except for proposition 7 (2.63), the average means for the five value propositions relative to preference for independence are higher, ranging from 3.00 (proposition 5) to 3.61 (proposition 3), than the average means for the first two propositions pertaining to the need to work hard (2.93 and 2.68, respectively). It is interesting to note that the respondents from the People's Republic of China and the former Soviet Union are the only ones surveyed that have a higher preference for independence for all of these five value propositions relative to the average mean for each. Except as dependency relates to better learning (proposition 4), the respondents from the other collectivist country (Yugoslavia) also show a higher preference for independence relative to the average means for this set of propositions. On the other hand, the respondents from the United States and Chile show a lower preference for independence as reflected in each of these five value propositions.

Except for a mean response only slightly higher than the average mean for proposition 1, the respondents from the United States place a lower emphasis on the overall work ethic as measured by the mean responses to all seven value proposition relative to the average means of each. In fact, these respondents have the lowest mean response for four of the seven value propositions.

Table 3.1 shows the overall emphasis on the work ethic values of respondents from each of the eight countries involved in our research survey. This overall emphasis is the combined total responses to the seven value propositions summarized. The chi square analysis indicates that there are some significant differences (.00 level) in the overall emphasis on the work ethic according to the country of the respondents (.65 coefficient of contingency). On the basis of the overall mean response, the respondents from the three collectivist countries, Yugoslavia, the People's Republic of China, and the former Soviet Union, place a greater emphasis on the work ethic (3.17, 3.44, and 3.45, respectively) than the respondents from the three market-oriented countries, Germany (2.91), Japan (2.90), and the United States (2.62), and the two Latin American countries, Venezuela (2.83) and Chile (2.74).

Table 3.1
Overall Emphasis on Work Ethic

A	Response Frequency (%)					N	X̄	Scheffe Test (B)							
	1	2	3	4	5			GER.	U.S.	JAPAN	YUG.	P.R.C.	F.S.U.	VEN.	CHILE
GER.	10.4	31.7	22.5	27.6	7.8	896	2.91		X					X	X
U.S.	15.3	40.4	18.6	19.1	6.7	1773	2.62								X
JAPAN	6.9	30.7	35.1	19.8	7.4	301	2.90		X						X
YUG.	7.5	23.6	27.0	28.4	13.5	719	3.17	X		X				X	X
P.R.C.	4.1	20.8	14.9	47.0	13.2	990	3.44	X		X	X			X	X
F.S.U.	4.1	16.5	25.5	38.4	15.5	1241	3.45	X		X	X			X	X
VEN.	14.0	35.8	15.6	22.8	11.9	953	2.83		X						
CHILE	13.7	35.5	21.4	22.0	7.5	311	2.74		X						
TOTAL	9.9	29.6	21.0	28.9	10.7	7184	3.01								

Total mean = average of eight means
Chi Square (Pearson) = 5133.35.64 (.00 level)
Coefficient of Contingency = .65
1 = Strongly Disagree; 5 = Strongly Agree

* = Significantly greater emphasis for each pair of countries
(.05 level)-A versus B

ANOVA F Ratio = 589.74 (.00 level)

The ANOVA Scheffe test results shown on Table 3.1 provide information on the specific comparisons of overall mean responses of respondents for each pair of countries in the research survey. The mean response of respondents of each country on the vertical axis (A) is compared to the mean response of respondents of each country on the horizontal axis (B). The asterisks indicate when the mean responses of the countries shown on the vertical axis (A) are significantly greater for each pair of countries (.05 level).

For example, the respondents from Germany (A) place a greater emphasis on the work ethic value than those from the United States, Venezuela, and Chile (B). As another example, the respondents from the People's Republic of China and the former Soviet Union place a greater emphasis on the work ethic value than those in all of the other six countries. It is interesting to note that on the basis of the comparison of overall mean responses, the respondents from the United States place the lowest emphasis on the work ethic value of all the respondents in the countries included in the research survey.

The results relating to the work ethic value seem somewhat counterintuitive. The lesser emphasis placed on the work ethic value by respondents from the three market-oriented countries, compared to that of respondents from the collectivist countries, seems unusual in terms of attributes such as risk taking, entrepreneurship, property rights, and freedom of choice commonly attributed to more capitalistic and market economies. One explanation may be that because the standard of living in the collectivist countries is much lower than in the market-oriented countries, the need for work in the collectivist countries is greater, thus the need for a greater work ethic value. Conversely, the less emphasis on the work ethic value by respondents in the market-oriented countries may be due to the greater amount of discretionary income in these countries, thus there is less emphasis on the work ethic value and more emphasis on noneconomic issues and needs, as well as on leisure activities.

Leisure Ethic Value

Buchholz's leisure ethic measures the relative importance that people place on leisure compared to work as a major value. In this context, leisure activities provide human fulfillment regarding the use of time. This includes pursuing activities of personal interest, and becoming involved in creative activities. Thus, the more time spent on leisure and the less on working, the better the individual and society. The leisure ethic value consists of the eight value proportions summarized later. The mean responses of respondents from each country surveyed, and the average mean (A.M.) of the eight means, are also shown for each value proposition. The eight value propositions were developed from similar dimensions of the leisure ethic used by Buchholz (1976).

1. Increased leisure time is good for society.

GER.	F.S.U.	JAPAN	U.S.	A.M.	YUG.	P.R.C.	VEN.	CHILE
3.93	3.84	3.83	3.81	**3.55**	3.46	3.17	3.17	3.17

2. Less work and more leisure time are better.

JAPAN	F.S.U.	GER.	A.M.	P.R.C.	YUG.	U.S.	CHILE	VEN.
3.64	3.12	2.90	**2.83**	2.75	2.74	2.54	2.49	2.45

3. Success means ample leisure time.

YUG.	U.S.	F.S.U.	P.R.C.	A.M.	JAPAN	GER.	CHILE	VEN.
3.47	3.26	2.95	2.78	**2.72**	2.50	2.46	2.21	2.16

4. Encourage shorter work week.

P.R.C.	F.S.U.	GER.	A.M.	JAPAN	YUG.	VEN.	CHILE	U.S.
3.85	3.71	3.63	**3.23**	3.17	3.10	3.08	2.76	2.56

5. Leisure activities are more interesting than work.

JAPAN	YUG.	P.R.C.	GER.	U.S.	A.M.	F.S.U.	CHILE	VEN.
3.81	3.43	3.42	3.27	3.16	**3.15**	3.12	2.60	2.40

6. Work is too time consuming.

JAPAN	F.S.U.	P.R.C.	GER.	YUG.	A.M.	U.S.	CHILE	VEN.
3.58	3.52	3.35	3.14	3.12	**3.10**	2.95	2.65	2.52

7. More leisure time is good for people.

F.S.U.	YUG.	JAPAN	U.S.	GER.	A.M.	P.R.C.	CHILE	VEN.
3.87	3.69	3.74	3.43	3.38	**3.33**	3.13	2.80	2.59

8. Providing more leisure time is good.

JAPAN	U.S.	YUG.	GER.	A.M.	F.S.U.	P.R.C.	CHILE	VEN.
3.88	3.60	3.50	3.49	**3.29**	3.12	3.08	2.85	2.80

The combined group of eight value propositions reflects the overall emphasis placed on the leisure ethic value by respondents from each country, and for the combined countries as measured by the average mean. As in the discussion of the work ethic value, the average mean is used as a general indicator of the overall emphasis on the leisure ethic value. Respondents from the following countries have mean responses that exceed the average mean for each of the eight value propositions: Japan (7 of 8); Germany and the former Soviet Union (6 of 8 each); the United States and Yugoslavia (5 of 8 each); and the People's Republic of China (4 of 8). This corresponds to 18 of 24 (75 percent) for the total respondents from the three market-oriented countries, compared to 15 of 24 (63 percent) and none for the three collectivist and two Latin American countries, respectively.

While the respondents from the market-oriented countries place a lower emphasis on the work ethic value and a higher emphasis on the leisure ethic value, the responses from the collectivist countries place a relatively higher emphasis on both work and leisure. On the other hand, the responses from the two Latin American countries reflect a lower emphasis on both work and leisure.

Table 3.2 shows the overall emphasis on the leisure ethic of respondents from each of the eight countries involved in our research survey. This overall emphasis is the combined responses to the eight value proportions pertaining to leisure as summarized previously. The chi square analysis indicates that there are significant differences (.00 level) in the overall emphasis on the leisure ethic according to the country of the respondents (.61 coefficient of contingency). The overall mean responses of respondents from all of the countries, except Venezuela and Chile exceed the average of the eight means (3.14).

The ANOVA Scheffe test results shown on Table 3.2 reflect a different pattern of differences than those shown on Table 3.1 for the work ethic value. The data show that respondents from Japan, followed by those from the former Soviet Union and Yugoslavia, place a greater emphasis on the leisure ethic value, while, on the basis of a comparison of overall mean responses, the emphasis placed on the leisure value by the respondents from Venezuela and Chile is substantially lower than that of the other six countries.

The greater emphasis on leisure by the respondents from Japan may reflect the long work week that traditionally many workers have had in that country. Moreover, the standard of living is very high in Japan, and this permits considerably more leisure activities. The greater emphasis placed on both the work ethic and leisure values by respondents from Yugoslavia and the former Soviet Union, which seems contrary to expectations, needs further analysis.

Table 3.2
Overall Emphasis on Leisure Ethic

	A								B							
	Response Frequency (%)								Scheffe Test							
A	1	2	3	4	5	N	$\overline{X}$	GER.	U.S.	JAPAN	YUG.	P.R.C.	F.S.U.	VEN.	CHILE
GER.	4.6	21.9	31.9	30.1	11.4	895	3.22							X	X
U.S.	5.5	22.6	27.3	32.6	12.0	1773	3.23					X		X	X
JAPAN	3.6	11.9	25.0	38.9	20.6	301	3.61	X	X		X	X	X	X	X
YUG.	4.5	18.7	31.6	31.7	13.5	719	3.31	X	X			X		X	X
P.R.C.	4.1	28.0	22.4	38.3	7.2	990	3.16							X	X
F.S.U.	3.5	19.2	27.1	36.5	13.6	1243	3.37	X	X			X		X	X
VEN.	16.8	38.1	22.2	15.8	7.1	953	2.58								
CHILE	10.5	38.7	28.0	19.4	3.3	310	2.66								
TOTAL	6.4	24.6	26.9	31.1	11.0	7184	3.14								

* = Significantly greater emphasis for each pair of countries (.05 level)-A versus B

ANOVA F Ratio = 504.50 (.00 level)

Total mean = average of eight means
Chi Square (Pearson) = 4485.64 (.00 level)
Coefficient of Contingency = .61
1 = Strongly Disagree; 5 = Strongly Agree

CULTURAL VALUES

Hofstede conducted empirical research on the importance of national cultures for management theory and practice. His research especially focused on the consequences of culture on work-related values (1980) and the interactions between national and organizational values (1985). Hofstede views national culture in terms of social information processing, or collective mental programming. Such programming reflects the way people view reality and their place in it, within a national setting. Language, tradition, espoused values, behavioral norms, and laws all bear on shaping the view of reality. Since it is embedded in a society's institutions and in the minds of people, national culture is slow to change. Moreover, traditions and ways of thinking about the world are mutually reinforcing within a society's legal, educational, religious, and other institutions. Adherence to cultural tenets is rewarded and deviance is discouraged.

Hofstede's work provides an important general argument against the ethnocentrist convergence hypothesis that reflects any impact of culture on management. His work was an important catalyst calling for greater cultural awareness in cross-cultural management research. While Hofstede acknowledged the existence and importance of regional or subcultural groups within and across national boundaries, his research focused on a national level of analysis of cultures. He studied work-related values in a major multinational firm spanning 50 different countries. Through extensive factor analyses, he developed a number of factors which explained the variances among cultures in different countries. These factors, which we can view as cultural values, are personal individualism (versus collectivism), masculinity (versus femininity), uncertainty avoidance, and power distance.

Individualism

Personal individualism reflects loose ties between individuals in a society, as well as in an organization. Members of society are expected to take care of their own affairs, and collective responsibilities extend only occasionally to immediate family members. In this type of society, considerably greater personal freedoms exist and are supported by the national cultural norms. On the other hand, a collectivist society relies on strong ties between individuals. Group membership is expected and intergroup social exchanges are common. The norms and values of the group provide the linking mechanism to guide individual behavior, action, and thought. Hofstede views more loosely integrated countries as individualist, in contrast to collectivist ones that are more tightly integrated wholes. He also contends that there is a strong positive correlation between country wealth, as expressed by gross national product, and individualism.

Personal individualism consists of the four value propositions summarized in the following. The mean responses of respondents for each country, and the average mean (A.M.) of the eight means, are also shown for each proposition. These individualist value propositions were developed from similar dimensions of individualism used by Hofstede (1980).

1. Encourage individual initiative rather than loyalty and sense of duty.

U.S.	YUG.	GER.	JAPAN	**A.M.**	F.S.U.	VEN.	CHILE	P.R.C.
3.44	3.41	3.38	3.22	**3.15**	3.10	3.10	2.98	2.60

2. Autonomy on the job is more important than group assistance.

U.S.	CHILE	JAPAN	F.S.U.	VEN.	**A.M.**	YUG.	GER.	P.R.C.
3.46	3.26	3.20	3.17	3.11	**3.11**	3.09	2.97	2.64

3. Individual rewards are as important as group welfare.

U.S.	YUG.	GER.	CHILE	**A.M.**	F.S.U.	JAPAN	VEN.	P.R.C.
3.46	3.35	3.32	3.20	**3.21**	3.12	3.10	3.06	2.96

4. Individual success is as important as group success.

U.S.	CHILE	VEN.	JAPAN	YUG.	**A.M.**	GER.	F.S.U.	P.R.C.
3.17	3.17	3.13	3.07	3.06	**3.02**	3.01	2.93	2.60

The combined group of these four value propositions reflects the overall emphasis placed on personal individualism by respondents from each country, and for the combined countries as measured by the average of the eight means (A.M.). Using the average mean as a general indicator of the emphasis on individualism, respondents from the following countries have mean responses that exceed (or equal) the average mean response of respondents from the eight countries surveyed for the four value propositions: United States (4 of 4); Japan, Yugoslavia, and Chile (3 of 4 each); Germany and Venezuela (2 of 4 each); and the former Soviet Union (1 of 4). This corresponds to 9 of 12 (75 percent) for the respondents from the three market-oriented countries, compared to 5 of 8 (63 percent) and 4 of 12 (33 percent) for the respondents from the three collectivist and two Latin American countries, respectively. The respondents from the United States tend to place the highest, and those from the People's Republic the lowest, emphasis on personal individualism as reflected by the mean responses for each of the four value propositions.

The responses from the market-oriented countries are consistent with intuitive expectations. For example, the socioeconomic and political freedoms in these three countries would suggest that personal individualism is an important cultural value. However, the higher emphasis on personal individualism in these countries seems to be somewhat contradictory to the responses pertaining to the work ethic value discussed earlier for these countries. One would expect that the greater emphasis on personal individualism should coincide with a similar emphasis on the work ethic, especially since five of the seven value propositions pertaining to the work ethic dealt with the importance of, and preference for, independence. However, this is not the case.

The responses by respondents from the People's Republic of China and the former Soviet Union also seem to be contradictory when compared to their work ethic responses, but in a different way (e.g., a lower emphasis on personal individualism with a higher emphasis on the work ethic). The lower emphasis on personal individualism seems to be consistent with what you would expect of respondents from collectivist countries, but the higher preference for independence as part of the work ethic seems to be inconsistent. The Yugoslav respondents' higher emphasis on personal individualism is consistent with their higher emphasis on the work ethic.

Turning to the Latin American countries, the respondents from Venezuela have lower than average emphasis on both personal individualism and the work ethic which is consistent. However, they have a lower emphasis on the leisure ethic as well, a finding which needs further analysis. Chile's respondents have a higher emphasis on personal individualism but a lower emphasis on the work ethic, similar to the market-oriented countries.

Table 3.3 shows the overall emphasis on personal individualism of respondents from each of the eight countries. This overall emphasis is the combined total responses to the four value propositions pertaining to personal individualism as summarized. The chi square analysis indicates that there are some significant differences (.00 level) in the overall emphasis on personal individualism according to the country of the respondents (.47 coefficient of contingency). Except for respondents

Table 3.3
Overall Emphasis on Personal Individualism

A	Response Frequency (%)					N	$\bar{X}$	Scheffe Test (B)							
	1	2	3	4	5			GER.	U.S.	JAPAN	YUG.	P.R.C.	F.S.U.	VEN.	CHILE
GER.	2.9	21.8	37.3	31.1	6.8	890	3.17					X	X		
U.S.	3.8	16.2	30.1	37.9	12.0	1770	3.28	X		X	X	X	X	X	X
JAPAN	4.4	22.0	35.6	30.3	7.7	281	3.15					X			
YUG.	4.7	22.2	31.8	28.4	12.9	703	3.22					X	X	X	X
P.R.C.	5.5	48.6	19.8	22.8	3.4	989	2.70								
F.S.U.	4.7	26.1	32.8	29.6	6.8	1226	3.08					X			
VEN.	8.3	24.5	26.8	30.0	10.4	948	3.10					X			
CHILE	2.5	27.1	29.0	35.5	5.9	304	3.15					X			
TOTAL	4.7	25.4	29.9	31.2	8.7	7111	3.11								

Total mean = average of eight means
Chi Square (Pearson) = 1985.44 (.00 level)
Coefficient of Contingency = .47
1 = Strongly Disagree; 5 = Strongly Agree

* = Significantly greater emphasis for each pair of countries (.05 level)-A versus B

ANOVA F Ratio = 163.50 (.00 level)

from the People's Republic of China (2.70), the former Soviet Union (3.08), and Venezuela (3.10), all overall mean responses were greater than the average of the eight means (3.11).

The ANOVA Scheffe test results shown on Table 3.3 reflect a greater emphasis on personal individualism by the respondents from the United States and the opposite emphasis of the respondents from the People's Republic of China. The respondents from the remaining countries reflect minimal emphases placed on personal individualism compared to the United States. The overall emphasis placed on personal individualism by the respondents from the combined eight countries, as measured by the average mean, is comparable to the overall emphasis on the leisure ethic.

Masculinity

The masculinity versus femininity scale used by Hofstede measures the division of sex roles in a society. Most of these sex roles are social and they are often derived arbitrarily. According to Hofstede, typical tasks for men and women vary considerably across cultures. He defines masculine societies as those in which masculine sex roles deeply permeate the entire society, its institutions and organizations, and this eventually affects the mental programming of both sexes. Common values attributed to masculine behavior are achievement, materialism, and individualism. On the other hand, values attributed to feminine behavior are the reverse-preference for quality of life over materialism, involvement in groups, and a concern for organizational issues rather than personal achievement.

Masculinity consists of the five values propositions summarized next. The mean responses of respondents for each country, and the average mean (A.M.) of the eight means, are also shown for each proposition. These five value propositions were developed from similar masculinity dimensions used by Hofstede (1980).

1. It is more important for men to have professional careers than women.

F.S.U.	P.R.C.	A.M.	GER.	JAPAN	CHILE	YUG.	VEN.	U.S.
3.59	3.29	2.52	2.37	2.33	2.27	2.18	2.12	2.01

2. Women do not value recognition and promotion for their work as much as men.

F.S.U.	P.R.C.	JAPAN	**A.M.**	CHILE	YUG.	GER.	VEN.	U.S.
3.58	3.01	2.53	**2.35**	2.20	2.06	1.89	1.81	1.74

3. Solving organizational problems requires the active forceful approach typical of men.

F.S.U.	P.R.C.	JAPAN	CHILE	**A.M.**	YUG.	U.S.	VEN.	GER.
3.43	2.70	2.68	2.54	**2.43**	2.29	1.95	1.95	1.91

4. It is preferable to have men in high level positions rather than women.

F.S.U.	P.R.C.	JAPAN	**A.M.**	CHILE	YUG.	U.S.	VEN.	GER.
3.69	3.39	2.56	**2.51**	2.36	2.20	2.00	1.96	1.90

5. A man can always do some jobs better than a woman.

F.S.U.	P.R.C.	JAPAN	**A.M.**	YUG.	VEN.	CHILE	U.S.	GER.
4.04	3.50	3.24	**3.22**	3.13	3.11	3.04	2.90	2.82

The combined group of these five value propositions reflects the overall emphasis placed on masculinity by respondents from each country, and from the combined countries as measured by the average mean. Using the average mean as a general indicator, the following countries have mean responses that exceed the average mean for each of the five propositions: People's Republic of China and the former Soviet Union (5 of 5 each); Japan (4 of 5); and Chile (1 of 5). This compounds to 10 of 15 (67 percent) for respondents from the three collectivist countries, compared to 4 of 15 (27 percent) for those from the three market-oriented countries, and 1 of 10 (10 percent) for those from the two Latin American countries. Except for value proposition 5, the average means are very low (ranging from 2.35 to 2.52).

In terms of the mean responses to the preceding five value propositions, the respondents from the former Soviet Union and the People's Republic of China place a much greater emphasis on masculinity in each of their respective societies. Moreover, the mean responses of these respondents tend to be much higher than the average means for the five value propositions.

It is interesting to note the lower emphasis placed on masculinity by the respondents from Yugoslavia compared to those from the other two collectivist countries. This lower emphasis on masculinity may be the result of the greater openness of Yugoslav society in terms of fewer restrictions on travel to the West. The mean responses of respondents from Germany, the United States, and Venezuela for the first four value propositions are lower, indicating less emphasis on masculinity and more pronounced femininity in these societies.

Table 3.4 shows the overall emphasis on masculinity of respondents from each of the eight countries. This overall emphasis is the combined responses to the five masculinity value propositions. The chi square analysis indicates that there are some significant differences (.00 level) in the overall emphasis on masculinity according to the country of the respondents (.74 coefficient of contingency). However, except for the respondents from the former Soviet Union (3.67) and, to a lesser extent, those from the People's Republic of China (3.18), the mean responses are low. Moreover, the average mean for all countries combined (2.61) is low. This indicates a general tendency toward less masculine, and more feminine, societies.

The ANOVA Scheffe test results shown on Table 3.4 reflect the greater emphasis placed on the masculinity value by the respondents from the former Soviet Union and the People's Republic of China. At the other extreme, the mean responses of respondents from Germany, the United States, and Venezuela tend to indicate that these societies are more feminine. The responses of the respondents from Japan, except when compared to those from the People's Republic of China and the former Soviet Union, reflect a more masculine society.

Uncertainty Avoidance

Hofstede's cultural dimension of uncertainty avoidance incorporates the notion of time as it relates to the future. He reasoned that time and uncertainty avoidance were related within the context of a person's expectations about future events, especially in terms of how these events will affect the person's well-being in a negative or positive sense. Hofstede discovered that people in different cultures reacted to uncertainty in different ways. People who simply accept an uncertain future have low uncertainty avoidance. On the other hand, people who strive to engineer uncertainty out of existence, or those who prefer certain situations, have high uncertainty avoidance.

Cultures with high uncertainty avoidance generally exhibit greater levels of anxiety, emotional behavior, and nervousness than those that accept or are resigned to uncertain situations. Moreover, cultures with high uncertainty avoidance generally develop institutions to reduce uncertainty for their members, thereby hoping to foster security and

Table 3.4
Overall Emphasis on Masculinity

A	Response Frequency (%)					N	$\overline{X}$	Scheffe Test							
	1	2	3	4	5			GER.	U.S.	JAPAN	YUG.	P.R.C.	F.S.U.	VEN.	CHILE
GER.	34.2	32.8	16.6	13.1	3.2	891	2.18								
U.S.	40.0	30.4	11.7	13.2	4.7	1766	2.12								
JAPAN	16.6	27.2	33.3	18.9	4.0	275	2.66	X	X		X			X	X
YUG.	32.6	27.3	16.2	17.5	6.3	710	2.38	X	X					X	
P.R.C.	5.7	28.0	15.3	44.7	6.3	986	3.18	X	X	X	X			X	X
F.S.U.	2.8	13.1	15.7	51.1	17.3	1233	3.67	X	X	X	X	X		X	X
VEN.	35.5	35.5	10.2	12.6	6.2	950	2.18								
CHILE	23.1	32.4	19.9	22.0	2.5	300	2.48	X	X					X	
TOTAL	25.3	27.8	14.9	24.9	7.1	7111	2.61								

B

* = Significantly greater emphasis for each pair of countries
(.05 level)-A versus B

ANOVA F Ratio = 1305.38 (.00 level)

Total mean = average of eight means
Chi Square (Pearson) = 8735.73 (.00 level)
Coefficient of Contingency = .74
1 = Strongly Disagree; 5 = Strongly Agree

reduce risks.

Uncertainty avoidance consists of the five value propositions summarized in the following discussion. The mean responses of respondents for each country, and the average mean (A.M.) of the eight means, are shown for each value proposition. These value propositions were developed from similar dimensions used by Hofstede (1980).

1. It is important to clearly specify job requirements/instructions so people know what is expected of them.

VEN.	YUG.	U.S.	A.M.	CHILE	P.R.C.	F.S.U.	JAPAN	GER.
4.12	3.96	3.85	3.67	3.63	3.60	3.50	3.38	3.30

2. Rules/regulations are needed so workers know what is expected of them.

U.S.	VEN.	CHILE	YUG.	A.M.	YUG.	U.S.	CHILE	VEN.
4.01	3.93	3.77	3.66	3.63	3.61	3.58	3.32	3.15

3. Better to have a certain bad situation than an uncertain better situation.

P.R.C.	CHILE.	U.S.	A.M.	JAPAN	YUG.	F.S.U.	GER.	JAPAN
3.37	2.90	2.81	2.69	2.68	2.61	2.56	2.55	2.07

4. Avoid making changes because things could get worse.

JAPAN	F.S.U.	P.R.C.	CHILE	A.M.	YUG.	U.S.	GER.	VEN.
2.46	2.45	2.33	2.19	2.12	1.96	1.87	1.84	1.83

5. Standardized work procedures are more important than opportunities to be innovative.

JAPAN	U.S.	CHILE	YUG.	A.M.	P.R.C.	GER.	F.S.U.	VEN.
2.57	2.55	2.53	2.33	2.32	2.30	2.14	2.12	2.00

The combined group of these propositions reflects the overall emphasis placed on uncertainty avoidance by respondents from each country, and from the combined countries as measured by the average mean. Using the average mean as a general indicator, respondents from the following countries have mean responses that exceed the average mean for each of the five propositions: the United States and Chile (4 of 5 each); Yugoslavia (3 of 5); Japan, the People's Republic of China, and Venezuela (2 of 5 each); and the former Soviet Union (1 of 5). This corresponds to 6 of 10 (60 percent) for the respondents from the two Latin American countries combined, compared to 6 of 15 (40 percent) each for the respondents from the three market-oriented and three collectivist countries. The respondents from Germany are the only ones with no mean response above the average mean for any of the value propositions, reflecting a lower uncertainty avoidance by these respondents.

The higher uncertainty avoidance of the respondents from the United States is somewhat surprising because of the historical emphasis on entrepreneurship and risk taking in this country. However, the sample of respondents from the United States consisted primarily of students, and this could reflect a generational value change that may be occurring. Propositions 1, 2, and 5 relate to the emphasis on the need for rules, regulations, procedures, and requirements, while 3 and 4 pertain to future uncertainty.

There appears to be no pronounced pattern of responses by respondents from the eight countries surveyed relating to these two groups of value propositions. However, some observations are in order concerning some of the responses to individual value propositions. For example, relating to proposition 1, the respondents from Venezuela feel strongly that job requirements and instructions are necessary (4.12), yet they feel less strongly about proposition 2, that deals with the need for rules and regulations (3.15). Similarly, the respondents from Japan are more risk averse than the other respondents on the basis of their responses to proposition 4 (2.46), yet they seem to disagree relative to the other respondents, that the status quo is preferable as reflected in proposition 3 (2.07). Moreover, these types of response inconsistencies are evident for other countries shown.

Table 3.5 shows the overall emphasis placed on uncertainty avoidance for respondents in each of the eight countries. This overall emphasis is the combined responses to the five uncertainty avoidance value propositions. The chi square analysis shows that there are some significant differences (.00 level) in the overall emphasis on uncertainty avoidance according to the country of the respondents (.49 coefficient of contingency). However, the combined mean responses of respondents from each country, as well as the average mean for the combined respondents, tend to be low.

The ANOVA Scheffe test results shown in Table 3.5 highlight the lower uncertainty avoidance of respondents from Germany compared to those from each of the other seven countries. The lower uncertainty avoidance of respondents from Germany seems counterintuitive when you consider that country's traditional emphasis on formal organizational

Table 3.5
Overall Emphasis on Uncertainty Avoidance

A	Response Frequency (%)					N	X̄	Scheffé Test (B)							
	1	2	3	4	5			GER.	U.S.	JAPAN	YUG.	P.R.C.	F.S.U.	VEN.	CHILE
GER.	17.5	38.0	21.5	19.3	3.7	893	2.54								
U.S.	11.3	28.0	19.2	30.5	11.0	1770	3.02	X		X	X		X	X	
JAPAN	8.0	26.9	40.2	21.2	3.7	285	2.86	X							
YUG.	14.4	26.5	21.5	29.8	7.9	702	2.90	X							
P.R.C.	7.7	31.2	14.0	42.1	5.1	990	3.06	X		X	X		X	X	
F.S.U.	8.7	35.1	22.6	28.6	5.1	1228	2.86	X							
VEN.	18.3	31.0	9.6	26.6	14.5	949	2.88	X							
CHILE	9.8	30.2	20.6	28.8	10.6	306	3.00	X					X		
TOTAL	12.2	31.2	19.1	29.3	8.2	7123	2.89								

X = Significantly greater emphasis for each pair of countries (.05 level)-A versus B

ANOVA F Ratio = 87.04 (.00 level)

Total mean = average of eight means
Chi Square (Pearson) = 2255.33 (.00 level)
Coefficient of Contingency = .49
1 = Strongly Disagree; 5 = Strongly Agree

concepts, operating policies, and procedures. On the other hand, the Scheffe Test results show higher levels of uncertainty avoidance for respondents from the United States, the People's Republic of China, and Chile, followed by those from Japan, Yugoslavia, Soviet Union, and Venezuela.

Power Distance

Power distance measures the extent people accept inequalities in authority and wealth in a given society. Hofstede relates the power distance dimension to the extent of centralization of authority in organizations. For example, he views power distance as an acceptance of a centralized and autocratic leadership structure that emanates from the mental frame of mind of the larger society. This mind-set reflects the general preferences of the leaders to lead and the followers to be led, and therefore, the value systems of the managers and workers are in tune. In other words, the dependency needs of the workers in this type of society are satisfied, along with managers' need for power to lead.

Power distance consists of the five value propositions summarized in the following. These five propositions were developed from similar dimensions of power distance used by Hofstede (1980). Moreover, the mean responses of respondents for each country, and the average mean (A.M.) of the eight means, are shown for each value proposition.

1. Asking opinions too often of subordinates may make managers seem weak or incompetent.

F.S.U.	P.R.C.	CHILE	JAPAN	A.M.	VEN.	YUG.	U.S.	GER.
2.72	2.57	2.48	2.35	2.32	2.19	2.16	2.11	1.99

2. Managers should make most decisions without consulting subordinates.

P.R.C.	F.S.U.	CHILE	A.M.	VEN.	U.S.	YUG.	GER.	JAPAN
2.80	2.78	2.48	2.40	2.39	2.28	2.23	2.14	2.07

3. Managers should perform difficult and important work and delegate repetitive and mundane work to subordinates.

P.R.C.	F.S.U.	GER.	YUG.	A.M.	CHILE	VEN.	U.S.	JAPAN
3.50	3.31	3.18	3.13	2.91	2.75	2.74	2.57	2.12

4. Social interaction with subordinates may decrease a manager's objectivity in dealing with them.

U.S.	F.S.U.	P.R.C.	A.M.	JAPAN	CHILE	GER.	YUG.	VEN.
2.75	2.74	2.63	2.47	2.45	2.45	2.35	2.27	2.08

5. Higher level managers deserve more privileges and benefits than lower level ones.

P.R.C.	VEN.	U.S.	CHILE	A.M.	JAPAN	YUG.	GER.	F.S.U.
3.40	3.20	3.14	2.92	2.83	2.76	2.70	2.43	2.07

This combined group of five value propositions reflects the overall emphasis placed on power distance by respondents from each country, and for the combined countries as measured by the average mean. Using the average mean as a general indicator, respondents from the following countries have mean responses that exceed the average mean for each of the five value propositions pertaining to power distance: the People's Republic of China (5 of 5); the former Soviet Union (4 of 5); Chile (3 of 5); the United States (2 of 5); and Germany, Japan, Yugoslavia, and Venezuela (1 of 5 each). Moreover, the combined respondents from the three collectivist countries place a greater emphasis on power distance, with the frequency of responses higher than the average means for each proposition in 10 of 15 cases (67 percent), compared to 3 of 10 cases (40 percent) for the respondents from the two Latin American countries and 4 of 15 cases (57 percent) for respondents from the three market-oriented countries.

However, in terms of their mean responses, respondents from all countries except the People's Republic of China and the former Soviet Union have a relatively lower emphasis placed on power distance. This can be seen more clearly on Table 3.6, which shows the overall emphasis on power distance by respondents for each of the eight countries. First, it should be noted that the average mean of respondents for the eight countries combined (2.59) is low, and none of the mean responses for respondents in any of the eight countries exceeds 3.00. Thus, respondents from all eight countries tend to have relatively low emphases on power distance. Even though the chi square analysis indicates that there are some significant differences (.00 level) in the overall emphasis placed on power distance (.45 coefficient of contingency), these differences occur within a generally lower emphasis overall on power distance by respondents from all of the countries.

The ANOVA Scheffe test results reflect where these differences

Table 3.6
Overall Emphasis on Power Distance

A — Response Frequency (%)

A	1	2	3	4	5	N	X̄
GER.	18.1	43.9	19.2	15.9	2.9	892	2.42
U.S.	17.4	39.5	16.7	21.7	4.7	1768	2.57
JAPAN	19.2	41.7	26.6	10.2	2.3	286	2.35
YUG.	18.0	38.2	23.4	16.8	3.6	695	2.50
P.R.C.	7.9	34.6	13.3	39.5	4.6	988	2.98
F.S.U.	11.5	37.8	22.4	23.6	4.7	1233	2.72
VEN.	16.7	45.6	14.0	16.5	7.3	948	2.52
CHILE	12.4	39.8	24.5	20.1	3.2	303	2.62
TOTAL	15.0	39.9	18.5	22.1	4.5	7113	2.59

Total mean = average of eight means
Chi Square (Pearson) = 1785.26 (.00 level)
Coefficient of Contingency = .45
1 = Strongly Disagree; 5 = Strongly Agree

B — Scheffe Test

A	GER.	U.S.	JAPAN	YUG.	P.R.C.	F.S.U.	VEN.	CHILE
GER.								
U.S.			X					
JAPAN								
YUG.			X					
P.R.C.	X	X	X	X		X	X	X
F.S.U.	X	X	X	X			X	
VEN.	X		X					
CHILE	X		X					

* = Significantly greater emphasis for each pair of countries (.05 level)-A versus B

ANOVA F Ratio = 127.08 (.00 level)

between various pairs of countries occur. The data in Table 3.6 show that the respondents from the People's Republic of China and the former Soviet Union, two of the collectivist countries, place a greater emphasis on power distance than respondents from the other six countries. At the other extreme, respondents from Japan, Germany, and Yugoslavia, and to some extent, those from the United States, Venezuela, and Chile, place a relatively lower emphasis on power distance. The relatively higher emphasis by respondents from the People's Republic of China seems consistent with its relatively high emphasis on uncertainty avoidance. For example, this society tends to accept the division of powers, status, and rewards between managers and subordinates (power distance), and it also supports the need for regulations, rules, procedures, and so forth (uncertainty avoidance). On the other hand, the answers of respondents from the remaining countries, except those from the United States and the former Soviet Union, reflect lower emphases placed on both power distance and uncertainty avoidance. This is consistent with expectations, but at the lower end. The United States' lower emphasis on power distance coupled with its higher emphasis on uncertainty avoidance, and the reverse emphasis for the former Soviet Union, need further analysis.

FAMILY VALUES

The types of family values analyzed in this research are (1) the emphasis placed on individualism within the family, (2) the economic orientation of the family, and (3) the emphasis placed on family cohesion and status. The first two of these values are analyzed in this chapter under the broad umbrella of the tendency toward individualism while the third one is analyzed in the next chapter within the topic of collectivism.

Individualism within the Family

The emphasis on individualism within the family is measured by responses to the four value propositions shown later. The mean responses of respondents from each country, and the average mean (A.M.) of the eight means, are also shown. These four value propositions were developed and patterned after similar propositions found throughout sociological literature. These four value propositions were presented to respondents within the context of how the emphasis placed on individualism, along with personal accomplishments, enhances the family.

1. Family members often need to spend more time by themselves.

U.S.	YUG.	VEN.	A.M.	GER.	P.R.C.	JAPAN	CHILE	F.S.U.
4.20	4.05	4.01	3.86	3.84	3.80	3.78	3.74	3.46

2. Each family member has a different personality and needs that should be respected by others.

VEN.	GER.	YUG.	U.S.	F.S.U.	A.M.	CHILE	P.R.C.	JAPAN
4.39	4.36	4.36	4.33	4.18	4.13	4.03	3.91	3.91

3. Personal accomplishments of family members influence the family's social status in the community.

YUG.	F.S.U.	U.S.	GER.	P.R.C.	A.M.	VEN.	CHILE	JAPAN
4.00	3.91	3.89	3.83	3.89	3.89	3.71	3.71	3.45

4. High ambition by each family member ensures the overall growth and well-being of the whole family.

YUG.	P.R.C.	F.S.U.	U.S.	A.M.	JAPAN	GER.	VEN.	CHILE
3.89	3.75	3.60	3.64	3.35	3.29	3.03	2.82	2.72

The combined group of these four value propositions reflects the overall emphasis on individualism within the family by respondents from each country, and for the combined countries as measured by the average mean. Using the average mean as a general indicator, respondents from the following countries have mean responses that exceed the average mean for each of the propositions pertaining to individualism within the family: the United States and Yugoslavia (4 of 4 each); the former Soviet Union (3 of 4); and Germany, the People's Republic of China, and Venezuela (2 of 4 each). This corresponds to 9 of 12 (75 percent) for the combined respondents from the three collectivist countries, compared to 6 of 12 (50 percent) and 2 of 8 (25 percent) for those from the combined three market-oriented countries and the two Latin American countries, respectively.

The first two value propositions refer to the necessity to recognize the individual needs of each family member, while propositions 3 and 4 support the notion that accomplishments of individual family members enhance the status of the family. The average means for all four propositions tend to be high. Moreover, this is true for the mean responses of respondents from each of the countries as well, except for

Venezuela (2.82) and Chile (2.72), for proposition 4 relating to individual growth versus family well-being. Moreover, the respondents from Japan and Chile tend to place a lower emphasis on individualism within the family relative to the respondents from the other countries on the basis of the mean responses for the four propositions.

Table 3.7 shows the overall emphasis placed on individualism within the family by respondents in each of the eight countries surveyed. This emphasis reflects the combined responses to the preceding four value propositions. The chi square analysis indicates that there are some significant differences (.00 level) in the overall emphasis placed on individualism within the family according to the country of the respondents (.44 coefficient of contingency). Moreover, the average means of respondents from all of the countries are high, ranging from 3.31 for Chile to 3.77 for Yugoslavia, with an average mean for the eight countries of 3.52.

The ANOVA Scheffe test results highlight the differences in the overall emphasis on individualism within the family within this generally high range of mean responses. On the basis of these results, the respondents from Yugoslavia and the United States place a greater emphasis on individualism within the family. Yet when comparing these results with those shown on Table 3.3 relating to overall individualism as a personal value, only the respondents from the United States show consistent results: that is, they tend to place a higher emphasis on both personal individualism and individualism within the family.

Economic Orientation of the Family

The importance of the economic orientation of the family is measured by responses to the six value propositions shown next. The mean responses of respondents from each country, and the average mean (A.M.) of the eight means, are also shown. These six value propositions were developed and patterned after similar propositions found throughout sociological literature, and they were presented to respondents within the context of the importance of the economic priorities of the family.

1. More education usually results in greater family well-being.

VEN.	U.S.	CHILE	YUG.	GER.	A.M.	P.R.C.	F.S.U.	JAPAN
4.23	4.04	4.02	3.89	3.85	3.71	3.46	3.20	2.95

Table 3.7
Overall Emphasis on Individualism in the Family

A	\(1\)	2	3	4	5	N	$\overline{X}$	GER.	U.S.	JAPAN	YUG.	P.R.C.	F.S.U.	VEN.	CHILE
			Response Frequency (%)								Scheffe Test (B)				
GER.	4.1	17.3	22.3	39.5	16.8	891	3.48			X				X	X
U.S.	4.7	14.0	13.6	44.3	23.4	1770	3.68	X		X		X	X	X	X
JAPAN	3.4	15.8	30.7	37.7	12.3	295	3.40								
YUG.	2.7	11.7	15.4	45.7	24.5	705	3.77	X	X	X		X	X	X	X
P.R.C.	3.7	18.7	10.4	56.5	10.6	990	3.52								X
F.S.U.	3.1	16.3	18.4	48.0	14.3	1232	3.54			X					X
VEN.	8.7	19.0	11.3	36.3	24.6	948	3.49								X
CHILE	5.7	24.7	18.5	35.1	16.0	303	3.31								
TOTAL	4.5	16.4	15.8	44.4	18.8	7134	3.52								

Total mean = average of eight means
Chi Square (Pearson) = 1754.92 (.00 level)
Coefficient of Contingency = .44
1 = Strongly Disagree; 5 = Strongly Agree

* = Significantly greater emphasis for each pair of countries (.05 level)-A versus B

ANOVA F Ratio = 55.41 (.00 level)

2. Work for material wealth is higher priority than physical/mental health of family.

VEN.	F.S.U.	P.R.C.	VEN.	A.M.	JAPAN	U.S.	GER.	YUG.
2.35	2.11	2.03	1.98	1.97	1.96	1.81	1.77	1.72

3. Higher family standard of living is higher priority than national security.

CHILE	U.S.	GER.	P.R.C.	A.M.	JAPAN	F.S.U.	VEN.	YUG.
3.17	2.98	2.94	2.90	2.86	2.81	2.76	2.68	2.63

4. Doing socially accepted work does not enhance the family's community status.

YUG.	F.S.U.	GER.	JAPAN	A.M.	CHILE	P.R.C.	U.S.	VEN.
2.72	2.62	2.60	2.54	2.42	2.35	2.24	2.21	2.09

5. Wealth enhances the family's community status.

GER.	U.S.	P.R.C.	YUG.	A.M.	VEN.	F.S.U.	JAPAN	CHILE
3.62	3.60	3.49	3.37	3.60	3.16	3.12	3.09	2.95

6. Opportunities to gain large material wealth are more important than economic security.

JAPAN	YUG.	F.S.U.	A.M.	GER.	U.S.	CHILE	P.R.C.	VEN.
2.65	2.48	2.39	2.35	2.33	2.32	2.32	2.29	2.02

The combined group of the six propositions reflects the overall importance of the economic orientation of the family of respondents from each country, and of respondents for all countries surveyed. Using the average mean for the eight countries as a general indicator, the respondents from the following countries have mean responses that exceed the average mean for each of the six value propositions: Germany and Yugoslavia (4 of 6 each); the United States, the People's Republic of China, the former Soviet Union, and Chile (3 of 6 each); and Japan and Chile (2 of 6 each). This corresponds to 10 of 18 (56 percent) for the combined respondents from the three collectivist countries, compared to 9 of 18 (50 percent) and 5 of 12 (42 percent) for the combined respondents from the three market-oriented and two Latin American countries, respectively.

Value propositions 2, 3, 5, and 6 deal specifically with a preference for wealth and material well-being. Proposition 1 advocates more education to acquire wealth, while proposition 5 views wealth as a means to enhance community status. The average means for these two propositions, 3.71 and 3.30, respectively, are very much higher than for the other four value propositions relating to the economic orientation of the family. The respondents from Germany, the United States, and Yugoslavia are the only ones that have higher mean responses than the average mean for both propositions 1 and 5.

Table 3.8 shows the overall economic orientation of the family by respondents in each of the eight countries. This overall orientation reflects the combined responses to the six value propositions. The chi square analysis indicates that there are some significant differences (.00 level) in the overall importance of the economic orientation of the family (.40 coefficient of contingency). However, all of the mean responses of the eight countries tend to be generally low, with a somewhat narrow range of means (Japan 2.67 to Chile 2.96), and with an average mean for the eight countries of 2.84.

However, the ANOVA Scheffe Test results on Table 3.8 shows some different levels of the family economic orientation between respondents from pairs of countries. For example, the respondents from the former Soviet Union and Japan place a lower emphasis on the economic orientation of the family than respondents from the other six countries. The respondents from the United States and Chile place greater importance on the economic orientation of the family than those from Japan, the People's Republic of China, the former Soviet Union, and Venezuela in terms of these paired comparison tests.

SUMMARY AND CONCLUSIONS

This chapter compares the relative overall tendency toward individualism of respondents in the eight countries surveyed. This comparison focuses on five specific values that reflect a higher emphasis on the tendency toward individualism as a general value. These include one workplace value relating to the work ethic, two cultural values relating to personal individualism and masculinity, and the two family values pertaining to individualism within the family and family economic orientation. Respondents who place more emphasis on these five values have a higher mean response to a set of value propositions that measures the extent of each value emphasized. For example, the attributes of a greater tendency toward individualism are an emphasis on work; a preference for personal independence; a masculine outlook that emphasizes work, achievement, and individualism; and an emphasis on economic

Table 3.8

Overall Emphasis on Family Economic Orientation

A

| | Response Frequency (%) | | | | | | |
	1	2	3	4	5	N	$\bar{X}$
GER.	12.8	29.5	21.5	28.7	7.5	892	2.89
U.S.	14.3	29.2	17.4	27.4	11.6	1770	2.93
JAPAN	13.8	31.5	33.2	17.0	4.5	295	2.67
YUG.	14.0	28.5	24.0	23.9	9.5	704	2.86
P.R.C.	8.5	41.4	15.5	29.2	5.4	989	2.82
F.S.U.	9.9	36.4	26.8	21.2	5.7	1234	2.76
VEN.	16.8	32.2	15.8	22.1	13.1	948	2.82
CHILE	8.8	34.5	20.9	22.9	12.8	303	2.96
TOTAL	12.6	32.8	20.5	25.1	9.0	7135	2.84

Total mean = average of eight means
Chi Square (Pearson) = 1322.86 (.00 level)
Coefficient of Contingency = .40
1 = Strongly Disagree; 5 = Strongly Agree

B

Scheffe Test

	GER.	U.S.	JAPAN	YUG.	P.R.C.	F.S.U.	VEN.	CHILE
GER.			X			X		
U.S.			X		X	X	X	
JAPAN								
YUG.			X			X		
P.R.C.			X					
F.S.U.								
VEN.			X					
CHILE			X		X	X	X	

* = Significantly greater emphasis for each pair of countries (.05 level)-A versus B

ANOVA F Ratio = 17.74 (.00 level)

and material rewards.

Persons who have a greater tendency toward individualism, as measured directly by the five specific values, are expected to place a lower emphasis on three other specific values: leisure ethic, uncertainty avoidance, and power distance. Thus, respondents who have higher mean responses for these five values that directly measure the tendency toward individualism are expected to have lower mean responses for these three indirect measures of individualism. For example, a higher work ethic should usually be accompanied by a lower leisure ethic. Similarly, persons with a higher work ethic, and who place a higher emphasis on personal individualism and masculinity, are expected to place a lower emphasis on uncertainty avoidance and power distance. These latter two values generally reflect a greater need for rules, regulations, and authority to enable people to feel more secure about the future and to understand better what is expected of them in an organization.

On the bases of the Scheffe test results comparing mean responses of respondents from each country with each of the other seven countries, Table 3.9 summarizes the overall tendency toward individualism as measured by the eight values discussed. The first five values directly measure the overall emphasis placed on individualism (the higher the mean response the greater tendency toward individualism). Values six through eight indirectly measure this emphasis (the lower the mean response, the less tendency toward individualism). The data on Table 3.9 are taken from Tables 3.1 through 3.8 for the eight values shown: values 1 through 8 relate to Tables 3.1 through 3.8, respectively.

The numerical data shown on Table 3.9 are the frequencies of significantly higher mean responses (.05 level) of each country's respondents when compared to mean responses for each of the other seven countries using the Scheffe Test of paired comparisons. A country with a greater overall tendency toward individualism will have a higher total frequency for values one through five and a lower frequency for values six through eight. On the basis of the frequency data shown on Table 3.9, the following section discusses each country's overall tendency toward individualism.

Keep in mind that this discussion focuses on the relative significant differences in the overall tendency toward individualism of respondents from pairs of countries rather than the strength of this tendency as measured by the actual size of the mean response. Moreover, the total frequency of significantly higher mean responses (.05 level) of respon-

Table 3.9
Summary of the Overall Tendency Toward Individualism

VALUES	GER.	U.S.	JAPAN	YUG.	P.R.C.	F.S.U.	VEN.	CHILE
1. Work Ethic	3	0	2	5	6	6	1	1
2. Personal Individualism	2	7	1	3	0	1	1	1
3. Masculinity	0	0	5	3	6	7	0	3
4. Individualism Within the Family	1	6	0	7	1	2	1	0
5. Family Economic Orientation	2	4	0	2	1	0	1	4
Combined Emphasis (1 - 5)	8	17	8	20	14	16	4	9
As a Percent of Maximum	23%	49%	23%	57%	40%	46%	11%	26%
6. Leisure Ethic	2	3	7	5	2	5	0	0
7. Uncertainty Avoidance	0	5	1	1	5	1	1	2
8. Power Distance	0	2	0	1	7	5	2	2
Combined Emphasis (6 - 8)	2	10	8	7	14	11	3	5
As a Percent of Maximum	10%	48%	38%	33%	67%	52%	14%	24%

Numbers equal frequency of significantly higher mean responses using ANOVA Scheffe test paired comparisons (0 - 7 are possible range of frequencies) for each of the eight values (maximum total frequency = 35 for values 1 - 5, and 21 for values 6 - 8).

dents from a given country measures the number of times their mean responses were significantly greater in a series of paired comparisons.

The respondents from Germany reflect a relatively lower tendency toward individualism, even though the percentage frequency of higher mean responses (23 percent) is higher for values one through five than the percentage frequency for values six through eight (10 percent). The relatively lower tendency toward individualism is supported by the fact that none of the frequencies of higher means exceeds 3 of a possible 7 for any of the first five values. While the lower response frequency for the last three values generally reflects a greater tendency toward individualism, it is somewhat inconsistent with the ressponses to the first five values that more directly measure this tendency.

Compared to Germany, the mean responses of the respondents from the United States reflect a greater tendency toward individualism, with a combined percentage frequency of 49 percent for the first five values, however, the percentage frequency for values six through eight is also relatively high (48 percent). These respondents tend to place a greater emphasis on individualism (both personal and within the family) when these two values are compared to the results from respondents from the other seven countries (values 2 and 4 on Table 3.9). While the respondents from the United States tend to place a greater emphasis on individualism, they also place a greater emphasis on uncertainty avoidance (value 7) compared to five of the seven other groups of respondents. This seems inconsistent.

For respondents from Japan, the percentage frequency of mean responses higher than in the other seven countries for the first five values is the same as for Germany (23 percent). However, Japan's respondents show a higher frequency (38 percent) for the last three values, indicating a lower tendency toward individualism than those respondents from Germany. As to the respondents from Japan, they seem to place a greater relative emphasis on the leisure ethic (value 6), and secondarily, on masculinity (value 3).

Except for the respondents from the United States to some extent, the combined respondents from the three market-oriented countries as a group do not show a higher overall tendency toward individualism when compared to the other groups of respondents. Some reasons for this may be that the higher standard of living in these countries encourages leisure or that the use of modern organizational and management concepts diminishes individual initiative. Thus, organizations tend to rely more on policies, procedures, rules, and formal authority arrangements.

Turning to the three collectivist countries, the respondents from Yugoslavia have the highest percentage frequency (57 percent) of mean responses significantly higher than for other countries on the basis of the Scheffe test results. The respondents from this country are the only ones surveyed with a frequency higher than 50 percent for the first five values. Moreover, the percentage frequency (33 percent) for values six through eight for the respondents from Yugoslavia is the fourth lowest of the eight countries. Therefore, as a whole, these respondents reflect a greater tendency toward individualism relative to the other seven countries surveyed. It is interesting to note that these respondents place a greater emphasis on both the work ethic and the leisure ethic (values 1 and 7) in five of the seven comparisons of mean responses.

The respondents from the former Soviet Union reflect a somewhat similar overall tendency toward individualism to those from the United States, with percentage frequencies of 46 percent for the combined first five values, and 52 percent for the combined last three values. These respondents from the former Soviet Union reflect a relatively greater tendency toward individualism than those from the other countries, excluding those from Yugoslavia and perhaps those from the United States to a lesser extent. In general, the respondents from the former Soviet Union tend to place a greater emphasis on the work ethic, masculinity, the leisure ethic, and uncertainty avoidance (values 1, 3, 6, and 8, respectively), when compared to the other groups of respondents.

The respondents from the People's Republic of China reflect a lower overall tendency toward individualism with a frequency of higher mean responses of 40 percent for the first five values combined, and a 67 percent higher mean responses for values 6 through 8. The responses to the last three values indicate a lower overall emphasis on individualism. In general, when compared to the other groups of respondents, these respondents tend to place a greater emphasis on the work ethic, masculinity, uncertainty avoidance, and power distance (values 1, 3, 7, and 8, respectively). This emphasis is somewhat similar to that of the respondents from the former Soviet Union.

When compared to the respondents from each of the other countries, the respondents from Venezuela and Chile tend to place a lower overall emphasis on individualism. Even though the mean responses of these respondents reflect a greater tendency toward individualism based on the lower percentage frequencies (14 percent and 24 percent) for the combined values 6 through 8, the percentage frequencies are lower for the first group of five values as well (11 and 26 percent, respectively).

This indicates a lesser emphasis on individualism as a general value. Except for higher mean responses for family economic orientation (value 5) for the respondents from Chile, none of the frequencies of higher means exceeds 3 of a possible 7 for respondents from either of these two countries.

Some final observations about the data shown on Table 3.9 should be made. These data focus on the relative emphases placed on those values that we traditionally associate with the overall tendency toward individualism as a general value. The frequencies of significantly higher mean responses are measures of the emphases placed on these values. The first five values are direct, while the last three are indirect measures of the overall tendency toward individualism.

Focusing first on the five direct measures, the respondents from Chile, Japan, Germany, and Venezuela place a lower emphasis on overall individualism than the respondents from the other four countries. On the other hand, those respondents from Yugoslavia place a higher emphasis on individualism than those from the United States, the former Soviet Union, and the People's Republic of China, as well as the respondents from the four countries referred to previously.

In terms of the last three values shown on Table 3.9, respondents from Germany, Venezuela, and Chile place a higher emphasis on overall individualism, and those from the People's Republic of China, followed by those from the former Soviet Union and the United States, place lower emphases on individualism.

When all of the eight values are considered, the following conclusions seem reasonable. The overall tendency toward individualism for the total sample of respondents is relatively low. Moreover, the responses to the individual values in the first group do not show a pronounced pattern for each country, except for two of the countries with the lower frequencies, Venezuela and Germany, and Yugoslavia to some extent as a country with the highest frequency.

4

Profile of Collectivism Values

Chapter 3 discussed the values that reflect a general tendency toward individualism. These values were discussed within three groups, workplace, cultural, and family, using value concepts of Buchholz, Hofstede, and those found in other sociological literature, respectively. This chapter presents an analysis of responses of respondents from the eight countries surveyed as they relate to the collectivism values. The pattern of analysis and discussion are similar to those pertaining to responses to individualism values in Chapter 3. For example, mean responses to individual value propositions within each of the following collectivism values are compared and discussed: Buchholz's (1976) organizational, humanistic, and Marxist work belief systems; Dorfman and Howell's (1988) cultural value of paternalism as an extension of Hofstede's (1980) research; and family social cohesion and status.

WORKPLACE VALUES

Two of Buchholz's values pertaining to individualism were analyzed in Chapter 3 within the context of the relative preference given to work versus leisure by the respondents from the eight countries. The following analysis focuses on the preferences given to values which encourage and support collectivism; organizational, humanistic, and Marxist work belief system.

Organizational Belief System

The organizational belief system value reflects the extent to which a person believes that the real meaning from work can come about only if it contributes to the group or overall organizational well-being and status.

In this view, work is not an end in itself, but a means to serve group interests. If this occurs, then work has value, and a person's success in the organization is enhanced. Moreover, this success is dependent on the person's ability to conform and to adapt to group and organizational norms, rather than on the person's individual effort and accomplishments, as an integral part of the work ethic value. Thus, individual productivity and initiative must be balanced with group expectations.

The organizational belief system value consists of nine value propositions summarized in the followiing. The mean responses of respondents from each country, and the average mean (A.M.) of the eight means, are also shown for each value proposition. The nine propositions were developed by using similar dimensions of the organizational belief system used by Buchholz (1976).

1. Groups make better decisions than individuals.

VEN.	CHILE	F.S.U.	A.M.	U.S.	YUG.	GER.	JAPAN	P.R.C.
4.12	3.76	3.65	3.51	3.42	3.31	3.30	3.29	3.21

2. Contribution to the group is the most important aspect of work.

F.S.U.	VEN.	P.R.C.	CHILE	YUG.	A.M.	U.S.	GER.	JAPAN
4.08	3.69	3.60	3.45	3.44	3.40	3.25	2.97	2.75

3. A person should take an active part in all group activities.

VEN.	F.S.U.	A.M.	CHILE	GER.	JAPAN	YUG.	P.R.C.	U.S.
3.94	3.91	3.55	3.53	3.47	3.45	3.41	3.38	3.28

4. The best job is as part of a group that leads to group recognition.

U.S.	P.R.C.	F.S.U.	JAPAN	A.M.	CHILE	GER.	YUG.	VEN.
3.03	3.01	2.89	2.86	2.83	2.78	2.70	2.69	2.68

5. Better to work in a group than alone.

VEN.	GER.	F.S.U.	CHILE	P.R.C.	A.M.	YUG.	U.S.	JAPAN
3.63	3.50	3.45	3.4	3.41	3.40	3.34	3.24	3.14

6. Group survival is very important to an organization.

VEN.	JAPAN	F.S.U.	U.S.	A.M.	P.R.C.	CHILE	GER.	YUG.
4.08	3.84	3.84	3.76	3.76	3.73	3.71	3.61	3.52

7. The group is the organization's most important entity.

F.S.U.	VEN.	P.R.C.	A.M.	JAPAN	YUG.	CHILE	GER.	U.S.
3.83	3.74	3.56	3.38	3.24	3.21	3.19	3.18	3.12

8. Work can foster group interest.

VEN.	YUG.	F.S.U.	CHILE	P.R.C.	U.S.	A.M.	GER.	JAPAN
3.78	3.61	3.56	3.55	3.49	3.48	3.47	3.18	3.13

9. Conformity is necessary for organizational survival.

F.S.U.	P.R.C.	JAPAN	YUG.	A.M.	U.S.	GER.	CHILE	VEN.
3.87	3.74	3.56	3.25	3.03	2.91	2.70	2.34	1.90

The combined group of these nine value propositions reflects the overall emphasis placed on the organizational belief system value by respondents from each country, and for the combined respondents from the eight countries as measured by the average mean. Using the average mean as a general indicator, the respondents from the following countries have mean responses that exceed the average mean for each of the nine propositions: the former Soviet Union (9 of 9); Venezuela (7 of 9); the People's Republic of China (6 of 9); Chile (4 of 9); the United States, Japan, and Yugoslavia (3 of 9 each); and Germany (1 of 9). This corresponds to 18 of 27 (67 percent) for the three collectivist countries, compared to 11 of 18 (61 percent) and 7 of 27 (26 percent) for the two Latin American and the three market oriented countries, respectively.

Each of the nine value propositions relating to the organizational belief system value focuses on the importance and central role of the group as it relates to the performance of work. Except for the average mean of proposition 4 pertaining to the importance of group recognition, and, to a lesser extent, proposition 9 pertaining to the necessity of conformity in an organization, all average means are very high (ranging from 3.38 to 3.76). This suggests a relatively high emphasis is placed on the organizational belief system value, and collectivism in general, by the respondents as a whole compared to the average mean responses to the work ethic discussed in Chapter 3.

Table 4.1 shows the overall emphasis placed on the organizational belief system value of respondents from each of the eight countries involved in our research survey. This overall emphasis is the combined responses to the nine value propositions summarized previously. The chi square analysis indicates that there are significant differences (.00 level) in the overall emphasis on the organizational belief system value according to the country of the respondents (.58 coefficient of contingency). On the basis of the overall mean responses shown on Table 4.1, two collectivist countries, the former Soviet Union (3.68) and the

Table 4.1
Overall Emphasis on the Organizational Belief System

A	Response Frequency (%)					N	X̄	Scheffe Test							B
	1	2	3	4	5			GER.	U.S.	JAPAN	YUG.	P.R.C.	F.S.U.	VEN.	CHILE
GER.	4.8	19.7	34.0	35.5	6.0	895	3.18								
U.S.	4.7	19.2	30.0	36.0	10.1	1773	3.28	X							
JAPAN	5.1	15.3	37.6	33.5	8.5	298	3.25								
YUG.	5.2	15.6	31.9	37.2	10.0	718	3.31	X							
P.R.C.	2.9	16.8	18.8	54.7	6.8	990	3.46	X	X	X	X				X
F.S.U.	2.4	10.2	20.4	51.2	15.8	1242	3.68	X	X	X	X	X		X	X
VEN.	7.5	14.1	18.0	40.9	19.5	953	3.51	X	X	X	X				X
CHILE	5.5	20.2	23.1	40.5	10.8	310	3.31	X							
TOTAL	4.5	16.3	25.9	42.0	11.3	7179	3.37								

Total mean = average of eight means
Chi Square (Pearson) = 3685.99 (.00 level)
Coefficient of Contingency = .58
1 = Strongly Disagree; 5 = Strongly Agree

* = Significantly greater emphasis for each pair of countries (.05 level)-A versus B

ANOVA F Ratio = 233.05 (.00 level)

People's Republic of China (3.46), and one Latin American country, Venezuela (3.51), place a greater emphasis on the organizational belief system value relative to the respondents from the other countries. The respondents from the three market-oriented countries, Germany, Japan, and the United States, and those from Yugoslavia and Chile place a lower relative emphasis on this value.

The ANOVA Scheffe test results shown on Table 4.1 further confirm these differences. In terms of these paired comparisons, the respondents from the former Soviet Union place a higher emphasis on the organizational belief system value than do the respondents from each of the other seven countries. Moreover, the respondents from Venezuela and the People's Republic of China place a higher emphasis on this value than those respondents from five of the seven comparison countries. Of the three collectivist countries, it seems unusual that the respondents from Yugoslavia, with the historical emphasis on worker management as an organizational work mechanism in that country, place a lower emphasis on the organizational belief system value. Moreover, the lower emphasis placed on this value by respondents from Japan is unexpected.

Humanistic Belief System

The humanistic belief system value focuses on the process of work itself, in addition to (or rather than) only the output of that process. This value reflects the extent to which a person believes that work is important to discover or fulfill oneself as a human being. Thus, opportunity for individual growth and development on the job can be a major incentive or motivator for performance. Since work is an indispensable human activity, which for most people cannot be eliminated, it must be made meaningful and fulfilling to those people working in organizational settings. This concept of humanistic belief system is similar in some respect to Maslow's (1954) self-actualization concept as a motivator of performance. Work must be redesigned, or a person must have mobility to seek more challenging jobs, so that the person can reach higher levels of development, rather than only fulfilling material or lower order needs and wants.

The humanistic belief system consists of 10 value propositions summarized later. The mean responses of respondents from each country surveyed, and the average mean (A.M.) of the eight means, are also shown for each proposition. These value propositions reflect similar dimensions of the humanistic belief system used by Buchholz (1976).

1. Work can be made satisfying.

YUG.	U.S.	VEN.	F.S.U.	GER.	CHILE	A.M.	P.R.C.	JAPAN
4.21	4.18	4.05	4.04	3.94	3.83	3.83	3.32	3.10

2. The workplace can be humanized.

F.S.U.	VEN.	YUG.	GER.	U.S.	A.M.	CHILE	JAPAN	P.R.C.
4.30	4.18	4.16	4.08	4.08	3.96	3.88	3.85	3.13

3. Work can be made interesting.

VEN.	U.S.	F.S.U.	GER.	CHILE	A.M.	YUG.	P.R.C.	JAPAN
4.24	4.15	4.10	3.92	3.92	3.90	3.73	3.58	3.52

4. Work can be a means of self-expression.

YUG.	U.S.	VEN.	GER.	A.M.	F.S.U.	CHILE	P.R.C.	JAPAN
4.15	4.09	4.03	3.90	3.85	3.77	3.72	3.65	3.05

5. Work can be organized to allow human fulfillment.

YUG.	U.S.	F.S.U.	GER.	A.M.	VEN.	CHILE	P.R.C.	JAPAN
4.19	4.05	3.95	3.91	3.87	3.86	3.72	3.71	3.60

6. A job can provide new experiences.

YUG.	U.S.	F.S.U.	GER.	VEN.	A.M.	CHILE	P.R.C.	JAPAN
4.07	4.06	4.03	3.92	3.92	3.92	3.84	3.77	3.73

7. Work should enable us to learn new things.

VEN.	U.S.	F.S.U.	YUG.	A.M.	GER.	P.R.C.	CHILE	JAPAN
4.23	4.16	4.15	4.09	4.06	4.03	4.01	3.89	3.88

8. Work should allow use of human capabilities.

F.S.U.	VEN.	U.S.	GER.	A.M.	P.R.C.	CHILE	YUG.	JAPAN
4.23	4.23	4.07	4.04	3.96	3.79	3.77	3.76	3.75

9. Jobs should provide opportunities to try new ideas.

F.S.U.	YUG.	U.S.	VEN.	A.M.	JAPAN	GER.	P.R.C.	CHILE
4.20	4.12	4.09	4.04	4.01	3.97	3.96	3.90	3.78

10. Work can be made meaningful.

VEN.	U.S.	YUG.	F.S.U.	GER.	A.M.	JAPAN	P.R.C.	CHILE
4.23	4.12	4.10	4.04	3.99	3.97	3.82	3.74	3.70

The combined group of these 10 value propositions reflects the overall emphasis placed on the humanistic belief system value by respondents from each country, and for the combined respondents from the eight countries as measured by the average mean. Using the average mean as a general indicator, the respondents from the following countries have mean responses which exceed (or equal) the average mean for each of the preceding value propositions: United States (10 of 10); the former Soviet Union and Venezuela (9 of 10 each); Germany and Yugoslavia (8 of 10 each); and Chile (2 of 10). Moreover, the frequency of mean responses higher than the average mean for respondents from the three market-oriented countries is 18 of 30 (60 percent), compared to 17 of 30 (57 percent) and 11 of 20 (55 percent) for the respondents from the three collectivist and the two Latin American countries, respectively.

Respondents from one country in each of these three groups of countries place a relatively lower emphasis on humanistic work belief system: Japan, the People's Republic of China, and Chile. The similar higher emphasis placed on the humanistic belief system by respondents from Germany, the United States, the former Soviet Union, Yugoslavia, and Venezuela is somewhat difficult to explain at this time in our analysis; therefore, this topic will be revisited later. However, at this time it should be noted that the mean responses for all respondent groups are very high for all of the 10 value propositions, compared to mean responses for the other value propositions discussed earlier, and especially for those relating to individualism in Chapter 1. Any differences that exist pertaining to the emphasis placed on the humanistic belief system value occur within a high range of mean responses.

Table 4.2 shows the overall emphasis on the humanistic belief system value by respondents from the countries surveyed. This emphasis is the combined responses to the ten value propositions summarized here. The chi square analysis indicates that there are some significant differences (.00 level) in the overall emphasis on the humanistic work belief system value according to the country of the respondents (.62 coefficient of contingency). As mentioned earlier, all of the overall mean responses are very high, indicating a high emphasis is placed on this value by all eight groups of respondents.

The ANOVA Scheff test results shown on Table 4.2 indicate where there are significant differences in responses by respondents from pairs of countries. The United States (5 of 7), and Yugoslavia, the former Soviet Union, and Venezuela (4 of 7 each), stand out as placing a somewhat higher overall emphasis on the humanistic work belief system value.

The humanistic work belief system results are different than those for the organizational work belief system. While respondents from Venezula

Table 4.2
Overall Emphasis on the Humanistic Work Belief System

| | Response Frequency (%) | | | | | | | Scheffe Test (B) | | | | | | | |
A	1	2	3	4	5	N	$\bar{X}$	GER.	U.S.	JAPAN	YUG.	P.R.C.	F.S.U.	VEN.	CHILE
GER.	0.8	3.7	11.8	65.3	18.4	895	3.97			X		X			X
U.S.	0.9	2.9	7.3	62.5	26.4	1773	4.11	X		X	X	X			X
JAPAN	2.2	7.9	24.2	51.2	14.4	300	3.67								
YUG.	1.5	2.6	9.9	60.2	25.8	717	4.06	X		X		X			X
P.R.C.	2.3	11.0	14.2	62.6	9.9	990	3.67								
F.S.U.	1.0	2.2	8.2	64.7	23.9	1242	4.08	X		X		X			X
VEN.	2.9	4.7	5.3	53.9	33.3	952	4.10	X		X		X			X
CHILE	3.2	7.6	13.6	57.8	17.8	310	3.79			X		X			
TOTAL	1.6	4.6	9.9	61.2	22.7	7179	3.93								

Total mean = average of eight means
Chi Square (Pearson) = 4430.79 (.00 level)
Coefficient of Contingency = .62
1 = Strongly Disagree; 5 = Strongly Agree

* = Significantly greater emphasis for each pair of countries (.05 level)-A versus B

ANOVA F Ratio = 424.35 (.00 level)

and the former Soviet Union place a higher emphasis on both, those from the United States and Yugoslavia do not (e.g., lower emphases on the organizational work belief system and a higher emphasis on the humanistic belief system.) Although we are treating both of these work belief values within the general umbrella of a collectivistic ethic, they are at best only indirectly related. While the organizational work belief system clearly fits into the collectivistic ethic, only some aspects of the humanistic work belief system can be classified as collectivist. These relate to the notion that the general consideration for people at work in terms other than primarily as an economic resource without social and human needs is a collectivist notion to some extent.

Marxist Belief System

The Marxist belief system value views productive activity or work as necessary for, or basic to, human fulfillment. Work is necessary to satisfy a person's physical needs. Moreover, through work a person creates an environment to keep in touch with his fellow human beings. However, the Marxist belief system contends that in noncollectivist countries, work does not allow a person to be fulfilled as a creative and social individual. Instead, the work of the average person mainly benefits the ownership class of society, rather than the workers themselves, and they become exploited and alienated from their productivity. Furthermore, the Marxist view contends that value comes from the work of the labor class, not the ownership class, and therefore organizational work systems must be structured so that workers reap the benefits of their productivity. Moreover, the distributors of rewards must be influenced primarily by inputs from the working class.

The Marxist belief system consists of the following 11 value propositions. The mean responses of respondents from each country surveyed, and the average mean (A.M.) of the eight means, are also shown for each proposition. These value propositions reflect similar dimensions used by Buchholz (1976) for the Marxist belief system.

1. Management does not understand workers' needs.

YUG.	P.R.C.	F.S.U.	CHILE	JAPAN	VEN.	A.M.	GER.	U.S.
3.58	3.31	3.22	3.20	3.19	3.15	3.14	2.89	2.60

2. Workers should be on boards of directors of business firms.

F.S.U.	P.R.C.	YUG.	CHILE	JAPAN	A.M.	GER.	U.S.	VEN.
3.95	3.87	3.80	3.76	3.75	3.75	3.65	3.61	3.61

3. Organizations run better if workers have a say in management.

F.S.U.	P.R.C.	U.S.	CHILE	A.M.	JAPAN	VEN.	YUG.	GER.
3.96	3.72	3.54	3.53	3.50	3.39	3.36	3.32	3.15

4. Society's most important work is done by the labor class.

P.R.C.	VEN.	F.S.U.	CHILE	JAPAN	A.M.	GER.	YUG.	U.S.
3.65	3.33	3.31	3.27	3.25	3.19	2.96	2.92	2.81

5. The labor class should have more say in running society.

P.R.C.	VEN.	JAPAN	F.S.U.	A.M.	JAPAN	CHILE	GER.	U.S.
3.84	3.66	3.58	3.45	3.40	3.33	3.19	3.16	3.00

6. Wealthy people do not carry their fair share of a country's burdens.

YUG.	F.S.U.	CHILE	A.M.	GER.	U.S.	VEN.	P.R.C.	JAPAN
3.86	3.62	3.44	3.38	3.32	3.24	3.23	3.22	3.07

7. Rich people do not make much of a contribution to society.

F.S.U.	JAPAN	YUG.	A.M.	VEN.	P.R.C.	CHILE	GER.	U.S.
3.65	3.04	2.98	2.96	2.95	2.90	2.81	2.80	2.54

8. Work of the labor class is exploited by rich people.

P.R.C.	CHILE	YUG.	JAPAN	A.M.	VEN.	F.S.U.	U.S.	GER.
3.41	3.34	3.13	3.10	3.08	3.04	2.97	2.83	2.82

9. Workers should be more involved in decisions about products, finance, and investment.

F.S.U.	P.R.C.	JAPAN	YUG.	A.M.	U.S.	GER.	VEN.	CHILE
3.80	3.60	3.49	3.37	3.29	3.21	2.94	2.94	2.94

10. The free enterprise system mainly benefits rich and powerful people.

JAPAN	P.R.C.	CHILE	A.M.	F.S.U.	YUG.	GER.	U.S.	VEN.
3.35	3.31	3.18	2.97	2.96	2.84	2.82	2.65	2.63

11. Workers do not get a fair share of society's economic rewards.

VEN.	CHILE	YUG.	F.S.U.	A.M.	P.R.C.	GER.	U.S.	JAPAN
3.92	3.82	3.79	3.71	3.34	3.12	3.06	3.03	2.25

The combined group of 11 value propositions reflects the overall emphasis placed on the Marxist belief system value by respondents from each country, and for the combined respondents from all of the countries as measured by the average mean. The respondents from the following countries have mean responses that exceed the average mean for each of the propositions: the former Soviet Union (9 of 11); Japan, the People's Republic of China, and Chile (8 of 11 each); Yugoslavia (7 of 11); Venezuela (4 of 11); and the United States (1 of 11).

Except for the respondents from Japan, the combined mean responses for each group of respondents, market-oriented, collectivist, and Latin American, tend to coincide with traditional expectations. For example, the combined respondents from the three collectivist countries have higher mean responses than the overall mean response for 24 of the possible 33 value propositions (73 percent), compared to 12 of 22 (55 percent) and 9 of 33 (27 percent) for the respondents from the two Latin American and three market-oriented countries, respectively.

The unusually higher response of the Japanese respondents (8 of 11) may be attributed to the historical emphasis on social and economic class divisions. Moreover, it is interesting to note that the mean response to value proposition 3 by the Japanese respondents is lower than the average mean response. One would expect that the Japanese respondents would more strongly support this value proposition--"Organizations run better if workers have a say in management"--given the historical emphasis on worker involvement provided by Japanese managers. These results suggest that the involvement may not be as meaningful as often publicized in the literature and in other general news media.

Conversely, the relatively higher mean response of those from the United States, compared to Japanese respondents for proposition 3, suggests more meaningful participative management practices are desired. It is also peculiar that Yugoslavia's worker-management system is not reflected in a higher mean response for this value proposition. by the respondents from this country. The Yugoslav respondents' mean response is the second lowest of the eight countries surveyed for this value proposition.

It is interesting to note the lower emphasis placed on value propositions 2, 3, and 9 by the respondents from Germany. These three propositions advocate that workers should be more involved in management decisions. Even though German business organizations by law are required to involve workers in decisions throughout all levels of the organization through the board of directors (industrial democracy), the respondents from Germany tend to place a lower emphasis on this general concept of worker involvement.

From an overall standpoint, except for propositions 7 and 10, dealing with the rich people's importance to society, the average mean responses tend to be high, ranging from 3.08 (proposition 8) to 3.75 (proposition 2). This tends to indicate that there is some support for the Marxist belief system value by the combined respondents, compared to the general tendency toward the individualism value discussed in Chapter 1.

Table 4.3 shows the overall emphasis placed on the Marxist belief system value of respondents from the eight countries surveyed. This overall emphasis is the combined responses to the 11 value propositions summarized earlier for each country. The chi square analysis indicates that there are significant differences (.00 level) in the overall emphasis placed on the Marxist belief system value according to the country of the respondents (.60 coefficient of contingency). The average mean of the eight countries is 3.28 (which ranged from 3.01 to 3.52) seems higher than expected. Since most of the data collected for this survey were obtained during 1990 - 1991, the period of considerable movement toward market and democratic societies throughout major parts of the world, you would expect less emphasis on Marxist values.

The ANOVA Scheffe test results shown on Table 4.3 indicate the significant differences in mean responses from the pairs of countries surveyed. Respondents from the People's Republic of China and the former Soviet Union place a higher relative emphasis on the Marxist value than those from the other six countries, as expected, while the respondents from Japan, Venezuela, Chile, and Yugoslavia place a greater emphasis on this value than those from Germany and the United States. The respondents from Yugoslavia also place a greater emphasis on the Marxist value than those from Japan and Venezuela.

PATERNALISM AS A CULTURAL VALUE

Closely related to Buchholz's organizational, humanistic, and Marxist work belief system, is paternalism. In an important extension of Hofstede's research, Dorfman and Howell (1988) investigated the four dimensions of national culture used by Hofstede, but added paternalism as a fifth basic cultural value. This value focuses on the responsibility of management of the firm for providing both economic and social support to resolve workplace and personal problems of workers. In this respect, the firm through its management structure has an obligation to

Table 4.3
Overall Emphasis on the Marxist Belief System

| A | Response Frequency (%) | | | | | | | Scheffe Test | | | | | | | |
	1	2	3	4	5	N	X̄	GER.	U.S.	JAPAN	YUG.	P.R.C.	F.S.U.	VEN.	CHILE
GER.	5.0	25.6	34.7	29.0	5.7	896	3.05								
U.S.	8.3	27.0	29.2	26.8	8.8	1773	3.01								
JAPAN	5.7	17.5	36.1	30.7	10.1	301	3.22	X	X						
YUG.	5.5	16.0	28.5	37.3	12.7	717	3.36	X	X	X					
P.R.C.	3.0	18.7	18.2	49.8	10.4	989	3.46	X	X	X	X			X	
F.S.U.	3.9	15.4	20.8	44.5	15.4	1242	3.52	X	X	X	X			X	
VEN.	7.9	20.0	24.3	34.3	13.6	953	3.26	X	X						
CHILE	5.1	19.1	25.9	38.6	11.3	311	3.32	X	X					X	
TOTAL	5.9	21.1	26.5	35.8	10.9	7182	3.28								

B

* = Significantly greater emphasis for each pair of countries
(.05 level)-A versus B

ANOVA F Ratio = 367.49 (.00 level)

Total mean = average of eight means
Chi Square (Pearson) = 4096.13 (.00 level)
Coefficient of Contingency = .60
1 = Strongly Disagree; 5 = Strongly Agree

look after workers and subordinates as both workers and persons with unique problems that often may be only indirectly related, or not related at all, to their jobs. Thus, paternalism as a cultural value fits into the overall collectivism value.

Paternalism as a cultural value consists of the five value propositions summarized next. The mean responses of respondents from each country surveyed, and the average mean (A.M.) of the eight means, are also shown for each proposition. These value propositions reflect similar dimensions used by Dorfman and Howell (1988) for the paternalism value.

1. Managers should be interested in the personal problems of subordinates.

F.S.U.	YUG.	VEN.	GER.	A.M.	P.R.C.	U.S.	CHILE	JAPAN
4.16	3.96	3.76	3.72	3.70	3.69	3.50	3.46	3.32

2. Managers should ensure that workers earn enough for food and clothing.

VEN.	F.S.U.	GER.	U.S.	A.M.	CHILE	P.R.C.	JAPAN	YUG.
4.16	4.15	3.99	3.93	3.92	3.89	3.84	3.78	3.62

3. Managers should take a personal interest in problems of employees that affect performance.

VEN.	F.S.U.	U.S.	A.M.	GER.	P.R.C.	YUG.	CHILE	JAPAN
4.16	4.15	3.96	3.90	3.87	3.85	3.84	3.76	3.61

4. The firm should look out for employees as both persons and workers.

VEN.	F.S.U.	GER.	CHILE	A.M.	YUG.	P.R.C.	JAPAN	U.S.
4.46	4.29	4.26	4.04	3.98	3.79	3.68	3.65	3.63

5. The firm should provide lifetime job security.

VEN.	F.S.U.	CHILE	YUG.	A.M.	JAPAN	GER.	U.S.	P.R.C.
4.28	4.16	3.87	3.76	3.76	3.74	3.60	3.46	3.24

The combined group of these five value propositions reflects the overall emphasis placed on paternalism as a cultural value by respondents from each country, and for the combined respondents from the eight countries as measured by the average mean. The respondents from the following countries have mean responses which exceed the average mean for each of the value propositions: the former Soviet Union and Venezuela (5 of 5); Germany (3 of 5); and the United States, Yugoslavia, and Chile (2 of 5 each). Moreover, the frequency of mean responses higher than the average mean for the two Latin American countries is 7 of 10 (70 percent), compared to 7 of 15 (47 percent) and 5 of 15 (33 percent) for combined respondents from the three collectivist and three market-oriented countries, respectively.

The mean responses of respondents from the three collectivist countries vary considerably. The respondents from the former Soviet Union tend to place a higher emphasis on paternalism than those from the People's Republic of China for all of the five value propositions. Venezuela's respondents seem to place a similar emphasis on paternalism to those from the former Soviet Union. There does not seem to be an unusual pattern of mean responses for any specific proposition related to paternalism as a cultural value.

Table 4.4 shows the overall emphasis on paternalism as a cultural value by respondents from the eight countries surveyed. This emphasis is the combined responses to the five value propositions summarized. The chi square analysis indicates there are some significant differences (.00 level) in the overall emphasis on paternalism as a cultural value according to the country surveyed (.52 coefficient of contingency). The overall emphasis on paternalism, as measured by the combined mean responses of respondents from each country, is quite high, ranging from 3.62 (Japan) to 4.18 (former Soviet Union), with an average mean of 3.85 for the eight countries.

The ANOVA Scheffe test results indicate where there are significant differences in the emphasis placed on paternalism as a cultural value as reflected in differences in mean responses of respondents in various pairs of countries. Table 4.4 shows the higher overall emphasis placed on paternalism by the respondents from the former Soviet Union and Venezuela compared to the respondents from the other six countries (mean responses of 4.18 and 4.17, respectively). The overall emphasis placed on paternalism by respondents from Germany, Yugoslavia, and Chile is relatively higher when compared to that of the respondents from Japan, the People's Republic of China, and the United States.

The average mean responses for all of the four collectivistic values discussed thus far in this chapter are quite high--organizational, 3.37 (Table 4.1); humanistic, 3.93 (Table 4.2); Marxist, 3.28 (Table 4.3); and paternalism, 3.85 (Table 4.4)--especially when compared to the set of values relating to individualism discussed in Chapter 1.

Table 4.4
Overall Emphasis on Paternalism

A	Response Frequency (%)					N	X̄	Scheffe Test (B)							
	1	2	3	4	5			GER.	U.S.	JAPAN	YUG.	P.R.C.	F.S.U.	VEN.	CHILE
GER.	3.2	7.0	14.3	48.8	26.6	892	3.89		X	X	X	X			
U.S.	3.6	10.5	19.8	44.8	21.2	1770	3.70								
JAPAN	3.1	9.6	25.6	45.7	16.1	285	3.62								
YUG.	3.6	7.4	14.5	54.8	19.6	702	3.80		X	X		X			
P.R.C.	3.0	11.5	12.2	62.5	10.7	989	3.66								
F.S.U.	1.1	2.5	5.9	58.6	32.0	1234	4.18	X	X	X	X	X			
VEN.	1.4	4.5	8.0	48.1	38.0	948	4.17	X	X	X	X	X			X
CHILE	4.0	10.4	13.6	45.4	26.6	306	3.80		X	X		X		X	
TOTAL	2.7	7.7	13.5	51.6	24.5	7126	3.85								

Total mean = average of eight means
Chi Square (Pearson) = 2660.41 (.00 level)
Coefficient of Contingency = .52
1 = Strongly Disagree; 5 = Strongly Agree

* = Significantly greater emphasis for each pair of countries (.05 level)-A versus B

ANOVA F Ratio = 256.86 (.00 level)

FAMILY SOCIAL COHESION AND STATUS AS A VALUE

The emphasis on family social cohesion and status as a family value is measured by responses to the five value propositions summarized next. The mean responses of those from each country, and the average mean (A.M.) of the eight means, are also shown. These five value propositions were developed and patterned after similar propositions found throughout sociological literature, and they were presented to respondents within the context of their overall importance to the family.

1. Time spent with the family is more important than time spent at work.

U.S.	VEN.	CHILE	GER.	YUG.	A.M.	JAPAN	F.S.U.	P.R.C.
3.93	3.82	3.68	3.65	3.65	3.59	3.56	3.39	3.04

2. Bearing and raising children is an essential goal in life.

VEN.	YUG.	GER.	P.R.C.	F.S.U.	CHILE	A.M.	U.S.	JAPAN
4.06	3.86	3.62	3.61	3.61	3.60	3.60	3.58	2.91

3. Family honor and community status are the most important family goals.

YUG.	P.R.C.	VEN.	F.S.U.	A.M.	CHILE	JAPAN	U.S.	GER.
3.63	3.57	3.36	3.17	3.09	3.06	2.80	2.61	2.50

4. Family members should care for each other and share experiences.

F.S.U.	U.S.	YUG.	GER.	VEN.	A.M.	P.R.C.	CHILE	JAPAN
4.34	4.33	4.28	4.15	4.14	4.12	4.01	3.94	3.79

5. Older family members should make sacrifices for education and advancement of younger members.

U.S.	VEN.	P.R.C.	YUG.	F.S.U.	A.M.	CHILE	GER.	JAPAN
3.55	3.49	3.26	3.25	3.21	3.20	3.15	3.06	2.62

The combined group of these five value propositions reflects the overall emphasis on family cohesion and status by respondents from each country, and for the combined respondents from the eight countries surveyed. With the average mean of the eight countries as a general indicator, the respondents from the following countries have mean responses that exceed (or equal) the average mean response for each of the value propositions: Yugoslavia and Venezuela (5 of 5 each); the former Soviet Union (4 of 5); Germany, the United States, and the

People's Republic of China (3 of 5 each); and Chile (2 of 5). This corresponds to 12 of 15 (80 percent) for the combined respondents from the three collectivist countries, compared to 7 of 10 (70 percent) and 6 of 15 (40 percent) for the combined respondents from the two Latin American and three market-oriented countries, respectively. The respondents from Yugoslavia, Venezuela, and the former Soviet Union tend to place a greater overall emphasis on social cohesion and status as a family value when compared to the respondents from the other countries surveyed.

Table 4.5 shows the overall emphasis on social cohesion and status as a family value by respondents from each of the eight countries surveyed. This emphasis reflects the combined responses to the five value propositions referred to previously. The chi square analysis indicates that there are some significant differences (.00 level) in the overall emphasis on family cohesion and status according to the country of the respondents (.43 coefficient of contingency). As in the case of the other four collectivism values discussed earlier in this chapter, all of the overall mean responses of respondents from each country are quite high, ranging from 3.14 (Japan) to 3.77 (Venezuela), with an average mean of 3.52 for the eight countries.

The ANOVA Scheffe test results indicate where differences in mean responses are significant. For example, respondents from Venezuela and Yugoslavia place a higher emphasis on social cohesion and status as a family value than do the respondents from the other six countries surveyed, with the United States showing the next highest emphasis when compared to respondents from Germany, Japan, the People's Republic of China, and Chile.

SUMMARY AND CONCLUSIONS

This chapter compares the relative overall emphasis placed on collectivism by the respondents from the eight countries surveyed. This comparison focuses on five specific values which reflect a general tendency toward collectivism as a general value. These include three workplace values relating to organizational, humanistic, and Marxist work belief systems; one cultural value relating to paternalism; and one value relating to social cohesion and status in the family. Respondents who emphasize these five values have a higher mean response to a set of value propositions which measures the extent to which each value is

Table 4.5
Overall Emphasis on Family Social Cohesion and Status

A	Response Frequency (%)					N	X̄
	1	2	3	4	5		
GER.	4.6	17.6	25.9	36.7	15.1	890	3.40
U.S.	5.4	14.3	18.9	37.7	23.7	1770	3.60
JAPAN	6.9	20.3	35.1	27.1	10.6	294	3.14
YUG.	2.2	10.0	22.1	43.3	22.4	704	3.73
P.R.C.	2.9	17.6	16.8	52.1	10.7	990	3.50
F.S.U.	2.9	13.3	28.3	37.1	18.4	1236	3.55
VEN.	3.7	12.9	14.4	41.4	27.7	948	3.77
CHILE	5.3	17.7	19.4	38.3	19.2	303	3.48
TOTAL	4.0	14.8	21.5	40.1	19.6	7135	3.52

Total mean = average of eight means
Chi Square (Pearson) = 1590.72 (.00 level)
Coefficient of Contingency = .43
1 = Strongly Disagree; 5 = Strongly Agree

B

Scheffe Test

A \ B	GER.	U.S.	JAPAN	YUG.	P.R.C.	F.S.U.	VEN.	CHILE
GER.			X					
U.S.	X		X		X			X
JAPAN								
YUG.	X	X	X		X	X		X
P.R.C.	X		X					
F.S.U.	X		X					
VEN.	X	X	X		X	X		X
CHILE			X					

* = Significantly greater emphasis for each pair of countries (.05 level)-A versus B

ANOVA F Ratio = 84.25 (.00 level)

emphasized. For example, the attributes of collectivism are preference for organizational/group arrangements relating to performance of work; preference for jobs that provide opportunities for learning and growth; recognition of the value of workers relative to managers/wealth holders; concern for personal problems of workers; and recognition of the importance of family social cohesion.

On the basis of the Scheffe test that compared mean responses of respondents from each country with those of each of the other seven countries, Table 4.6 summarizes the overall tendency toward collectivism as measured by the preceding five values. The values 1 through 5 are taken from Tables 4.1 through 4.5, respectively. The numerical data shown on Table 4.6 are the frequencies of significantly higher mean responses, ranging from 0 to 7, when each country's respondents' mean responses are compared to respondents' mean responses from each of the other seven countries using the Scheffe test of paired comparisons. A group of respondents with a higher overall emphasis on collectivism will have higher frequencies for values one through five, indicating a greater number of times their mean responses were higher than those of the other countries in the survey. In terms of the frequency data shown on Table 4.6, the following paragraphs discuss each country's overall emphasis on collectivism.

As a group, the respondents from the three market-oriented countries place a lower overall emphasis on collectivism than those from the other two groups of countries. The frequencies of higher mean responses are 23 percent, 29 percent, and 6 percent for respondents from Germany, the United States, and Japan, respectively.

As you would expect, the respondents from the three collectivist countries place a greater overall emphasis on collectivism: Yugoslavia 51 percent and the former Soviet Union 71 percent. Except for value 5 dealing with family cohesion and status, the frequency of mean responses for the former Soviet Union's respondents was very high. The respondents from the People's Republic of China have only two relatively high frequencies of responses, organizational belief system (5 of 7) and Marxist belief system (6 of 7).

Venezuela's respondents are quite similar to those of the former Soviet Union in terms of frequency of mean responses significantly higher for paired comparisons (66 percent). However, these respondents from Venezuela have a lower frequency of mean response for the Marxist belief system (2 of 7) and a higher frequency for family cohesion and status (6 of 7), which are the reverse of the frequencies of

Table 4.6
Summary of the Overall Tendency Toward Collectivism

VALUES	GER.	U.S.	JAPAN	YUG.	P.R.C.	F.S.U.	VEN.	CHILE
1. Organizational Belief System	0	1	0	1	5	7	5	1
2. Humanistic Belief System	3	5	0	4	0	4	4	2
3. Marxist Belief System	0	0	2	4	6	6	2	2
4. Paternalism	4	0	0	3	0	6	6	3
5. Family Social Cohesion and Status	1	4	0	6	2	2	6	1
Combined Emphasis (1-5)	8	10	2	18	13	25	23	9
As a Percent of Maximum	23%	29%	6%	51%	37%	71%	66%	26%

Numbers equal frequency of significantly higher mean responses using ANOVA Scheffe test paired comparisons (0 - 7 is possible range of frequencies) for each of the five values (maximum total frequency = 35).

the former Soviet Union. Chile's respondents' overall emphasis on collectivism is similar to that of those from Germany and the United States as measured by the frequency of mean responses (26 percent).

In conclusion, the respondents from the former Soviet Union, Venezuela, and Yugoslavia place a greater overall emphasis on collectivism as a general value compared to those from the other five groups of respondents surveyed. It is somewhat surprising that the respondents from Japan reflect the lowest overall tendency toward collectivism on the basis of the data shown on Table 4.6. Even though Japan is viewed as a market-oriented country, except for the Marxist belief system value, these respondents' relative emphasis on organizational and humanistic belief systems (values 1 and 2), as well as paternalism and family status (values 4 and 5), seems to be somewhat unexpected.

5

Profile of Value Priorities

An analysis of significantly different values according to the country of the respondents was presented in Chapter 3 (individualism values) and Chapter 4 (collectivism values). This analysis focused on the significant differences in mean responses between pairs of countries surveyed using chi square and ANOVA procedures. Moreover, the analysis focused on mean responses to individual value propositions that pertained to a number of values falling within the two broad value tendencies, individualism and collectivism. This chapter continues this analysis by contrasting the value preferences pertaining to individualism and collectivism to ascertain the extent of congruence of the responses of respondents from each country involved. Then an analysis of the ranking of a set of values by respondents in each country follows. Finally, a value profile is developed for the respondents from each of the eight countries.

CONGRUENCE OF VALUES

There are certain expected relationships between preferences for individualism versus collectivism as major values. For example, you would expect a person who places a greater emphasis on individualism to have a lower preference for collectivism, and vice versa. In the previous two chapters the analysis focused on comparing the differences in mean responses according to the country of the respondents. These overall mean responses relating to the five values that directly reflect an overall tendency toward individualism are shown in Tables 3.1 through 3.5 of Chapter 3. Similarly, those overall mean responses relating to the five values that reflect an overall tendency toward collectivism are shown in Tables 4.1 through 4.5 of Chapter 4. Table 5.1 summarizes the value preferences of the eight groups of respondents using the data from those

Table 5.1
Summary of Value Preferences in Terms of Overall Mean Responses

VALUES	GER.	U.S.	JAPAN	YUG.	P.R.C.	F.S.U.	VEN.	CHILE	A.M.
Individualism									
3.1 Work Ethic	2.91	2.62	2.90	3.17	3.44	3.45	2.83	2.74	3.01
3.2 Personal Individualism	3.17	3.28	3.15	3.22	2.70	3.08	3.10	3.15	3.11
3.3 Masculinity	2.18	2.12	2.66	2.38	3.18	3.67	2.18	2.48	2.61
3.4 Family Individualism	3.48	3.68	3.40	3.77	3.52	3.54	3.49	3.31	3.52
3.5 Family Economic Orientation	2.89	2.93	2.67	2.86	2.82	2.76	2.82	2.96	2.84
Combined (3.1 - 3.5)	2.93	2.93	2.96	3.08	3.13	3.30	2.88	2.93	3.04
Collectivism									
4.1 Organizational Belief System	3.18	3.28	3.25	3.31	3.46	3.68	3.51	3.31	3.37
4.2 Humanistic Belief System	3.97	4.11	3.67	4.06	3.67	4.08	4.10	3.79	3.93
4.3 Marxist Belief System	3.05	3.01	3.22	3.36	3.46	3.52	3.26	3.32	3.28
4.4 Paternalism	3.89	3.70	3.62	3.80	3.66	4.18	4.17	3.80	3.85
4.5 Family Social Cohesion/Status	3.40	3.60	3.14	3.73	3.50	3.55	3.77	3.48	3.52
Combined (4.1 - 4.5)	3.50	3.54	3.38	3.65	3.55	3.80	3.76	3.54	3.61

Note: Mean responses in bold type equal or exceed the average mean (A.M.).

10 tables. Moreover, a combined mean of the five mean responses for each of the five groups of values that provides a general measure of the overall tendency toward individualism and collectivism by respondents from each country is shown. These two combined mean responses for each country are as follows (bold type indicates that the mean response is greater than the average mean):

	Individualism	Collectivism
Germany	2.93	3.50
United States	2.93	3.54
Japan	2.96	3.38
Yugoslavia	**3.08**	**3.65**
People's Republic of China	**3.13**	3.55
The former Soviet Union	**3.30**	**3.80**
Venezuela	2.88	**3.76**
Chile	2.93	3.54
Average Mean	3.04	3.61

The respondents from all countries place a lower emphasis on individualism compared to collectivism as a value priority if we consider only the previous combined mean responses. In other words, the combined mean responses are lower for individualism than for collectivism for respondents in each country. Furthermore, the combined mean responses for all of the three collectivist countries are higher for both the individualism and collectivism values, with the exception of Venezuela's for collectivism (3.76). Therefore, in a general way, the respondents from the three collectivist countries as a group tend to place a greater emphasis on both individualism and collectivism than do respondents from the other countries, with the exception of Venezuela, as noted, for collectivism.

To ascertain the general congruence of value preferences, we can compare the five values pertaining to individualism to the five values pertaining to collectivism that are shown on Table 5.1. The mean responses for two sets of five values each by the respondents from each country should be inversely related. For example, we would expect respondents with a higher overall emphasis on individualism to have a lower overall emphasis on collectivism, and vice versa. The latter is generally the case as shown on Table 5.1 in that there tends to be a greater emphasis on collectivism compared to individualism for all of the respondent groups: that is, a difference exists for each country's relative emphasis on each of the two general values.

We now want to summarize the differences in each respondent group's emphasis on individualism or collectivism when compared to each of the other seven groups of respondents using the Scheffe test of paired comparison of mean responses. This information was shown earlier on Table 3.9 (individualism) and Table 4.6 (collectivism). A summary of these frequencies of significantly different mean responses for respondents from each country is as follows for each of the two values:

	Individualism	Collectivism
Germany	8	8
United States	17	10
Japan	8	2
Yugoslavia	20	18
People's Republic of China	14	13
The Former Soviet Union	16	25
Venezuela	4	23
Chile	10	9

In terms of the frequency data, in a general way, the frequencies of significantly higher mean responses of respondents from the United States and Japan for each of the two ethics are different: 17 versus 10, and 8 versus 2 for individualism versus collectivism for each of the two countries, respectively. Moreover, the relationships are what you would expect for these two market-oriented countries, in that higher emphasis is placed on individualism and lower emphasis on collectivism. However, even though their value preferences seem to be generally congruent, the frequencies of significantly higher mean responses for the five values that directly reflect individualism are somewhat low, especially for Japan, on the basis of 35 paired comparisons (5 values times 7 paired comparisons). Moreover, the combined mean responses for the first five individualism values discussed earlier tend to be lower than for the five collectivism values, 2.93 versus 3.54 (United States) and 2.96 versus 3.38 (Japan), respectively.

The respondents from two other countries that have different frequencies of higher mean responses are those from the former Soviet Union and Venezuela, but with reverse emphasis from that of the respondents from the United States and Japan. The mean responses of the respondents from the former Soviet Union and Venezuela reflect a higher emphasis on collectivism and a lower emphasis on individualism, with frequencies of significantly higher mean responses of 25 versus 16 and 23 versus 4 for each country, respectively. The frequencies of significantly higher mean responses for the five values that reflect collectivism are higher for both countries (25 for the former Soviet Union and 23 for Venezuela), in terms of 35 paired comparisons. Moreover, as shown on Table 5.1, the combined mean responses for the five collectivism values are higher than the first five individualism values, 3.80 versus 3.30 (the former Soviet Union) and 2.88 versus 2.66 (Venezuela), respectively.

The respondents from the remaining four countries surveyed showed no or only slight differences in their overall emphasis on the individualism versus the collectivism values, based on the frequencies of significantly higher mean responses: Germany, 8 versus 8; Yugoslavia, 20 versus 18; People's Republic of China, 14 versus 13; and Chile, 10 versus 9. However, the mean responses of these respondents are higher for collectivism than those for individualism as shown in Table 5.1 and discussed earlier.

VALUE PRIORITIES

The final segment of the survey of values includes a ranking of 10 values by the respondents from each of the eight countries. Respondents ranked these 10 values as follows: "1" indicates the highest priority and "10" the lowest priority. The values were selected jointly by members of the research group, and the rankings generally show the relative priority of importance of each one. These values can also be viewed as basic needs of each group of respondents. The mean ranks of respondents from each country and the average mean rank (A.M.) of the eight means are shown next for each of the 10 values. These values are listed in the rank order or priority, based on the average mean rank: for example, a "happy and healthy family" is ranked as the highest priority or value (1), and to "own and operate my own business" is ranked as the lowest (10) on the basis of the rankings submitted in the survey. Keep in mind that the lower the mean rank, the higher the ranking.

1. Happy and healthy family.

U.S.	YUG.	F.S.U.	VEN.	JAPAN	A.M.	GER.	CHILE	P.R.C.
1.89	2.15	2.16	2.23	2.32	2.34	2.56	2.57	2.87

2. Satisfying and enjoyable job.

GER.	U.S.	YUG.	JAPAN	A.M.	P.R.C.	F.S.U.	CHILE	VEN.
3.00	3.33	3.40	3.47	3.54	3.69	3.72	3.76	3.96

3. Children's education and success.

CHILE	U.S.	VEN.	YUG.	GER.	F.S.U.	A.M.	P.R.C.	JAPAN
3.49	4.24	4.28	4.36	4.43	4.48	4.48	5.25	5.34

4. Higher wages or salaries.

F.S.U.	CHILE	VEN.	A.M.	P.R.C.	U.S.	JAPAN	GER.	YUG.
3.78	3.99	4.40	4.93	5.01	5.17	5.49	5.63	5.98

5. Personal autonomy and independence.

YUG.	GER.	CHILE	A.M.	F.S.U.	JAPAN	P.R.C.	VEN.	U.S.
4.45	4.67	4.86	5.21	5.41	5.45	5.48	5.66	5.71

6. Personal achievement and power.

P.R.C.	CHILE	VEN.	F.S.U.	A.M.	U.S.	JAPAN	YUG.	GER.
4.83	5.17	5.31	5.60	5.61	5.68	5.87	6.08	6.36

7. Social status and acceptance by the group.

VEN.	CHILE	F.S.U.	GER.	A.M.	P.R.C.	JAPAN	YUG.	GER.
4.70	4.79	5.31	5.49	5.79	6.11	6.23	6.77	6.88

8. Reward for individual productivity.

CHILE	GER.	VEN.	U.S.	JAPAN	A.M.	YUG.	P.R.C.	F.S.U.
4.78	4.99	5.30	5.70	5.76	5.81	6.28	6.61	7.04

9. More leisure time.

JAPAN	GER.	CHILE	YUG.	A.M.	F.S.U.	U.S.	VEN.	P.R.C.
5.18	5.57	6.16	6.36	6.71	6.77	6.93	8.14	8.56

10. Own and operate my own business.

CHILE	P.R.C.	VEN.	A.M.	GER.	JAPAN	YUG.	U.S.	F.S.U.
5.31	6.23	6.34	6.86	6.96	7.34	7.43	7.50	7.81

The three most important values of all of the respondents combined as reflected in the average means are as follows: 1-happy and health family, 2-satisfying and enjoyable job, and 3-children's education and success. Thus, two of the highest values deal with family well-being, while the other pertains to job satisfaction. Two of the three lowest values pertain to individualism (8-reward for individual productivity, and 10-own and operate own business) while 9-more leisure time-is not a relatively high value.

The 10 values fall within three general somewhat related sets. The first set pertains to the individualism and economic needs of respondents, and it consists of the following five values: 4-higher wages/salaries; 5-personal autonomy/independence; 6-personal achievement/power; 8-reward for individual productivity; and 10-own and operate own business. Only the respondents from Chile have a mean response lower than the average mean (lower means higher rank or priority in terms of importance) for all five of these values. Next were the respondents from Venezuela (4 of 5), followed by those from Germany, the People's Republic of China, and the former Soviet Union (2 of 5 each, respectively), and then those from the United States, Japan, and Yugoslavia (1 of 5 each). The combined respondents from the two Latin American countries have 9 of 10 (90 percent) lower mean responses (thus a higher priority) for this set of five values, compared to 5 of 15 (33 percent) and 4 of 15 (27 percent) for the combined respondents from the three collectivist and market-oriented countries, respectively.

Table 5.2 shows the overall rank of the individualism and economic values by respondents from each of the eight countries surveyed. This overall rank reflects the combined responses to the five values referred to previously (4, 5, 6, 8, and 10). The chi square analysis indicates that there are some significant differences (.00 level) in the overall rank of these five combined values according to the country of the respondents (.37 coefficient of contingency).

The ANOVA Scheffe test results indicate where differences in mean rank responses are significantly lower (.05 level). Keep in mind that a lower mean rank response reflects a higher priority for this value. Respondents from the two Latin American countries, Chile and Venezu-

Table 5.2
Overall Rank of the Individualism and Economic Value

A	Response Frequency (%)					N	X̄
	1	2	3	4	5		
GER.	13.0	24.0	22.1	20.7	20.1	886	5.72
U.S.	10.5	21.6	24.4	22.8	20.8	1763	5.96
JAPAN	14.2	18.0	21.5	22.4	23.9	284	5.97
YUG.	14.2	17.2	20.4	23.3	24.9	663	6.03
P.R.C.	16.9	17.9	22.8	24.6	17.7	986	5.62
F.S.U.	16.4	16.5	21.2	20.9	25.1	1236	5.92
VEN.	22.0	17.3	21.1	22.3	17.4	958	5.40
CHILE	26.2	21.5	21.9	18.5	12.0	294	4.82
TOTAL	15.4	19.4	22.3	22.2	20.7	7070	5.68

B

Scheffe Test

A	GER.	U.S.	JAPAN	YUG.	P.R.C.	F.S.U.	VEN.	CHILE
GER.		X	X	X				
U.S.								
JAPAN								
YUG.		X	X	X		X		
P.R.C.		X	X	X		X		
F.S.U.								
VEN.	X	X	X	X	X	X		
CHILE	X	X	X	X	X	X	X	

* = Significantly greater emphasis for each pair of countries (.05 level)-A versus B

ANOVA F Ratio = 52.74 (.00 level)

Total mean = average of eight means
Chi Square (Pearson) = 1087.25 (.00 level)
Coefficient of Contingency = .37
1 = Strongly Disagree; 5 = Strongly Agree

la, place a higher priority on this value (lower mean rank) than do the respondents from the other countries surveyed (7 of 7 and 6 of 7, respectively). The respondents from the People's Republic of China place a relatively higher priority on the individualism and economic value than those respondents in 4 of the 7 countries, followed by those from Germany with 3 of 7 higher priority comparisons.

The second set of values pertains to family and leisure needs of respondents and consists of the following three values: 1-happy and healthy family, 3-children's education/success, and 9-more leisure time. The respondents from Yugoslavia have mean ranks lower than the average mean ranks for these three values (3 of 3 cases), thus higher value ranks. Respondents from six of the remaining countries have the next lowest mean rank (2 of 3 each), thus higher value ranks, than those from the People's Republic of China (0 of 3).

This corresponds to 6 of 9 (67 percent), 4 of 6 (67 percent) mean ranks significantly lower than the average mean rank for the respondents from the three market-oriented and the two Latin American countries, respectively, compared to 5 of 9 (56 percent) for respondents from the combined three collectivist countries. As a whole, however, the family and leisure value tends to be a relatively important priority for respondents from all of the countries, with the exception of those from the People's Republic of China.

Table 5.3 shows the overall rank of the family and leisure value by respondents from each of the eight countries. This overall rank reflects the combined responses to the three values referred to previously (1, 3, and 9). The chi square analysis indicates that there are some significant differences (.00 level) in the mean rank of these three values combined according to the country of the respondents (.40 coefficient of contingency).

The ANOVA Scheffe test results indicate where differences in mean rank responses are significantly lower (.05 level), therefore of a higher value priority. For this set of three family and leisure values, respondents from the People's Republic of China have a significantly lower priority (higher mean rank comparisons) than those from all of the remaining seven countries, followed by those from Venezuela (6 of 7 higher mean rank comparisons). Thus these two respondent groups place a lower overall emphasis on the family and leisure value in terms of the Scheffe test results than to the respondents from the other countries.

The third set of values pertains to social and satisfaction needs of respondents and consists of the following two values: 2-satisfying and

Table 5.3
Overall Rank of the Family and Leisure Value

A	Response Frequency (%)					N	$\overline{X}$	B — Scheffe Test							
	1	2	3	4	5			GER.	U.S.	JAPAN	YUG.	P.R.C.	F.S.U.	VEN.	CHILE
GER.	37.4	22.0	17.0	12.3	10.9	886	4.24					X		X	
U.S.	42.8	13.7	13.2	13.8	16.5	1761	4.32					X		X	
JAPAN	37.6	19.6	17.7	12.7	12.5	276	4.37					X		X	
YUG.	37.4	20.7	16.6	12.5	12.8	663	4.34					X		X	
P.R.C.	24.1	19.5	15.2	14.3	26.9	987	5.54							X	
F.S.U.	38.1	17.4	13.8	15.2	15.6	1237	4.46					X		X	
VEN.	41.4	13.4	6.8	11.7	26.7	957	4.86					X			
CHILE	47.1	14.5	12.0	10.0	16.4	293	4.09					X		X	
TOTAL	38.0	17.0	13.7	13.3	17.9	7060	4.53								

Total mean = average of eight means
Chi Square (Pearson) = 1311.20 (.00 level)
Coefficient of Contingency = .40
1 = Strongly Disagree; 5 = Strongly Agree

* = Significantly greater emphasis for each pair of countries (.05 level)-A versus B

ANOVA F Ratio = 57.06 (.00 level)

enjoyable job and 7-social status and acceptance by the group. The respondents from Germany place the highest emphasis on this value set in terms of the frequency of significantly lower mean rank responses (2 of 2), than the respondents from all of the remaining countries (1 of 2 each, except those from the People's Republic of China with 0 of 2). The respondents from the three market-oriented countries have 4 of 6 (67 percent) significantly lower mean responses, thus a higher emphasis on the social status and satisfaction value, compared to 2 of 4 (50 percent) for the respondents from the two Latin American countries and 2 of 6 (33 percent) for those from the three collectivist countries.

Table 5.4 shows the overall rank of the social status and satisfaction value by respondents from each of the eight countries, as reflected in the combined mean rank responses to the two values mentioned (2 and 7). The chi square analysis indicates that there are some significant differences (.00 level) in the mean rank responses to the two values combined according to the country of the respondents (.29 coefficient of contingency).

The ANOVA Scheffe test results indicate where differences in mean rank responses are significant. The respondents from Germany and the former Soviet Union place the highest priority on this value, having significantly lower mean responses (.05 level) than five of the six other countries surveyed. The respondents from Chile place a higher priority on this value than those from the United States, Yugoslavia, and the People's Republic of China.

SUMMARY AND CONCLUSIONS

This chapter develops a profile of value priorities for each of the eight countries surveyed. These value priorities are based on the results of the analysis of individualism and collectivism in Chapters 3 and 4, and the ranking of 10 values by the respondents discussed.

In terms of the summary of value preferences shown in Table 5.1, general profiles of values for the eight countries surveyed are summarized next. These profiles reflect those values that have four or more mean responses that are significantly higher than the average mean responses (shown in bold type on Table 5.1).

Germany: Higher emphasis on paternalism

United States: Higher emphasis on personal and family individualism, family economic orientation, uncertainty avoidance, humanistic beliefs,

Table 5.4
Overall Rank of the Social Status and Satisfaction Value

A

A	Response Frequency (%)					N	X̄
	1	2	3	4	5		
GER.	35.3	25.8	15.4	14.6	8.9	887	4.24
U.S.	23.2	26.7	16.2	15.8	18.1	1763	5.10
JAPAN	26.4	24.3	19.8	16.5	13.1	277	4.90
YUG.	17.0	20.7	17.7	16.6	17.9	660	5.07
P.R.C.	23.9	26.1	19.8	16.9	13.3	985	4.93
F.S.U.	30.8	28.7	21.8	11.6	7.0	1236	4.27
VEN.	23.0	30.1	23.7	13.2	10.1	956	4.71
CHILE	31.9	23.0	23.4	13.6	8.3	294	4.34
TOTAL	27.0	26.5	19.2	14.7	12.6	7058	4.70

Total mean = average of eight means
Chi Square (Pearson) = 647.52 (.00 level)
Coefficient of Contingency = .29
1 = Strongly Disagree; 5 = Strongly Agree

B

Scheffe Test

A	GER.	U.S.	JAPAN	YUG.	P.R.C.	F.S.U.	VEN.	CHILE
GER.		X	X	X	X		X	
U.S.								
JAPAN								
YUG.								
P.R.C.								
F.S.U.		X	X	X	X		X	
VEN.		X		X	X			
CHILE		X		X	X			

* = Significantly greater emphasis for each pair of countries (.05 level)-A versus B

ANOVA F Ratio = 35.36 (.00 level)

and family social cohesion/status

Japan: Higher emphasis on masculinity and leisure ethics

Yugoslavia: Higher emphasis on work ethic, family individualism, leisure ethic, humanistic beliefs, Marxist beliefs, and family social cohesion/status

People's Republic of China: Higher emphasis on work ethic, masculinity, uncertainty avoidance, power distance, organizational beliefs and Marxist beliefs

Former Soviet Union: Higher emphasis on work ethic, masculinity, leisure ethic, power distance, organizational beliefs, humanistic beliefs, Marxist beliefs, and paternalism

Venezuela: Higher emphasis on organizational beliefs, humanistic beliefs, paternalism, and family social cohesion/status

Chile: Higher emphasis on family economic orientation

On the other hand, the value priorities as shown in the preceding discussion of value ranks are shown in the following. The frequencies of significantly lower mean rank responses for the three categories of values-individualism and economic (I&E), family and leisure (F&L), and social status and job satisfaction (SS&JS)-are summarized as follows. These numbers are the significantly lower mean rank responses using the Scheffe test of paired comparison of means with a possible range of frequencies of 0 - 7. A lower mean rank response indicates a higher value priorty (numbers in bold type reflect at least 4 of the 7 possible frequencies).

	I&E (Table 5.2)	F&L (Table 5.3)	SS&JS (Table 5.4)
Germany	3	2	**5**
United States	0	2	0
Japan	0	2	0
Yugoslavia	0	2	0
People's Republic of China	**4**	0	0
Former Soviet Union	0	2	**5**
Venezuela	**6**	1	2
Chile	**7**	2	3

Compared to the respondents from the other countries, the value ranks of the respondents from Germany show a higher priority for social status and job satisfaction (5 of 7 paired mean rank comparisons). This is consistent with their higher emphasis on paternalism presented in the summary of value preferences based on the data in Table 5.1. The value ranks of the respondents from the United States show a slightly higher priority for the family and leisure value (2 of 7), and this is consistent with the earlier summary, except for leisure. The respondents from the third market-oriented country, Japan, also show a slightly higher priority for the family and leisure value (2 of 7), which somewhat coincides with their previous emphasis on the leisure ethic.

The results of the Yugoslav respondents are similar to those of the respondents from the United States and Japan, in that they reflect a slightly higher priority for the family and leisure value. Moreover, this is consistent in part with the previous value profile of Yugoslav respondents. The higher priority for the individualism and economic value by the respondents from the People's Republic of China (4 of 7) is also consistent with their previous profile of values. The respondents from the other collectivist country, the former Soviet Union, place a higher priority on the social status and job satisfaction value (5 of 7), similarly to their previous value profile, but a lower priority on the individualism and economic value that is somewhat opposite to their earlier value profile.

The respondents from the two Latin American countries show a high priority for the individualism and economic value (Chile 7 of 7, and Venezuela 6 of 7), and this is quite opposite to the earlier profiles of values developed for these two countries, except for Chile's emphasis on family economic orientation.

6

Profile of Organizational Issues

The cross-cultural analysis of values presented in the previous three chapters focused on the first segment of the "values-attitudes-behavior" model. This analysis included comparisons of selected cultural, workplace, and family values within the overall context of their general orientation toward individualism versus collectivism. From this analysis, general value profiles for respondents in each of the eight countries surveyed were eventually developed in Chapter 5.

A person's orientation toward individualism versus collectivism reflects the values that person has developed over time in response to his or her environment. This environment consists of three fundamental levels -- organizational, national, and international. Within each of these levels, various social and political organizations are created to provide both economic and noneconomic goods and services needed and desired by people in a society. Within this context, values shape the needs and desires of a society, as well as the political economy infrastructure that is created to fulfill these needs and desires.

In the next four chapters, the various political economy issues that people perceive to exist at the organizational, national, and international levels are analyzed for the eight countries surveyed. This chapter focuses an organizational issues, while Chapters 7 and 8 deal with national and international issues, respectively. Chapter 9 develops a general profile of issues priorities for each of the eight countries.

Keep in mind that our focus is on people's perceptions of, or attitudes toward, these political economy issues. In this context, the focus is on the middle segment of the "values-attitudes-behavior" model. Five organizational issues are analyzed in this chapter, relating to participation, communications, motivation, standard of living, and productivity.

OPPORTUNITY FOR PARTICIPATION

The perceived opportunity for participation in work organizations is reflected in the seven issue propositions summarized next. The mean response of respondents from each country surveyed, and the average mean (A.M.) of the eight means, are shown for each proposition. The seven issue propositions reflect those that are traditionally used when assessing the opportunity for participation in work organizations.

1. Employees have adequate opportunities to work in groups.

U.S.	JAPAN	VEN.	P.R.C.	YUG.	A.M.	F.S.U.	GER.	CHILE
3.73	3.55	3.49	3.47	3.36	3.35	3.10	3.04	3.02

2. Employees have sufficient opportunities to participate in decisions.

U.S.	JAPAN	P.R.C.	A.M.	GER.	VEN.	CHILE	F.S.U.	YUG.
3.07	2.82	2.70	2.61	2.55	2.52	2.46	2.44	2.29

3. Employees have sufficient opportunities to try new ideas and make suggestions.

U.S.	JAPAN	P.R.C.	GER.	CHILE	A.M.	VEN.	F.S.U.	YUG.
3.29	3.14	2.91	2.80	2.79	2.76	2.71	2.44	2.02

4. Management is flexible.

F.S.U.	U.S.	P.R.C.	VEN.	A.M.	GER.	JAPAN	CHILE	YUG.
3.34	3.18	3.17	2.95	2.90	2.80	2.80	2.76	2.20

5. Committees make the most important decisions.

JAPAN	VEN.	P.R.C.	A.M.	YUG.	U.S.	F.S.U.	GER.	CHILE
3.62	3.42	3.19	3.01	2.96	2.75	2.75	2.72	2.63

6. Committees make salary level decisions.

P.R.C.	VEN.	JAPAN	YUG.	A.M.	F.S.U.	U.S.	CHILE	GER.
3.20	3.07	2.98	2.92	2.81	2.71	2.68	2.56	2.38

7. Power is decentralized in organizations.

U.S.	GER.	JAPAN	P.R.C.	A.M.	CHILE	F.S.U.	YUG.	VEN.
2.91	2.69	2.62	2.46	2.42	2.36	2.30	2.05	1.99

The combined group of seven issue propositions reflects the overall perceived opportunity for participation in work organizations by respondents from each country, and for the combined countries as measured by the average mean. Using the average mean as a general indicator, respondents from the following countries have mean responses that exceed the average mean for each of the seven issues propositions: the People's Republic of China (7 of 7); Japan (6 of 7); the United States (5 of 7); Venezuela (4 of 7); Germany and Yugoslavia (2 of 7); and the former Soviet Union (1 of 7). Moreover, the frequency of mean responses higher than the average mean for the respondents from the three market-oriented countries is 13 of 21 (62 percent), compared to 10 of 21 (48 percent) and 5 of 14 (35 percent) for those from the three collectivist and two Latin American countries, respectively.

On the basis of the preceding data, the respondents from the People's Republic of China, Japan, the United States, and Venezuela tend to perceive a greater level of opportunity to participate in work organizations in their countries when compared to the respondents from the remaining four countries. The relatively lower perceived opportunity for participation by respondents from two of the collectivist countries, Yugoslavia and the former Soviet Union, seems somewhat surprising in view of the inherent features supporting collaborative type decision making in collectivist societies.

The average mean for proposition 1 (3.35) indicates a higher perceived opportunity to work in groups than the perceived level of participation in decision making (2.61 for proposition 2). In other words, opportunities for participation are perceived to exist, however, actual levels of participation are perceived to be lower. Moreover, the average means for propositions 2 through 6, relating to various types of opportunities for involvement, are considerably lower (ranging from 2.61 to 3.01) when compared to that of issue proposition 1. From an overall viewpoint, the locus of power in the organization as reflected in proposition 7 (2.42 average mean) reflects that although there may be some perceived opportunities to participate in organizational activities and decisions, power is still perceived to be quite centralized in work organizations in all of the eight countries (range of mean responses from 1.99 to 2.91).

Table 6.1 shows the overall perceived level of opportunity for participation in work organizations by respondents from each of the eight countries surveyed. This overall perception is the combined responses to the seven issue propositions summarized previously. The chi square analysis indicates that there are some significant differences (.00 level) in the overall perception of an opportunity to participate in work organizations according to the country of the respondents (.45 coefficient of contingency). In terms of the mean responses, respondents from

Table 6.1
Overall Perceived Level of Participation in Organizations

A	Response Frequency (%)					N	$\bar{X}$	Scheffe Test B							
	1	2	3	4	5			GER.	U.S.	JAPAN	YUG.	P.R.C.	F.S.U.	VEN.	CHILE
GER.	17.7	27.0	26.4	23.1	5.8	851	2.72				X				
U.S.	11.3	23.1	22.8	30.7	12.1	1762	3.09	X			X	X	X	X	X
JAPAN	10.1	19.9	32.0	28.1	9.9	243	3.08	X			X		X	X	X
YUG.	21.6	34.2	21.3	18.5	4.4	737	2.50								
P.R.C.	11.7	28.7	16.3	33.6	9.6	919	3.01	X			X		X	X	X
F.S.U.	14.0	33.5	23.4	24.1	5.1	1236	2.73				X				
VEN.	16.9	27.9	17.7	26.8	10.8	961	2.87	X			X		X		X
CHILE	16.3	33.5	24.5	19.8	5.8	313	2.65				X				
TOTAL	14.5	28.2	22.0	26.7	8.5	7022	2.83								

Total mean = average of eight means
Chi Square (Pearson) = 1752.16 (.00 level)
Coefficient of Contingency = .45
1 = Strongly Disagree; 5 = Strongly Agree

* = Significantly greater perceived level for each pair of countries (.05 level)-A versus B

ANOVA F Ratio = 172.30 (.00 level)

the United States (3.09), Japan (3.08), and the People's Republic of China (3.01) perceive a greater overall opportunity to participate than those from the remaining five countries. The average mean of the total sample of respondents (2.83) appears low.

The ANOVA Scheffe test results shown on Table 6.1 provides information on the specific comparisons of mean responses for each pair of countries in the research survey. These comparisons show the significantly higher perceived opportunity to participate in organizations in their countries by respondents from the United States (6 of 7), Japan and the People's Republic of China (5 of 7 each), and Venezuela (4 of 7). However, as mentioned, the mean responses of all respondent groups indicate a somewhat lower level of perceived opportunity to participate by respondents from all of the countries surveyed.

ADEQUACY OF COMMUNICATIONS

The perceived adequacy of communications in work organizations is reflected in the five issue propositions summarized next. The mean responses of respondents from each of the eight countries surveyed, and the average mean (A.M.) of the eight means, are shown for each proposition. The five issue propositions reflect those that are often used when assessing the adequacy of communications in work organizations.

1. Employees understand their organization's goals.

U.S.	GER.	P.R.C.	JAPAN	F.S.U.	A.M.	CHILE	VEN.	YUG.
3.37	3.36	3.22	3.17	3.15	3.08	2.99	2.77	2.66

2. Employees clearly understand the requirements of their job.

U.S.	GER.	JAPAN	VEN.	F.S.U.	A.M.	CHILE	P.R.C.	YUG.
3.65	3.47	3.47	3.34	3.29	3.29	3.19	3.02	2.86

3. Communications between managers and employees are effective.

U.S.	JAPAN	GER.	P.R.C.	VEN.	A.M.	CHILE	F.S.U.	YUG.
3.42	3.32	3.05	2.96	2.95	2.92	2.64	2.56	2.42

4. Employee grievance policies and procedures are satisfactory.

U.S.	JAPAN	P.R.C.	GER.	A.M.	CHILE	VEN.	F.S.U.	YUG.
3.35	2.89	2.72	2.69	2.62	2.54	2.41	2.35	1.98

5. Managers/supervisors are interested in personal problems of employees.

U.S.	JAPAN	GER.	P.R.C	A.M.	VEN.	CHILE	F.S.U.	YUG.
3.30	3.21	2.80	2.75	2.71	2.64	2.62	2.48	1.88

The combined group of five issue propositions reflects the overall
perception of the adequacy of communications by respondents from each
country, and for the combined countries as measured by the average
mean. Using the average mean as a general indicator, the following
countries have mean responses that exceed (or equal) the average mean
for each of the five issue propositions: Germany, the United States, and
Japan (5 of 5 each); the People's Republic of China (4 of 5); and the
former Soviet Union and Venezuela (2 of 5 each). This corresponds to
15 of 15 (100 percent) for the respondents from the three market-oriented
countries, compared to 6 of 15 (40 percent) and 2 of 10 (20 percent) for
the three collectivist and two Latin American countries, respectively.

Respondents from the three market-oriented countries and the
People's Republic of China appear to perceive a greater adequacy of
communications in work organizations in their countries compared to the
other four respondent groups. As in the case of opportunity for
participation, the lower perceived adequacy of communications by the
respondents from the former Soviet Union and Yugoslavia seems
somewhat unexpected.

The first two issue propositions pertain to understanding organizational and job expectations, while propositions 3 through 5 deal generally
with the adequacy of ongoing communications concerning performance
of work and related access to management issues. On the basis of the
comparison of average means, the respondents as a whole seem to
perceive a better understanding of organizational goals (3.08) and job
requirements (3.29), compared to their lower perceptions of the
effectiveness of communications and grievance procedures, and the level
of interest by managers in personal problems as reflected in propositions
3 through 5, respectively (average means of 2.92, 2.62, and 2.71).

Table 6.2 shows the overall perceived adequacy of communications
in work organizations by respondents from each of the countries
surveyed. This overall perception is the combined mean response to the
five issue propositions summarized previously. The chi square analysis
indicates that there are some significant differences (.00 level) in the
overall perceived adequacy of communications in work organizations

Table 6.2
Overall Perceived Adequacy of Communications in Organizations

A	Response Frequency (%)					N	$\overline{X}$	Scheffe Test (B)							
	1	2	3	4	5			GER.	U.S.	JAPAN	YUG.	P.R.C.	F.S.U.	VEN.	CHILE
GER.	10.8	19.0	29.3	32.8	8.1	842	3.08	X			X	X	X	X	X
U.S.	5.9	15.7	22.6	41.9	13.8	1761	3.42			X	X	X	X	X	X
JAPAN	5.6	17.9	33.8	34.6	8.0	225	3.21				X	X	X	X	X
YUG.	24.2	34.0	26.4	13.0	2.4	729	2.35								
P.R.C.	10.1	30.5	20.6	32.7	6.1	910	2.94				X		X	X	X
F.S.U.	12.8	29.2	28.4	26.5	3.1	1229	2.78				X				
VEN.	16.0	29.5	19.1	27.0	8.4	957	2.82				X				
CHILE	11.9	30.9	28.5	22.5	6.2	313	2.80				X				
TOTAL	11.7	24.8	24.6	31.0	7.9	6966	2.57								

Total mean = average of eight means
Chi Square (Pearson) = 3078.62 (.00 level)
Coefficient of Contingency = .55
1 = Strongly Disagree; 5 = Strongly Agree

* = Significantly greater perceived level for each pair of countries (.05 level)-A versus B

ANOVA F Ratio = 391.93 (.00 level)

according to the country of the respondents (.55 coefficient of contingency). In terms of the mean responses, respondents from the United States (3.42), Japan (3.21), and Germany (3.08), the three market-oriented countries, perceive a higher overall level of communications in work organizations than respondents from the other five countries surveyed.

The ANOVA Scheffe test results shown on Table 6.2 reflect the higher perceived level of adequacy of communications for the three market-oriented countries. In terms of the frequency of significantly higher mean responses, the respondents from the United States have a higher perceived level of adequate communications when compared to the perceptions of respondents from each of the seven other countries (7 of 7), followed by the respondents from Japan and Germany (5 of 7 each), and those from the People's Republic of China (4 of 7). Respondents from these four countries, except Germany, also perceive higher levels of opportunities to participate in work organizations (Table 6.1). For the total sample, the average mean pertaining to perceptions of the adequacy of communications is lower (2.57) than for the perceived opportunity to participate in work organizations (2.96).

LEVEL OF MOTIVATION

The perceived level of motivation in work organizations is reflected in the 10 issue propositions summarized next. These propositions encompass various organizational factors that generally lead to a higher level of motivation of people in the workplace. The mean responses of respondents from each of the eight countries surveyed, and the average mean (A.M.) of the eight means, are shown for each proposition.

1. Wages and salaries are fair/equitable.

U.S.	GER.	JAPAN	P.R.C	A.M.	CHILE	F.S.U.	VEN.	YUG.
3.11	2.88	2.80	2.56	**2.39**	2.03	2.02	1.99	1.69

2. Individual productivity is rewarded.

P.R.C.	U.S.	GER.	JAPAN	A.M.	VEN.	F.S.U.	CHILE	YUG.
3.31	3.27	2.92	2.87	**2.73**	2.66	2.44	2.38	2.02

3. Opportunities for promotion are good.

JAPAN	U.S.	VEN.	GER.	A.M.	P.R.C.	CHILE	F.S.U.	YUG.
3.12	3.02	2.94	2.75	**2.72**	2.66	2.66	2.42	2.21

4. Seniority is not the most important promotion criterion.

GER.	U.S.	YUG.	CHILE	A.M.	F.S.U.	VEN.	P.R.C.	JAPAN
3.53	3.39	3.30	3.30	3.18	3.10	3.05	3.04	2.75

5. Sufficient job opportunities exist for those who want to work.

U.S.	GER.	JAPAN	A.M.	F.S.U.	VEN.	P.R.C.	YUG.	CHILE
3.71	3.49	3.00	2.95	2.87	2.81	2.69	2.53	2.47

6. There are sufficient opportunities to change jobs.

U.S.	GER.	JAPAN	F.S.U.	A.M.	P.R.C.	VEN.	CHILE	YUG.
3.06	2.86	2.78	2.78	2.51	2.37	2.24	2.22	1.75

7. There are sufficient opportunities for training and development.

U.S.	JAPAN	GER.	VEN.	A.M.	F.S.U.	CHILE	P.R.C.	YUG.
3.46	3.30	3.27	3.06	3.02	2.99	2.81	2.77	2.50

8. Physical working conditions are satisfactory.

U.S.	VEN.	GER.	A.M.	CHILE	P.R.C.	F.S.U.	JAPAN	YUG.
3.91	3.44	3.12	3.04	3.01	2.83	2.79	2.70	2.50

9. Amount of available leisure time is satisfactory.

VEN.	YUG.	U.S.	GER.	A.M.	P.R.C.	CHILE	F.S.U.	JAPAN
3.73	3.33	3.32	3.30	3.17	3.13	3.13	2.81	2.62

10. Employee morale is high.

GER.	F.S.U.	U.S.	P.R.C.	A.M.	CHILE	VEN.	YUG.	JAPAN
3.56	3.36	3.30	3.10	3.05	3.01	2.87	2.62	2.59

The combined group of 10 issue propositions reflects the overall perception of the level of motivation of respondents from each country, and for the combined countries as measured by the average mean. Using the average mean as a general indicator, the following countries have mean responses that exceed the average mean for each of the 10 propositions: the United States and Germany (10 of 10); Japan (6 of 10); Venezuela (4 of 10); the People's Republic of China (3 of 10); Yugoslavia and the former Soviet Union (2 of 10 each); and Chile (1 of 10). This corresponds to 26 of 30 (87 percent) for respondents from the three market-oriented countries, compared to 7 of 30 (23 percent) and 5 of 20 (25 percent) for respondents from the three collectivistic and two Latin American countries, respectively. The relative perceived level of motivation by respondents in the three market-oriented countries is higher than for those respondents in the other five respondent groups.

The perceived level of motivation as reflected in the first three issue propositions pertaining to the level of satisfaction with direct economic rewards seems low for the combined sample of respondents from all countries as reflected in the average means (2.39, 2.73, and 2.72, respectively). This is somewhat puzzling since the overall perceived level of morale as shown for proposition 10 is higher (3.05). Perhaps the noneconomic incentives, such as those reflected in issue propositions 9 (3.17-leisure), 8 (3.02-working conditions), and 7 (3.02-training and development), are more important than economic factors for motivating people at work.

It is interesting to note that opportunities for promotion (proposition 3) are perceived to be somewhat low (2.72) when compared to proposition 4 that views seniority as not the most important criterion for promotion (3.18). Moreover, while the respondents from Japan have the highest perceived opportunity for promotion (3.12), they are the ones that most strongly disagree that seniority is not important for promotion (2.75).

Table 6.3 shows the overall perceived level of motivation in work organizations by respondents from each of the countries surveyed as reflected in the combined mean response to the 10 issue propositions summarized. The chi square analysis indicates there are some significant differences (.00 level) in the overall perceived level of motivation in work organizations according to the country of the respondents (.65 coefficient of contingency). On the basis of the mean responses, respondents from the United States (3.36) and Germany (3.17) perceive a higher level of motivation in work organizations than do the respondents from the other six countries. The average mean (2.87) for the eight countries seems low as a general indicator of the level of motivation that is perceived to exist in work organizations in these countries.

The ANOVA Scheffe test results shown on Table 6.3 clearly reflect the significantly higher overall perceived level of motivation in work organizations by respondents from the United States (7 of 7 paired comparisons) and those from Germany (6 of 7 paired comparisons). At the other extreme, respondents from Yugoslavia have the lowest overall perceived level of motivation (0 of 7), followed by those from the former Soviet Union and Chile (1 of 7), Japan (2 of 7), and the People's Republic of China and Venezuela (3 of 7). On the basis of these comparisons of mean responses with those shown in Tables 6.1 and 6.2, the respondents from the United States also have a higher perceived level of opportunity for participation and adequacy of communications, where-

Table 6.3

Overall Perceived Level of Motivation in Organizations

A	Response Frequency (%)					N	X̄	Scheffe Test (B)							
	1	2	3	4	5			GER.	U.S.	JAPAN	YUG.	P.R.C.	F.S.U.	VEN.	CHILE
GER.	10.0	19.3	26.4	32.5	11.8	847	3.17			X	X	X	X	X	X
U.S.	8.7	17.6	18.4	39.7	15.5	1764	3.36	X		X	X	X	X	X	X
JAPAN	11.6	29.4	28.1	24.1	6.7	240	2.85				X				X
YUG.	25.4	32.6	20.1	16.4	5.5	738	2.44								
P.R.C.	13.3	34.5	15.7	27.1	9.5	921	2.85				X		X		X
F.S.U.	14.0	31.5	24.3	25.4	4.8	1238	2.75				X				
VEN.	16.6	27.9	17.8	26.9	10.9	961	2.88				X		X		X
CHILE	16.6	31.4	23.3	23.5	5.1	313	2.69				X				
TOTAL	13.6	26.3	20.6	29.4	10.0	7022	2.87								

Total mean = average of eight means
Chi Square (Pearson) = 5014.73 (.00 level)
Coefficient of Contingency = .65
1 = Strongly Disagree; 5 = Strongly Agree

* = Significantly greater perceived level for each pair of countries (.05 level)-A versus B

ANOVA F Ratio = 584.18 (.00 level)

as the respondents from Germany have higher perceived levels of motivation and adequacy of communications. The respondents from Japan have higher perceived levels of opportunity for participation and adequacy of communications, while the respondents from the People's Republic of China perceive higher opportunities to participate, with a moderate adequacy of communications, and level of motivation, relative to the other respondent groups.

LEVEL OF JOB SECURITY AND STANDARD OF LIVING

The perceived level of job security and standard of living in work organizations are reflected in the four issue propositions summarized next. These propositions focus on both current and future employment security as well as the overall standard of living. The mean responses of respondents from each of the countries surveyed, and the average mean (A.M.) of the eight means, are shown for each proposition.

1. There is adequate job security.

JAPAN	VEN.	U.S.	P.R.C.	A.M.	GER.	CHILE	F.S.U.	YUG.
3.86	3.51	3.44	3.24	3.23	3.19	3.05	2.98	2.56

2. Stability of employment is satisfactory.

U.S.	VEN.	GER.	P.R.C.	A.M.	JAPAN	F.S.U.	CHILE	YUG.
3.54	3.28	3.23	3.22	3.08	3.07	3.07	2.93	2.32

3. Long range future employment potential is good.

GER.	U.S.	JAPAN	P.R.C.	CHILE	A.M.	F.S.U.	VEN.	YUG.
3.56	3.50	3.20	2.92	2.92	2.92	2.87	2.68	1.74

4. Standard of living is high.

GER.	U.S.	JAPAN	A.M.	CHILE	P.R.C.	VEN.	F.S.U.	YUG.
3.84	3.66	3.54	2.81	2.65	2.55	2.16	2.07	2.03

The total set of four issue propositions reflects the overall perception of the level of job security and standard of living of respondents from each country, and for the combined countries as measured by the average mean. On the basis of the average mean as a general indicator, the respondents from the following countries have mean responses that exceed (or equal) the average mean for each of the four propositions: United States (4 of 4); Germany, Japan, and the People's Republic of

China (3 of 4 each); and Venezuela (2 of 4). This translates into 10 of 12 (83 percent) for the three market-oriented countries, compared to 3 of 8 (38 percent) and 3 of 12 (25 percent) for the two Latin American and three collectivist countries, respectively. For the respondents as a whole as reflected in the average mean, there is a higher perceived level of job security (3.23-proposition 1) and employment stability (3.08-proposition 2) than the perceived level future employment potential (2.92-proposition 3) and standard of living (2.81-proposition 4).

Table 6.4 shows the overall perceived level of job security and standard of living in work organizations by respondents from the countries surveyed, as reflected in the combined mean response to the four issue propositions summarized previously. The chi square analysis indicates that there are some significant differences (.00 level) in the overall perceived level of job security and standard of living in work organizations according to the country of the respondents (.62 coefficient of contingency). In terms of the mean responses shown on Table 6.4, the respondents from the three market-oriented countries have higher perceived levels of job security and standard of living than do the respondents from the remaining five countries. The average mean for the total sample of respondents (3.10) is considerably higher than the average means for the other three organizational climate indicators: opportunity for participation (2.83), adequacy of communications (2.57), and level of motivation (2.87).

The ANOVA Scheffe test results shown on Table 6.4 reflect the significantly higher perceived level of job security and standard of living of the respondents from the other three market-oriented countries when compared to the other five respondent groups. This is generally consistent with the Scheffe paired comparison results for these three countries for the other three organizational climate issues.

LEVEL OF PRODUCTIVITY

The overall perceived level of productivity in work organizations is reflected in the 14 issue propositions summarized. These propositions focus on four broad groups of propositions relating to (1) technology (propositions 1 through 3); (2) management (propositions 4 through 7); (3) labor (propositions 7 through 11); and (4) employee behavior (propositions 12 through 14).

The combined group of 14 issue propositions reflects the overall

Table 6.4
Overall Perceived Adequacy of Job Security and Standard of Living in Organizations

A	Response Frequency (%)							Scheffe Test (B)							
	1	2	3	4	5	N	X̄	GER.	U.S.	JAPAN	YUG.	P.R.C.	F.S.U.	VEN.	CHILE
GER.	4.4	13.2	25.4	39.8	17.2	899	3.52			X	X	X	X	X	X
U.S.	5.5	11.5	20.6	43.1	19.4	1770	3.59			X	X	X	X	X	X
JAPAN	4.2	16.9	34.2	32.2	12.4	279	3.32				X	X	X	X	X
YUG.	28.4	31.8	19.6	15.5	4.7	744	2.36								
P.R.C.	8.6	31.5	19.0	33.0	7.8	988	3.00				X		X		
F.S.U.	14.9	29.4	21.4	29.1	5.1	1245	2.80				X				
VEN.	14.7	21.6	14.1	32.0	17.6	962	3.16				X	X	X		
CHILE	7.8	25.7	27.9	31.3	7.3	314	3.05				X	X	X		
TOTAL	11.0	21.5	20.9	33.8	12.8	7201	3.10								

* = Significantly greater perceived level for each pair of countries (.05 level)-A versus B

ANOVA F Ratio = 549.95 (.00 level)

Total mean = average of eight means
Chi Square (Pearson) = 4462.62 (.00 level)
Coefficient of Contingency = .62
1 = Strongly Disagree; 5 = Strongly Agree

perceived level of productivity in work organizations of the respondents from each country, and for the combined countries, as measured by the average mean of the eight means. Using the average mean as a general indicator, the respondents from the following countries have higher mean responses that exceed (or equal) the average mean response for each of the 14 issue propositions: United States (14 of 14); Germany (12 of 14); Japan (11 of 14); Chile (10 of 14); Venezuela (9 of 14); the People's Republic of China (5 of 14); the former Soviet Union (3 of 14); and Yugoslavia (2 of 14). This translates into 37 of 42 (88 percent) for the combined respondents from the three market-oriented countries, compared to 19 of 28 (68 percent) and 10 of 42 (24 percent) for those respondents from the two Latin American and three collectivist countries, respectively.

The respondents from the three market-oriented countries, as in the case of the other organizational climate issues discussed earlier, perceive a higher overall level of productivity for their work organizations than do the other five respondent groups. However, the respondents from the two Latin American countries also perceive higher levels of productivity in their work organizations when compared to those from the three collectivist countries.

1. There is a high level of work automation.

GER.	JAPAN	U.S.	VEN.	CHILE	A.M.	P.R.C.	YUG.	F.S.U.
3.34	3.29	3.28	3.00	2.99	2.89	2.69	2.37	2.19

2. There is an appropriate use of technology in the workplace.

U.S.	GER.	P.R.C.	VEN.	JAPAN	A.M.	CHILE	F.S.U.	YUG.
3.67	3.42	3.18	3.11	3.05	3.03	2.95	2.55	2.30

3. The speed of technological change is satisfactory.

U.S.	GER.	JAPAN	CHILE	VEN.	A.M.	P.R.C.	F.S.U.	YUG.
3.25	3.02	2.82	2.76	2.64	2.63	2.57	2.04	1.96

4. Management is efficient and effective.

U.S.	GER.	JAPAN	CHILE	VEN.	P.R.C.	A.M.	F.S.U.	YUG.
3.20	3.09	3.07	2.98	2.97	2.89	2.83	2.49	1.92

5. Supply of good managers is adequate.

F.S.U.	U.S.	VEN.	A.M.	CHILE	JAPAN	GER.	P.R.C.	YUG.
3.69	3.21	2.98	2.97	2.94	2.90	2.85	2.73	2.44

6. The level of organizational growth is satisfaction.

GER.	U.S.	VEN.	CHILE	JAPAN	A.M.	F.S.U.	P.R.C.	YUG.
3.46	3.23	3.03	2.99	2.95	2.91	2.75	2.72	2.15

7. An adequate supply of well trained labor exists.

YUG.	GER.	U.S.	CHILE	A.M.	P.R.C.	JAPAN	VEN.	F.S.U.
3.48	3.23	3.21	2.99	2.99	2.98	2.94	2.61	2.46

8. Quality of work force is good.

U.S.	JAPAN	GER.	CHILE	A.M.	VEN.	YUG.	P.R.C.	F.S.U.
3.63	3.41	3.38	3.30	3.16	3.08	3.03	2.84	2.62

9. Productivity of labor is high.

JAPAN	GER.	U.S.	CHILE	A.M.	VEN.	P.R.C.	F.S.U.	YUG.
3.43	3.39	3.35	3.19	2.87	2.82	2.71	2.26	1.84

10. Mobility of labor is high.

VEN.	U.S.	F.S.U.	JAPAN	CHILE	A.M.	GER.	YUG.	P.R.C.
3.12	3.07	2.91	2.85	2.84	2.82	2.71	2.62	2.47

11. Influence of labor unions is not excessive.

F.S.U.	U.S.	YUG.	GER.	P.R.C.	A.M.	GER.	YUG.	P.R.C.
3.90	3.84	3.74	3.68	3.59	3.54	3.48	3.14	2.94

12. Employee absenteeism is low.

JAPAN	U.S.	CHILE	GER.	VEN.	P.R.C.	A.M.	F.S.U.	YUG.
3.89	3.38	3.34	3.11	3.11	3.09	3.09	2.92	1.90

13. Level of employee theft is low.

JAPAN	U.S.	GER.	P.R.C	A.M.	F.S.U.	CHILE	VEN.	YUG.
3.74	3.70	3.51	3.39	3.21	3.11	3.11	3.05	2.03

14. Ethical behavior of employees is satisfactory.

U.S.	JAPAN	CHILE	GER.	VEN.	A.M.	P.R.C.	F.S.U.	YUG.
3.64	3.20	3.13	3.04	3.03	3.03	3.02	2.83	2.31

The responses to the first three issue propositions pertaining to the use of technology in the workplace seem to be consistent with expectations: perceived higher level of use in the three market-oriented countries relative to the other five respondent groups' perceptions of use. The responses that pertain to the perceived level of management efficiency/ effectiveness (proposition 4) compared to the perceived adequacy of supply of good managers (proposition 5) by respondents from the former

Soviet Union seem inconsistent. The perceived managerial efficiency/ effectiveness by these respondents is low (2.49) when compared to their perceptions of the adequacy of supply of good managers (3.69). Respondents from Germany, on the other hand, show somewhat opposite perceptions, with mean responses of 3.09 versus 2.85 for propositions 4 and 5, respectively.

Concerning the labor force (propositions 9 through 11), for the total responses as measured by the average mean, respondents perceive a higher quality of work force exists (3.16-proposition 8), but they perceive a lower productivity of labor (2.87-proposition 9) and mobility of labor (proposition 10). The perceived influence of labor unions (proposition 11) is not considered excessive as reflected by the highest average mean (3.54) of the 14 issue propositions.

Table 6.5 shows the overall perceived level of productivity in work organizations by respondents from the countries surveyed as reflected in the combined mean response to the 14 issue propositions summarized previously. The chi square analysis indicates that there are some significant differences (.00 level) in the overall perceived level of productivity in work organizations according to the country of the respondents (.72 coefficient of contingency). On the basis of the mean responses, respondents from the three market-oriented countries perceive a higher level of productivity than respondents from the other countries, and these results are consistent with the other four indicators of a favorable organizational climate relating to participation, communications, motivation, and job security/standard of living. However, the respondents from Chile perceive a somewhat higher level of productivity in work organizations (3.08) than they did for the other four indicators.

The ANOVA Scheffe test results shown on Table 6.5 reflect the significant differences in mean responses of respondents between alternating pairs of countries. These results show the respondents from the United States with a higher perceived level of productivity as reflected in the number of significantly higher mean responses (7 of 7) on one extreme, and those respondents from Yugoslavia with the lowest perceived level of productivity on the other extreme (0 of 7). Respondents from Germany and Japan, each with 5 of 7 significantly higher mean responses, along with the respondents from Chile (4 of 7), are the other countries that perceive somewhat higher levels of productivity in work organizations.

Table 6.5
Overall Perceived Level of Productivity in Organizations

A	Response Frequency (%)							Scheffe Test B							
	1	2	3	4	5	N	X̄	GER.	U.S.	JAPAN	YUG.	P.R.C.	F.S.U.	VEN.	CHILE
GER.	7.4	18.5	29.3	33.3	11.5	847	3.23				X	X	X	X	X
U.S.	6.2	16.0	24.4	38.1	15.2	1763	3.40	X		X	X	X	X	X	X
JAPAN	5.9	19.9	34.9	29.1	10.2	239	3.18				X	X	X	X	X
YUG.	21.1	36.6	22.3	14.8	5.2	738	2.46								
P.R.C.	9.8	36.6	16.7	28.5	8.4	917	2.89				X		X		
F.S.U.	13.4	33.9	20.9	25.1	6.6	1237	2.78				X				
VEN.	11.6	27.0	22.9	28.2	10.2	961	2.99				X	X	X		
CHILE	6.8	23.2	32.5	30.3	7.2	313	3.08				X	X	X	X	
TOTAL	10.3	26.1	23.7	29.7	10.2	7015	3.00								

Total mean = average of eight means
Chi Square (Pearson) = 7406.63 (.00 level)
Coefficient of Contingency = .72
1 = Strongly Disagree; 5 = Strongly Agree

* = Significantly greater perceived level for each pair of countries (.05 level)-A versus B

ANOVA F Ratio = 867.88 (.00 level)

SUMMARY AND CONCLUSIONS

This chapter compares the overall favorable organizational climate as perceived by respondents from the eight countries surveyed. This comparison focuses on five broad issues that reflect the respondents' perceptions of the existence of favorable factors that tend to enhance organizational effectiveness and efficiency, including the satisfaction of people's needs and wants as related to the workplace. These five issues are (1) opportunity to participate in decision making, (2) adequacy of communications within the organization, (3) level of favorable motivational factors and incentives, (4) level of job security and standard of living, and (5) overall productivity of the organization.

In terms of the Scheffe test results that compared mean responses of respondents from each country with the mean responses of respondents from each of the other seven countries, Table 6.6 summarizes the perception of the overall work organization climate as measured by the preceding five issues. The numerical data shown on Table 6.6 are taken from Tables 6.1 through 6.5. These data reflect the frequencies of significantly higher mean responses (.05 level), when each country's respondents' mean responses are individually compared to the mean responses of respondents from each of the other seven countries using the Scheffe test of paired comparisons. The focus of these comparisons is on the significant differences in the perceived organizational climate, rather than simply on the level of perception as measured by a special mean response score.

The data shown on Table 6.6 reflect that the respondents from the United States, compared to those respondents from the other seven countries, perceive a significantly more favorable organizational climate in 33 of 35 (94 percent) of paired comparisons. Respondents from the other two market-oriented countries, Germany and Japan, perceive a more favorable organizational climate in 23 of 35 (66 percent) and 21 of 35 (60 percent) of paired comparisons, relative to the respondents from the three collectivist and two Latin American countries. Concerning the respondents from the other five countries, those from the People's Republic of China have significantly higher mean responses in 16 of 35 cases (46 percent), and Venezuela in 14 of 35 cases (40 percent). However, as a group, the respondents from the two Latin American countries have a higher frequency of significantly higher mean responses in 23 of 70 cases (33 percent) compared to 21 of 105 cases (20 percent) for the three collectivist countries.

Table 6.6
Summary of the Perceived Favorable Organizational Climate

ISSUES	GER.	U.S.	JAPAN	YUG.	P.R.C.	F.S.U.	VEN.	CHILE
1. Participation	1	6	5	0	5	1	4	1
2. Communications	5	7	5	0	4	1	1	1
3. Motivation	6	7	2	0	3	1	3	1
4. Job Security/Standard of Living	6	6	5	0	2	1	3	2
5. Productivity	5	7	4	0	2	1	3	4
Combined Emphasis (1 - 5)	23	33	21	0	16	5	14	9
As a Percent of Maximum	66%	94%	60%	0%	46%	14%	40%	26%

Numbers equal frequency of significantly higher mean responses using ANOVA Scheffe test paired comparisons (0 - 7 is possible range of frequencies) for each of the five issues (maximum total frequency = 35).

The perceived opportunity to participate by the respondents from Germany (1 of 7) and the perceived level of motivation by the respondents from Japan (2 of 7) seem unexpectedly low. The perceived opportunity to participate and the adequacy of communications by respondents from Yugoslavia (0 of 7 for each issue) and for those respondents from the former Soviet Union (1 of 7 for each issue) also seem lower than expected, especially with worker management and more collectivist systems within work organizations. Moreover, this seems true for the issue relating to job security and standard of living for these two countries (recall that for this issue, 3 of the 4 propositions dealt with job security and employment).

In a general way, and to some extent, the perceived favorableness of the organizational climate may reflect the general level of economic development in each country, plus other selected socioeconomic factors may bear on the respondents in different situations. These later factors are still undefined.

7

Profile of National Issues

The analysis in Chapter 6 focused on the overall organizational climate as perceived by respondents from each of the eight countries surveyed. Responses to a number of issue propositions grouped within five broad issues provide a general and overall insight of the significant differences in the perceived organizational climate in work organizations in each respondent group's country. The analysis in this chapter uses a similar approach as that used in Chapter 5, except that the focus is on the overall national climate in terms of perceptions of issues by each group of respondents surveyed. The overall perceived national climate consists of issues relating climate for productivity and growth, national standard of living, and sociopolitical climate. Each of these three issues consists of a number of issue propositions. Again, our focus is on the relative significant differences in perceived issues, rather than on a particular level of perception as measured by a specific numerical value.

ECONOMIC CLIMATE FOR PRODUCTIVITY AND GROWTH

The perceived national economic climate for productivity and growth is reflected in the overall socioeconomic and political infrastructure that exists in each country as it relates to improving national productivity and growth. This national economic climate is reflected in the 19 issue propositions summarized next, which pertain to various monetary/fiscal, government support programs or policies, demographic factors, and other socioeconomic and political factors. The mean response of respondents from each country surveyed, and the average mean (A.M.) of the eight means, are shown for each of the 19 issue propositions. These propositions reflect those that are commonly used when assessing the general national economic climate for productivity and growth.

1. The inflation rate is satisfactory.

GER.	CHILE	JAPAN	A.M.	U.S.	YUG.	P.R.C.	F.S.U.	VEN.
3.76	3.59	3.33	2.94	2.72	2.23	2.21	1.99	1.84

2. Domestic interest rates are satisfactory.

P.R.C.	F.S.U.	JAPAN	A.M.	GER.	CHILE	U..S.	YUG.	VEN.
3.43	3.14	3.07	2.83	2.81	2.72	2.68	2.68	2.14

3. Government fiscal and monetary policies are effective.

GER.	CHILE	JAPAN	P.R.C.	U.S.	A.M.	VEN.	YUG.	F.S.U.
3.15	3.01	2.69	2.69	2.62	2.58	2.45	2.15	1.90

4. National economic development programs are effective.

GER.	CHILE	JAPAN	P.R.C.	U.S.	A.M.	VEN.	YUG.	F.S.U.
3.18	3.03	2.95	2.78	2.70	2.66	2.37	2.24	2.06

5. Regional economic development programs are effective.

P.R.C.	GER.	U.S.	CHILE	JAPAN	A.M.	YUG.	VEN.	F.S.U.
3.20	3.17	2.91	2.77	2.67	2.65	2.23	2.20	2.02

6. Private-public sector economic development cooperation is effective.

F.S.U.	P.R.C.	U.S.	A.M.	GER.	CHILE	JAPAN	YUG.	VEN.
4.02	3.38	3.12	3.01	3.00	2.89	2.83	2.49	2.33

7. Expansion of private enterprise is encouraged.

U.S.	CHILE	GER.	P.R.C.	A.M.	JAPAN	YUG.	VEN.	F.S.U.
3.76	3.67	3.52	3.41	3.30	3.28	3.25	2.92	2.55

8. Government supports small business.

P.R.C.	CHILE	U.S.	YUG.	A.M.	GER.	JAPAN	VEN.	F.S.U.
3.59	3.15	3.08	3.00	2.96	2.86	2.73	2.73	2.57

9. Regulation of economic activity is not excessive.

CHILE	F.S.U.	GER.	P.R.C.	A.M.	U.S.	YUG.	JAPAN	VEN.
3.45	3.43	3.36	3.20	3.19	3.15	3.12	3.03	2.74

10. National defense expenditures are not too high.

P.R.C.	F.S.U.	VEN.	YUG.	A.M.	JAPAN	CHILE	U.S.	GER.
3.22	2.72	2.70	2.57	2.56	2.53	2.44	2.43	1.88

11. Competition exists among domestic firms.

CHILE	U.S.	VEN.	GER.	A.M.	JAPAN	P.R.C.	YUG.	F.S.U.
3.54	3.39	2.91	2.88	2.75	2.72	2.44	2.10	2.04

12. Labor laws have a positive influence on industrial development.

U.S.	JAPAN	P.R.C.	GER.	CHILE	A.M.	VEN.	F.S.U.	YUG.
3.22	3.16	3.15	3.10	2.94	**2.85**	2.51	2.40	2.33

13. Rate of population growth is not too high.

GER.	F.S.U.	YUG.	JAPAN	CHILE	A.M.	U.S.	VEN.	P.R.C.
3.72	3.62	3.51	3.17	3.11	**3.07**	2.68	2.52	2.21

14. Population migration to cities is not too great.

GER.	U.S.	F.S.U.	P.R.C.	A.M.	CHILE	JAPAN	VEN.	YUG.
3.25	2.78	2.46	2.43	**2.37**	2.29	2.06	1.89	1.77

15. Existing transportation infrastructure is satisfactory.

GER.	U.S.	CHILE	JAPAN	A.M.	P.R.C.	VEN.	F.S.U.	YUG.
3.79	3.08	2.98	2.86	**2.68**	2.56	2.15	2.12	1.89

16. Domestic distribution/marketing systems are adequate.

U.S.	GER.	CHILE	JAPAN	A.M.	VEN.	P.R.C.	YUG.	F.S.U.
3.67	3.57	3.21	3.08	**2.79**	2.66	2.50	2.06	1.64

17. Domestic markets are not too small relative to productive capacity.

F.S.U.	YUG.	JAPAN	CHILE	P.R.C.	U.S.	A.M.	VEN.	GER.
3.30	3.21	3.09	3.09	3.08	3.05	**3.02**	2.84	2.51

18. Environmental protection is not a high priority.

YUG.	JAPAN	VEN.	CHILE	A.M.	GER.	U.S.	P.R.C	F.S.U.
3.98	3.76	3.51	3.08	**3.00**	2.91	2.75	2.66	1.36

19. Cultural values that promote economic development are encouraged.

F.S.U.	P.R.C.	U.S.	GER.	A.M.	JAPAN	CHILE	VEN.	YUG.
3.83	3.63	3.36	3.25	**3.14**	3.05	3.04	2.42	2.41

The combined group of 19 propositions reflects the overall favorable perception of the national economic climate for productivity and growth of respondents from each country, and for the combined countries as measured by the average mean. With the average mean as a general indicator, the respondents from the following countries have mean responses that exceed the average mean for each of 19 issue propositions: Chile (14 of 19); Germany, the United States, and the People's Republic of China (13 of 19); Japan (11 of 19); the former Soviet Union (8 of 19); Yugoslavia (5 of 19); and Venezuela (3 of 19). This translates into 37 of 57 (65 percent) for the combined respondents from the three market-oriented countries, compared to 26 of 57 (46 percent) and 17 of 38 (45 percent) for the combined respondents from the three collectivist and two Latin American countries, respectively. On the basis of these comparisons with the average means, the respondents from the three market-oriented countries, plus those from Chile and the People's Republic of China, tend to perceive a higher overall favorable national economic climate.

The first three propositions reflect the perceptions of respondents about the effectiveness of monetary and fiscal policies and their impact on inflation and interest rates. Because of the wide range of perceptions about each of these three propositions, the average means are low (2.94, 2.83, and 2.58, respectively, for propositions 1 through 3). In a general way, the inflation rate and domestic interest rates (propositions 1 and 2) reflect the perceived effectiveness of government fiscal and monetary policies (proposition 3). Thus, those respondent groups that perceive greater effectiveness in government and fiscal policies should also perceive more satisfactory levels of inflation and interest rates. This only seems to be true for the respondents from Chile and Japan.

Propositions 4 through 9 in a general way pertain to the effectiveness of government in enhancing business operations and development. The perceived effectiveness of national and regional economic development programs (propositions 4 and 5) is low as reflected in the responses of the combined respondents with average means of 2.66 and 2.65, respectively. Only the respondents from Germany and Chile (proposition 4), and those from the People's Republic of China and Germany (proposition 5), have mean responses greater than 3.00. Of the respondents from the three collectivist countries, those from the People's Republic of China tend to perceive a greater level of effectiveness of national and economic development programs compared to those respondents from Yugoslavia and the former Soviet Union. Similarly, the respondents from Chile, when compared to those from Venezuela, tend to perceive a greater level of effectiveness for these types of programs.

Propositions 6 through 9 pertain to the general support of business through cooperative and regulative dimensions of government at the national level. There seems to be a greater favorable perception by the respondents as a whole about the effectiveness of these cooperative and regulative endeavors to the first five propositions. This is especially reflected in the high average mean of 3.30 for proposition 7 relating to the encouragement of the expansion of private enterprises, and 3.01 for proposition 6 relating to the effectiveness of public-private sector cooperation. Similarly, the respondents perceive a satisfactory level of regulation of economic activity (3.19-proposition 9).

On the basis of comparisons with the average means, the respondents from Japan and Venezuela tend to perceive lower effectiveness of government relations with business as related to propositions 6 through 9. All of the mean responses of these two respondent groups for these four propositions are less than the average mean, whereas all of the mean responses of the respondents from the People's Republic of China exceed the average mean. The relatively lower overall perception of government effectiveness of the respondents from Japan is unexpected in view of that country's tradition of strong government support of business. Similarly, the relatively greater overall perception of government effectiveness by the Chinese respondents seems somewhat unexpected, unless it stems from a tradition of the acceptance of authority.

The responses to the remaining issue propositions 10 through 18 are mixed. In terms of the average means, there seems to be a perception that national defense expenditures are too high (proposition 10), population migration to cities is too great (proposition 14), competition among domestic firms needs to be improved (proposition 11), and the general transportation infrastructure needs improvement (proposition 15). On the basis of proposition 19, there is a stronger perception that cultural values that promote economic development are encouraged (overall mean of 3.14, with mean responses above 3.00 for respondents from six of the eight countries).

Table 7.1 shows the overall perceived favorable level of the national economic climate for productivity and growth by respondents from each country surveyed. This overall perception is the combined total responses to the 19 issue propositions summarized. The chi square analysis indicates that there are some significant differences (.00 level) in the overall perception of the national economic climate for productivity and growth according to the country of the respondents (.74 coefficient of contingency). On the basis of the mean responses, respondents from Germany (3.15), Chile (3.06), and the United States (3.00) perceive a greater favorable national economic climate for productivity and growth.

The ANOVA Scheffe test results shown on Table 7.1 provide information on the specific paired comparisons of mean scores for this issues category. The perceived national economic climate for productivity and growth by respondents from Germany is significantly higher than

Table 7.1
Overall Perception of Favorable National Economic Climate for Productivity and Growth

A	Response Frequency (%)					N	X̄	Scheffe Test — B							
	1	2	3	4	5			GER.	U.S.	JAPAN	YUG.	P.R.C.	F.S.U.	VEN.	CHILE
GER.	9.0	19.5	28.0	33.6	9.8	906	3.15		X	X	X	X	X	X	X
U.S.	11.3	23.4	27.3	29.8	8.2	1773	3.00				X	X	X	X	
JAPAN	9.1	23.8	36.2	24.2	6.7	303	2.96				X		X	X	
YUG.	21.1	32.0	22.9	16.9	7.0	747	2.57							X	
P.R.C	12.1	32.7	16.6	31.4	7.2	990	2.89				X		X	X	
F.S.U.	23.5	34.1	13.9	21.0	7.5	1246	2.55							X	
VEN.	24.2	34.3	16.7	16.8	8.0	964	2.50								
CHILE	9.0	25.1	26.3	31.3	8.4	316	3.06			X	X	X	X	X	
TOTAL	15.7	28.4	22.1	25.9	8.0	7245	2.84								

Total mean = average of eight means
Chi Square (Pearson) = 8748.22 (.00 level)
Coefficient of Contingency = .74
1 = Strongly Disagree; 5 = Strongly Agree

* = Significantly greater perceived level for each pair of countries (.05 level)-A versus B

ANOVA F Ratio = 793.76 (.00 level)

that perceived by respondents from each of the other countries (7 of 7). Respondents from Chile and the United States perceive a more favorable national economic climate in 5 of 7 and 4 of 7 paired comparisons, respectively. Respondents from Japan and the People's Republic of China are next, with significantly higher perceptions of a favorable national economic climate in 3 of 7 pair comparisons. In terms of these paired comparisons, the respondents from Chile perceive the least favorable overall national economic climate, followed by those from the former Soviet Union as perceiving the next least favorable economic climate.

ADEQUACY OF STANDARD OF LIVING

The national standard of living measures include such factors as income levels, availability of housing, access to consumer goods and services, effectiveness of social welfare programs, and general level of confidence about the future. The perceived adequacy of the standard of living is reflected in the 11 issue propositions summarized next. The mean response of respondents from each country surveyed, and the average mean (A.M.) of the eight means, are shown for each of these 11 propositions. These propositions reflect those commonly used when assessing the general standard of living for a particular country.

1. Poverty level is low.

JAPAN	P.R.C.	F.S.U.	GER.	A.M.	U.S.	YUG.	VEN.	CHILE
3.53	3.25	3.20	2.87	2.76	2.57	2.29	2.21	2.12

2. Per capita income is satisfactory.

GER.	JAPAN	U.S.	A.M.	CHILE	VEN.	P.R.C.	F.S.U.	YUG.
3.45	3.13	2.73	2.52	2.50	2.28	2.25	1.98	1.85

3. Equality of income distribution is satisfactory.

GER.	U.S.	P.R.C.	A.M.	CHILE	JAPAN	YUG.	F.S.U.	VEN.
2.96	2.62	2.42	2.35	2.31	2.25	2.17	2.07	2.00

4. Unemployment level is satisfactory.

JAPAN	F.S.U.	P.R.C.	U.S.	CHILE	A.M.	VEN.	GER.	YUG.
3.94	3.52	3.26	2.93	2.89	2.88	2.48	2.31	1.72

5. Adequate housing exists.

P.R.C.	U.S.	CHILE	A.M.	JAPAN	YUG.	VEN.	GER.	F.S.U.
2.89	2.57	2.50	2.10	1.97	1.96	1.85	1.57	1.47

6. Qualify of consumer products is good.

GER.	JAPAN	U.S.	CHILE	A.M.	YUG.	VEN.	P.R.C.	F.S.U.
4.19	4.08	3.78	3.42	3.07	2.79	2.37	2.27	1.64

7. Quality of consumer products and services is satisfactory.

GER.	U.S.	CHILE	JAPAN	A.M.	YUG.	VEN.	P.R.C.	F.S.U.
3.90	3.61	3.41	3.39	2.93	2.48	2.44	2.36	1.88

8. Sufficient opportunities to own property exist.

GER.	YUG.	U.S.	P.R.C.	A.M.	CHILE	VEN.	F.S.U.	JAPAN
3.39	3.35	3.27	3.11	2.71	2.57	2.17	2.15	1.65

9. Social welfare programs are effective.

GER.	P.R.C.	CHILE	A.M.	U.S.	JAPAN	VEN.	F.S.U.	YUG.
3.74	3.19	2.77	2.72	2.69	2.65	2.38	2.22	2.14

10. Government social welfare expenditures are satisfactory.

JAPAN	U.S.	A.M.	CHILE	GER.	P.R.C.	VEN.	YUG.	F.S.U.
3.92	2.93	2.68	2.68	2.61	2.61	2.45	2.16	2.10

11. Level of confidence about the future is high.

GER.	U.S.	P.R.C.	CHILE	JAPAN	A.M.	F.S.U.	VEN.	YUG.
3.47	3.28	3.25	3.22	3.13	3.00	2.67	2.64	2.35

The combined group of 11 propositions reflects the overall favorable perception of the national standard of living by respondents from each country, and for the eight countries combined, as measured by the average mean. When the average mean is used as a general indicator, the following countries have mean responses that exceed the average mean for each of the 11 issue propositions: the United States (9 of 11), Germany (8 of 11 each), Japan and the People's Republic of China (7 of 11 each), Chile (6 of 11), the former Soviet Union (2 of 11), and Yugoslavia (1 of 11). This translates into 24 of 33 (73 percent) for the combined respondents from the three market-oriented countries, compared to 10 of 33 (30 percent) and 6 of 22 (27 percent) for the combined respondents from the three collectivist and the two Latin American countries, respectively.

The five respondent groups with the higher overall perceived adequacy of the standard of living are the three market-oriented countries, as you would expect, plus those respondents from the People's Republic of China and Chile. These perceptions are similar to those relating to the perceptions of overall productivity in these countries.

The first five propositions deal generally with the economic conditions that are perceived in each country. Looking first at the respondents from the three market-oriented countries, and using the average mean as a basic benchmark, the following observations about differences are made. Relative to respondents from Germany and Japan, those from the United States perceive a greater level of poverty (proposition 1), greater satisfactory level of income distribution (proposition 3) relative to the respondents from Japan, more satisfactory level of unemployment (proposition 4) compared to respondents from Germany, and more adequate housing (proposition 5) compared to respondents from Japan and Germany.

The respondents from the People's Republic of China and the former Soviet Union have similar perceptions: lower poverty level, lower per capita income, and a more satisfactory unemployment level, with higher than the average mean responses for these propositions (1, 2, and 4). However, the respondents from the People's Republic of China perceive a greater equality of income (proposition 4) and more adequate housing (proposition 5) than do the respondents from the former Soviet Union. The respondents from the other collectivist countries perceive a lower standard of living as reflected in all of these five propositions. The respondents from Chile are the only other group that perceives a higher standard of living relating to any of these first value propositions: more adequate housing (propositions 4 and 5, respectively).

As might be expected, there is a wide range of perceptions by respondents as they pertain to the quality of consumer goods and services (propositions 6 and 7). Except for the respondents from Venezuela, the People's Republic of China, and the former Soviet Union, in terms of their mean responses, the perceived level of satisfaction with the quality of consumer products and services is less when services are included in the issue proposition (proposition 7 versus 6).

The perceptions of social welfare program effectiveness (proposition 9) and satisfactory government expenditures for welfare (proposition 10) are summarized as follows. The respondents from Germany, the People's Republic of China, and Chile perceive more effective social welfare programs than do the other five respondent groups using the average mean as a basic benchmark. On the other hand, only the respondents from Japan and the United States perceive that government expenditures on social welfare are at a satisfactory level. The mean responses from all countries except the former Soviet Union, Venezuela, and Yugoslavia to proposition 11 (high confidence about the future) in general reflect a somewhat more favorable overall perception of the national standard of living.

Table 7.2 shows the overall perceived favorable level of the national standard of living by respondents from each country surveyed as reflected by the combined responses to the 11 issue propositions summarized. The chi square analysis indicates that there are some significant differences (.00 level) in the overall perception of the level of the national standard of living according to the country of the respondents (.71 coefficient of contingency). On the basis of the mean responses, the respondents from Germany (3.13), Japan (3.08), and the United States (3.08), as we might expect, perceive a higher national standard of living exists in their countries.

The ANOVA Scheffe test results shown on Table 7.2 provide information on the specific paired comparisons of mean scores for this issue. This information shows that the perceived national standard of living by respondents from Germany is higher in 6 of 7 paired comparisons, followed by those respondents from Japan and the United States (5 of 7 each). The paired comparison results for the remaining countries seem consistent with what one might expect, with the respondents from the People's Republic of China and Chile next, each with 3 of 7 significantly higher mean scores. The results shown on Table 7.2 are generally comparable with those pertaining to perceptions of national economic climate for productivity and growth as summarized earlier on Table 7.1.

FAVORABLE SOCIOPOLITICAL CLIMATE

The perceived favorable sociopolitical climate is reflected in the nine issue propositions summarized. These propositions include such factors as the opportunities for citizens to influence government, level of government corruption, support for family and ethnic values, and level of sociopolitical unrest within society. The mean responses of respondents from each country surveyed, and the average mean (A.M.) of the eight means, are shown for each of the nine issues propositions. These propositions reflect some of those commonly used when assessing the

Table 7.2
Overall Perception of Favorable Level of the National Standard of Living

A	Response Frequency (%)					N	X̄	Scheffe Test (B)							
	1	2	3	4	5			GER.	U.S.	JAPAN	YUG.	P.R.C.	F.S.U.	VEN.	CHILE
GER.	12.6	20.5	20.2	34.3	12.5	906	3.13		X		X	X	X	X	X
U.S.	13.1	26.4	18.5	31.3	10.7	1773	3.00				X	X	X	X	X
JAPAN	13.8	18.4	26.0	29.3	12.6	304	3.08				X	X	X	X	X
YUG.	28.5	36.7	16.2	14.1	4.6	748	2.30								
P.R.C.	13.7	35.3	15.8	27.9	7.2	990	2.80				X		X	X	
F.S.U.	30.6	36.9	14.8	13.1	4.6	1245	2.24								
VEN.	32.4	34.2	12.6	13.0	7.8	964	2.30								
CHILE	15.8	31.7	20.4	25.2	6.9	316	2.76				X		X	X	
TOTAL	20.3	30.6	17.1	23.6	8.3	7246	2.70								

Total mean = average of eight means
Chi Square (Pearson) = 7280.75 (.00 level)
Coefficient of Contingency = .71
1 = Strongly Disagree; 5 = Strongly Agree

* = Significantly greater perceived level for each pair of countries (.05 level)-A versus B

ANOVA F Ratio = 945.00 (.00 level)

general sociopolitical climate in a country.

1. The extent of centralized government is satisfactory.

GER.	U.S.	CHILE	P.R.C.	A.M.	YUG.	JAPAN	F.S.U.	VEN.
3.53	3.11	3.00	2.73	2.66	2.61	2.43	1.99	1.89

2. Sufficient opportunities exist for citizens to influence government policies.

U.S.	JAPAN	P.R.C.	CHILE	A.M.	GER.	F.S.U.	YUG.	VEN.
2.83	2.45	2.43	2.36	2.29	2.25	2.03	2.02	1.91

3. Communications between government agencies and citizens are effective.

CHILE	U.S.	P.R.C.	JAPAN	A.M.	F.S.U.	GER.	VEN.	YUG.
2.76	2.69	2.69	2.44	2.40	2.36	2.26	2.09	1.89

4. Government corruption is low.

CHILE	GER.	P.R.C.	A.M.	U.S.	JAPAN	YUG.	F.S.U.	VEN.
3.33	3.18	2.89	2.46	2.45	2.26	2.10	2.04	1.45

5. Crime rate is low.

JAPAN	P.R.C.	GER.	A.M.	YUG.	CHILE	U.S.	VEN.	F.S.U.
3.32	2.81	2.35	2.28	2.14	2.14	1.90	1.78	1.77

6. Recognition of ethnic cultures is an important priority.

F.S.U.	P.R.C.	U.S.	A.M.	GER.	YUG.	CHILE	VEN.	JAPAN
4.02	3.65	3.17	3.05	3.04	3.00	2.69	2.47	2.34

7. Family activities are encouraged.

U.S.	P.R.C.	GER.	CHILE	A.M.	JAPAN	F.S.U.	VEN.	YUG.
3.41	3.18	2.89	2.82	2.82	2.67	2.61	2.50	2.44

8. Serious conflicts between social/ethnic groups do not exist.

P.R.C.	JAPAN	VEN.	CHILE	A.M.	GER.	F.S.U.	U.S.	YUG.
3.46	3.44	3.37	3.18	2.89	2.75	2.44	2.39	2.06

9. Level of political/social unrest is low.

GER.	JAPAN	U.S.	P.R.C.	A.M.	CHILE	F.S.U.	VEN.	YUG.
3.21	3.21	3.05	2.69	2.63	2.59	2.47	1.99	1.80

The preceding nine issue propositions as a whole reflect the overall perception of the favorableness of the sociopolitical climate within each country, and for the eight countries as measured by the average mean.

Using the average mean as a general indicator, respondents from the following countries have mean responses that exceed the average mean for each of the nine propositions: the People's Republic of China (9 of 9); the United States and Chile (6 of 9 each); Germany and Japan (5 of 9); and the former Soviet Union and Venezuela (1 of 9 each). This translates into 16 of 27 (59 percent) for the combined respondents from the three market-oriented countries, compared 7 of 18 (39 percent) and 10 of 27 (37 percent) for the combined respondents from the two Latin American and three collectivist countries, respectively.

The first three issue propositions deal generally with the opportunities to influence government. Taken as a whole, and as reflected by the average means, the perceived level of access to government by respondents tends to be generally low as regards their access to, and ability to influence, government. Except for the mean responses of the respondents from Germany (3.53), the United States (3.11), and Chile (3.00) regarding the extent of centralized government (proposition 1), all respondents tend to perceive a low overall effectiveness of government as measured by the first three issues propositions (all other mean responses are below 2.83 and as low as 1.89). The average means for these propositions are quite low, 2.66, 2.29, and 2.40 for propositions 1 through 3, respectively.

This low perception of the level of effectiveness of government continues when you look at the mean responses for propositions 4 and 5, that deal with the level of government corruption and the crime rate, respectively. Except for Chile (3.33) and Germany (3.18) in regard to government corruption, and Japan (3.32) for the crime rate, all perceptions by respondents from the other countries are below a 2.89 mean response, and as low as 1.45. Moreover, the average means for propositions 4 and 5 are very low, 2.46 and 2.78, respectively.

The remaining propositions 6 through 9 pertain more to the social environment in each country. The perceptions of respondents for these five propositions taken as a whole reflect a more favorable social climate, as reflected in the higher average mean scores. However, there are important lower perceptions of the social environment as reflected in these last four propositions when you look at specific countries. For example, using the average mean as a basic benchmark, the respondents from Yugoslavia and the former Soviet Union tend to perceive a higher level of social unrest (lower mean responses) than those respondents from the People's Republic of China as reflected in propositions 7 through 9. It is interesting to note the lower perceived encouragement of family activities by the respondents from Japan (proposition 7). There seem to be conflicting views by both groups of respondents from the United States and the former Soviet Union regarding their higher perceived recognition of ethnic cultures (proposition 6) compared to their higher perceived level (lower mean responses) of social/ethnic conflicts (proposition 8). Moreover, both groups of respondents from Germany and the United States perceive more serious social/ethnic conflicts (proposition 8), yet they perceive a lower level of political/social unrest (proposition 9).

Table 7.3 shows the overall perceived favorableness of the sociopolitical climate by respondents from each country surveyed as reflected by the combined response to the nine issue propositions summarized. The chi square analysis indicates that there are some significant differences (.00 level) in the overall perceived sociopolitical climate according to the country of the respondents (.65 coefficient of contingency). Compared to the average means for the two other national issues categories, economic climate (2.84-Table 7.1) and standard of living (2.70-Table 7.2), the average mean for responses about the sociopolitical climate shown on Table 7.3 is the lowest (2.60) of the three issues categories. Moreover, none of the mean responses for respondents from any of the eight countries exceeds 2.95 (the People's Republic of China), with the lowest being 2.15 (Venezuela).

Within this generally low range of mean responses, the ANOVA Scheffe test results shown on Table 7.3 provide information on the relative perceived favorableness of the sociopolitical climate using individual paired comparisons of mean responses for this issue. This analysis shows that the respondents from the People's Republic of China perceive a more favorable sociopolitical climate in their country, compared to respondents from all of the other seven countries. Respondents from the three market-oriented countries, along with Chile, perceive the next most favorable sociopolitical climate (3 of 7 paired comparisons each). The respondents from Yugoslavia and Venezuela (0 of 7 paired comparisons) are at the other extreme. The higher perceived overall favorableness of the sociopolitical climate by the respondents from the People's Republic of China is somewhat unexpected considering that the responses were received at about the time of the sociopolitical unrest in 1989. However, keep in mind that this higher perception is relative to the perceptions of other respondent groups, rather than an absolute measure of the sociopolitical climate.

Table 7.3
Overall Perceived Sociopolitical Climate

| | Response Frequency (%) | | | | | | | Scheffe Test (B) | | | | | | | |
A	1	2	3	4	5	N	$\bar{X}$	GER.	U.S.	JAPAN	YUG.	P.R.C.	F.S.U.	VEN.	CHILE
GER.	11.6	30.8	27.4	24.0	6.2	906	2.82				X		X	X	
U.S.	16.0	28.7	23.9	24.3	7.0	1773	2.78				X		X	X	
JAPAN	12.2	33.6	28.5	19.2	6.4	304	2.74				X		X	X	
YUG.	29.3	37.3	19.0	10.5	3.9	747	2.22								
P.R.C.	12.4	28.7	18.1	33.1	7.6	990	2.95	X	X	X	X		X	X	X
F.S.U.	23.7	39.5	14.8	16.3	5.7	1246	2.41				X			X	
VEN.	38.3	32.1	12.5	10.0	7.0	963	2.15								
CHILE	14.7	30.2	26.1	21.7	7.2	316	2.76				X		X	X	
TOTAL	20.4	32.4	20.3	20.5	6.5	7245	2.60								

* = Significantly greater perceived level for each pair of countries (.05 level)-A versus B

ANOVA F Ratio = 510.05 (.00 level)

Total mean = average of eight means
Chi Square (Pearson) = 5279.87 (.00 level)
Coefficient of Contingency = .65
1 = Strongly Disagree; 5 = Strongly Agree

SUMMARY AND CONCLUSIONS

This chapter compares the perceived relative overall favorableness of the national climate by respondents from the eight countries surveyed. This comparison focuses on three broad issues that reflect the respondents' perceptions of the existence of favorable factors that tend to enhance the overall national sociopolitical and economic climate in each country surveyed: (1) economic climate for productivity and growth, (2) standard of living, and (3) sociopolitical climate.

Using the Scheffe test results that compared the mean responses of respondents from each country with the mean responses of respondents for each of the other seven countries, Table 7.4 summarizes the perceived overall favorableness of the national climate as measured by the three issues. The numerical data shown on Table 7.4 are taken from Tables 7.1 through 7.3, and they reflect the frequencies of significantly higher mean responses (.05 level), using the Scheffe test of paired comparisons. The focus of these comparisons is on the significant differences in the perceived national climate, rather than simply the level of perceptions as measured by a mean response score.

On the basis of 21 paired comparisons of mean responses for the combined three issues, the respondents from Germany perceive a higher overall favorable level of the national climate in 16 of 21 cases (76 percent), followed by the respondents from the People's Republic of China in 13 of 21 cases (62 percent), the United States in 12 of 21 cases (57 percent), and Japan and Chile in 11 of 21 cases (52 percent for each). The combined respondents from three market-oriented countries have the highest perception of an overall favorable national climate (39 of 51, or 76 percent), compared to the combined respondents from the three collectivist countries (17 of 51, or 33 percent) and the two Latin American countries (11 of 42, or 26 percent).

The relative perceptions of an overall favorable national climate as shown on Table 7.4 in a general way reflect the sociopolitical and economic problems that currently exist in each of these eight countries. The three market-oriented countries, plus the People's Republic of China and Chile, have more favorable economic climates and standards of living. The relatively lower perceptions of a favorable sociopolitical climate in Yugoslavia, Venezuela, and the former Soviet Union seem consistent with current conditions in these countries.

Table 7.4
Summary of Perceived Overall National Climate

ISSUES	GER.	U.S.	JAPAN	YUG.	P.R.C.	F.S.U.	VEN.	CHILE
1. Economic Climate	7	4	3	1	3	1	0	5
2. Standard of Living	6	5	5	0	3	0	0	3
3. Social and Political Climate	3	3	3	0	7	2	0	3
Combined Issues, 1 - 3	16	12	11	1	13	3	0	11
As a Percent of Possible	76%	57%	52%	5%	62%	14%	0%	52%

Note: Numbers equal frequency of significantly higher mean responses using ANOVA Scheffe test of paired comparisons (0 - 7 are the possible frequencies) for each of the three issues categories (maximum total frequency = 21).

8

Profile of International Issues

Continuing our cross-cultural discussion of issues, this chapter focuses on the international environment using a similar analytical approach to that used in Chapter 6 (organizational issues) and Chapter 7 (national issues). The international issues addressed in this chapter are related to (1) the economic climate for trade and development, (2) the need to develop resources, (3) the effectiveness of world governance/cooperative organizations, and (4) the emphasis on nationalism. The focus of our analysis is on the significant differences in perceived issues of respondents from each of the eight countries surveyed.

ECONOMIC CLIMATE FOR TRADE AND DEVELOPMENT

The perceived international economic climate for trade and development as an issue is reflected in the overall socioeconomic and political infrastructure that exists in each country and throughout the international community. This economic climate is reflected in the 17 issue propositions summarized in the following discussion that pertain to various factors such as opportunities for free trade, levels of imports and exports, export incentives, and international facilitators/limiters of trade. The mean response of respondents from each country surveyed, and the average mean (A.M.) of the eight means, are shown for each of the 17 issue propositions. These propositions are among those commonly used when assessing the general international economic climate for trade and development.

1. There are no serious trade barriers for exports.

GER.	CHILE	P.R.C.	**A.M.**	F.S.U.	JAPAN	U.S.	YUG.	VEN.
3.21	2.69	2.55	**2.55**	2.50	2.47	2.37	2.37	2.25

2. There are adequate opportunities for free trade.

P.R.C.	GER.	CHILE	U.S.	**A.M.**	YUG.	VEN.	JAPAN	F.S.U.
3.47	3.43	3.27	3.19	**3.04**	2.99	2.96	2.71	2.29

3. Dependence on imports is low.

P.R.C.	GER.	CHILE	F.S.U.	**A.M.**	YUG.	JAPAN	U.S.	VEN.
2.84	2.76	2.60	2.56	**2.45**	2.42	2.36	2.19	1.83

4. The level of exports is high.

GER.	JAPAN	CHILE	**A.M.**	P.R.C.	U.S.	F.S.U.	VEN.	YUG.
4.01	3.69	3.39	**2.96**	2.71	2.65	2.57	2.57	2.10

5. The balance of trade payments deficit is not too large.

JAPAN	GER.	CHILE	**A.M.**	P.R.C.	F.S.U.	YUG.	VEN.	U.S.
3.73	3.55	3.22	**2.75**	2.57	2.44	2.33	2.11	2.06

6. The level of foreign trade is satisfactory.

GER.	CHILE	JAPAN	VEN.	**A.M.**	U.S.	P.R.C.	YUG.	F.S.U.
3.80	3.08	2.97	2.83	**2.80**	2.63	2.62	2.32	2.18

7. New markets for domestic products are needed.

JAPAN	GER.	CHILE	F.S.U.	**A.M.**	P.R.C.	U.S.	YUG.	VEN.
2.59	2.38	2.25	2.22	**2.21**	2.18	2.16	2.02	1.88

8. There is sufficient export assistance to domestic producers.

GER.	P.R.C.	CHILE	YUG.	**A.M.**	U.S.	JAPAN	VEN.	F.S.U.
3.24	2.99	2.89	2.78	**2.78**	2.77	2.67	2.52	2.40

9. Export incentives should not be provided to domestic firms.

GER.	JAPAN	YUG.	U.S.	**A.M.**	CHILE	VEN.	P.R.C.	F.S.U.
3.47	3.34	2.76	2.73	**2.69**	2.55	2.46	2.12	2.09

10. The domestic currency is stable.

GER.	U.S.	JAPAN	CHILE	**A.M.**	VEN.	P.R.C.	F.S.U.	YUG.
4.22	3.28	3.25	2.96	**2.76**	2.21	2.09	2.05	2.02

11. High level domestic development does not require extensive regulation of imports.

GER.	VEN.	JAPAN	U.S.	**A.M.**	CHILE	YUG.	P.R.C.	F.S.U.
3.63	3.28	3.11	2.98	**2.90**	2.84	2.62	2.36	2.34

12. The European Economic Community is necessary.

F.S.U.	VEN.	YUG.	GER.	A.M.	P.R.C.	U.S.	CHILE	JAPAN
4.04	3.91	3.88	3.74	3.67	3.58	3.51	3.49	3.21

13. The influence of the Organization of Petroleum Exporting Countries (OPEC) is not too extensive.

VEN.	F.S.U.	P.R.C.	GER.	A.M.	JAPAN	CHILE	U.S.	YUG.
3.00	2.71	2.65	2.63	2.57	2.56	2.37	2.33	2.27

14. Economic imperialism is not a continuing threat.

F.S.U.	U.S.	GER.	JAPAN	A.M.	CHILE	YUG.	P.R.C.	VEN.
3.31	3.12	2.97	2.90	2.80	2.73	2.61	2.51	2.26

15. Tourism as a source of revenue is important.

YUG.	VEN.	U.S.	CHILE	P.R.C.	A.M.	F.S.U.	JAPAN	GER.
4.29	4.22	4.03	3.72	3.68	3.68	3.40	3.27	2.81

16. Confidence in the dollar is high.

F.S.U.	YUG.	A.M.	VEN.	P.R.C.	U.S.	CHILE	JAPAN	GER.
4.17	3.33	3.15	3.09	3.02	3.01	3.00	2.90	2.66

17. The ability of the world monetary system to provide for growth is good.

F.S.U.	P.R.C.	JAPAN	U.S.	A.M.	YUG.	GER.	VEN.	CHILE
3.56	3.42	3.15	3.09	3.08	3.05	2.87	2.78	2.68

The combined group of 17 issue propositions reflects the overall favorable perception of the national economic climate for trade and development by respondents from each country, and for the eight countries as measured by the average mean. On the basis of the average mean as a general indicator, respondents from the following countries have mean responses that exceed (or equal) the overall mean response for each of the 17 propositions: Germany (14 of 17); Chile (10 of 17); Japan (9 of 17); the United States, the People's Republic of China, and the former Soviet Union (7 of 17 each); and Yugoslavia and Venezuela (5 of 17 each). This corresponds to 30 of 51 (59 percent) for the three market-oriented countries, compared to 15 of 34 (44 percent) for the two Latin American countries and 19 of 51 (39 percent) for the respondents from the three collectivist countries.

The first two issue propositions relate to the existence of trade barriers and free trade opportunities. The average means to these two issues differ, 2.55 (proposition 1) versus 3.04 (proposition 2). This tends to indicate some perceived dissatisfaction with existing trade barriers compared to the adequacy of opportunities for free trade. This is especially true for the respondents from the United States, who disagree that no serious trade barriers exist (2.37), yet perceive relatively higher opportunities for free trade (3.19). These opportunities may exist for other reasons than the nonexistence of trade barriers.

Propositions 3 through 9 deal with import and export levels and the level of foreign trade. In the combined responses from all of the countries, respondents appear to have a low perceived level of satisfaction with the balance of trade and the overall level of foreign trade (average means range from 2.45 to 2.96). For each of the four propositions 3 through 6, more of the respondents from Germany, Japan, and Chile consistently perceive a more favorable overall foreign trade situation for their respective countries than do the respondents from the other countries surveyed, except for Japan's dependency on imports (proposition 3). The respondents as a whole do not perceive a need to find new markets for domestic products (2.21-proposition 7), yet disagree that export assistance (2.78-proposition 8) and export incentives (2.69-proposition 9) are not needed.

Propositions 10 and 11 reflect the level of perceived satisfaction with the domestic economy, especially in relation to the international trade situation. The total respondents generally disagree that the domestic currency is stable (2.76-proposition 10) and that domestic development does not require regulation of imports (2.90-proposition 11).

Propositions 12 through 14 relate to the impact of international economic cooperative ventures. The respondents as a whole perceive that the European Economic Community is needed (3.67-proposition 12), but do not agree that the influence of the Organization of Petroleum Exporting Countries (OPEC) is not too extensive (2.57-proposition 13), and that economic imperialism is not a continuing threat (2.80-proposition 14). There seems to be greater general support among respondents as a whole that tourism is an important source of revenue (3.68-proposition 15), and they tend to have confidence in the dollar (3.15-proposition 16). Moreover, they perceive that the world's monetary system is somewhat able to provide for growth (3.08-proposition 17).

Table 8.1 shows the overall perceived international climate for trade and development of respondents from each country surveyed. This overall perception is the combined responses to the 17 issue propositions summarized. The chi square analysis indicates that there are some

Table 8.1
Overall Perceived Economic Climate for Trade and Development

A	Response Frequency (%)					N	X̄	Scheffe Test							
	1	2	3	4	5			GER.	U.S.	JAPAN	YUG.	P.R.C.	F.S.U.	VEN.	CHILE
GER.	5.6	21.9	26.0	33.7	12.7	904	3.26		X	X	X	X	X	X	X
U.S.	11.5	30.9	27.6	22.9	7.0	1769	2.83				X	X	X	X	
JAPAN	7.3	25.7	34.1	25.5	7.5	302	3.00		X		X	X	X	X	
YUG.	13.6	34.7	24.7	19.4	7.6	739	2.73								
P.R.C.	9.1	41.1	17.4	28.4	4.1	988	2.77							X	
F.S.U.	12.8	38.9	16.2	23.5	8.6	1241	2.76								
VEN.	17.6	34.8	16.8	20.2	10.6	954	2.71								
CHILE	8.1	31.8	25.6	28.1	6.3	314	2.93				X	X	X	X	
TOTAL	11.4	33.1	22.7	24.8	8.1	7211	2.87								

Total mean = average of eight means
Chi Square (Pearson) = 5304.02 (.00 level)
Coefficient of Contingency = .65
1 = Strongly Disagree; 5 = Strongly Agree

* = Significantly greater perceived level for each pair of
countries (.05 level)-A versus B

ANOVA F Ratio = 340.42 (.00 level)

significant differences (.00 level) in the overall perception of the international climate for export trade and development according to the country of the respondents (.65 coefficient of contingency). On the basis of the mean responses shown on Table 8.1, respondents from Germany (3.26) perceive a better economic climate exists, followed by respondents from Japan (3.00) and Chile (2.93), all with a mean response higher than the average mean.

The ANOVA Scheffe test results shown on Table 8.1 indicate that the respondents from Germany perceive a better economic climate for trade and development than the respondents from each of the other seven countries (7 of 7 paired comparisons). The respondents from Japan and Chile perceive the next best economic climate (5 of 7 paired comparisons), followed by those from the United States (4 of 7 paired comparisons). The respondents from the remaining four countries perceive a less favorable economic climate for trade and development.

NEED TO DEVELOP RESOURCES

The need to develop resources is an issue that has an international dimension, and in a general way, affects the overall international climate. The perceived need to develop resources is reflected in the four issue propositions summarized next. The mean response of respondents from each country surveyed, and the average mean (A.M.) of the eight means, are shown for each of the four issue propositions.

1. Development of nuclear energy for nonmilitary uses is necessary.

P.R.C.	CHILE	VEN.	U.S.	JAPAN	F.S.U.	A.M.	GER.	YUG.
4.06	3.88	3.82	3.48	3.40	3.39	**3.39**	2.70	2.35

2. There is not sufficient access to energy resources.

YUG.	JAPAN	GER.	P.R.C.	A.M.	CHILE	U.S.	F.S.U.	VEN.
3.78	3.56	3.47	3.22	**3.19**	3.04	2.92	2.77	2.75

3. Space exploration is needed to provide future resource needs.

F.S.U.	YUG.	JAPAN	P.R.C.	U.S.	A.M.	VEN.	CHILE	GER.
3.95	3.75	3.64	3.57	3.47	**3.46**	3.23	3.21	2.87

4. Highly qualified people are leaving our country.

YUG.	VEN.	P.R.C.	F.S.U.	JAPAN	CHILE	A.M.	U.S.	GER.
4.47	3.89	3.58	3.53	3.45	3.40	**3.39**	2.69	2.11

The combined group of four issue propositions reflects the overall need to develop resources as perceived by respondents from each country surveyed, and for the combined countries as measured by the average mean. Using the average mean as a general indicator, respondents from the following countries have mean responses that exceed the average mean for each of the four issue propositions: Japan and the People's Republic of China (4 of 4 each); Yugoslavia and the former Soviet Union (3 of 4 each); the United States, Venezuela, and Chile (2 of 4 each); and Germany (1 of 4). This corresponds to 10 of 12 (83 percent) for the combined respondents from the three collectivist countries, compared to 7 of 12 (58 percent) and 4 of 8 (50 percent) for the combined respondents from three market-oriented and two Latin American countries, respectively.

The first three propositions deal with energy and physical resource needs, while proposition 4 relates to the need for human capital. The average means for the combined respondents are all above 3.00, indicating relatively high support for the development of resources. It is interesting to note that, except for the respondents from Germany and Yugoslavia, all respondents support the development of nuclear energy for nonmilitary purposes (proposition 1). Moreover, even though the United State is a world leader in space exploration, the respondents from the United States do not perceive this as important (3.47) compared to respondents from four other countries (proposition 3). The international mobility of labor is perceived to be very high in six of the eight countries (proposition 4), excluding the United States and Germany.

Table 8.2 shows the overall perceived need to develop resources by respondents form each country surveyed, as reflected in the combined responses to the four issue propositions summarized. The chi square analysis indicates that there are some significant differences (.00 level) in the overall perception of the need to develop resources according to the country of the respondents (.46 coefficient of contingency). However, except for the respondents from Germany, all mean responses are 3.15 or higher. This indicates relatively high support for the development of resources. Besides the respondents from Germany, those from the United States have a lower mean response (3.15) than the average mean.

The ANOVA Scheffe test results shown on Table 8.2 indicate that respondents from the People's Republic of China and Yugoslavia perceive the greatest need to develop resources when compared to the other countries (5 of 7 paired comparisons). Except for the respondents

Table 8.2
Overall Perceived Need to Develop Resources

A	Response Frequency (%)					N	X̄	Scheffe Test (B)							
	1	2	3	4	5			GER.	U.S.	JAPAN	YUG.	P.R.C.	F.S.U.	VEN.	CHILE
GER.	16.9	28.4	22.0	23.6	9.1	904	2.80								
U.S.	9.2	23.5	23.1	31.8	12.3	1767	3.15	X							
JAPAN	4.6	13.3	27.3	35.8	19.0	300	3.51	X	X						
YUG.	10.6	11.8	14.6	34.1	28.9	738	3.59	X	X				X	X	X
P.R.C.	2.9	17.5	12.7	49.2	17.7	988	3.61	X	X				X	X	X
F.S.U.	5.1	18.4	20.3	37.2	18.9	1231	3.46	X	X						
VEN.	7.4	17.5	19.2	36.0	19.9	954	3.44	X	X						
CHILE	4.6	20.1	23.4	36.0	15.9	314	3.39	X	X						
TOTAL	8.2	19.9	19.9	35.2	16.9	7196	3.37								

Total mean = average of eight means
Chi Square (Pearson) = 1898.81 (.00 level)
Coefficient of Contingency = .46
1 = Strongly Disagree; 5 = Strongly Agree

* = Significantly greater perceived level for each pair of countries (.05 level)-A versus B

ANOVA F Ratio = 187.76 (.00 level)

from Germany (0 of 7) and the United States (1 of 7), the relative perceived need to develop resources of respondents from the remaining countries is similarly lower (2 of 7).

EFFECTIVENESS OF WORLD GOVERNANCE/COOPERATIVE ORGANIZATIONS

The perceived effectiveness of world governance and/or cooperative organizations as an issue is reflected in the following 12 issue propositions. These propositions pertain to various institutions and initiatives that tend to affect the overall international socioeconomic and political climate.

1. The United Nations is effective.

P.R.C.	GER.	F.S.U.	A.M.	U.S.	VEN.	JAPAN	YUG.	CHILE
3.28	3.16	3.15	**3.10**	3.09	3.09	3.07	3.03	2.89

2. More use of United Nations is needed to resolve international disputes.

VEN.	YUG.	F.S.U.	P.R.C.	A.M.	U.S.	CHILE	GER.	JAPAN
4.01	3.99	3.98	3.89	**3.74**	3.54	3.54	3.50	3.47

3. A world government is needed to resolve international social, economic, and political problems.

F.S.U.	YUG.	P.R.C.	JAPAN	A.M.	CHILE	VEN.	GER.	U.S.
3.59	3.14	3.03	3.01	**2.96**	2.85	2.78	2.65	2.62

4. Multinational security organizations are necessary.

U.S.	VEN.	JAPAN	CHILE	P.R.C.	A.M.	GER.	F.S.U.	YUG.
3.76	3.52	3.44	3.44	3.39	**3.14**	2.93	2.51	2.16

5. Multinational economic/political alliances do not endanger national identity.

GER.	U.S.	JAPAN	A.M.	CHILE	VEN.	YUG.	F.S.U.	P.R.C.
3.82	3.41	3.24	**3.17**	3.10	3.05	3.01	2.91	2.81

6. International legal/judicial systems are effective.

P.R.C.	CHILE	GER.	JAPAN	YUG.	A.M.	F.S.U.	VEN.	U.S.
3.12	3.09	2.97	2.88	2.88	**2.88**	2.72	2.69	2.68

7. The General Agreement on Tariffs and Trade (GATT) is effective.

P.R.C.	VEN.	GER.	A.M.	U.S.	CHILE	F.S.U.	JAPAN	YUG.
3.43	3.35	3.13	3.00	2.87	2.86	2.84	2.82	2.72

8. The International Monetary Fund is effective.

P.R.C.	F.S.U.	YUG.	A.M.	GER.	VEN.	U.S.	JAPAN	VEN.
3.52	3.00	2.99	2.99	2.97	2.97	2.94	2.94	2.61

9. Reform of international monetary system is not needed.

GER.	VEN.	U.S.	A.M.	F.S.U.	JAPAN	YUG.	P.R.C.	VEN.
3.27	2.81	2.77	2.65	2.55	2.51	2.49	2.42	2.36

10. More international regulations are needed to safeguard the natural environment.

GER.	F.S.U.	YUG.	A.M.	CHILE	VEN.	U.S.	JAPAN	P.R.C.
4.44	4.44	4.14	4.12	4.09	4.06	4.02	3.88	3.88

11. Cultural exchanges between nations are needed to reduce international stress/conflicts.

F.S.U.	U.S.	A.M.	P.R.C.	GER.	VEN.	JAPAN	YUG.	CHILE
4.40	3.95	3.93	3.91	3.90	3.88	3.87	3.87	3.62

12. There are not too many restrictions on international travel.

GER.	VEN.	U.S.	CHILE	A.M.	JAPAN	YUG.	P.R.C.	F.S.U.
3.84	3.60	3.51	3.30	3.09	3.05	3.02	3.43	1.98

The combined group of 12 issue propositions reflects the overall perceived effectiveness of world governance/cooperative organizations by respondents from each country, and for the combined countries as measured by the average mean (A.M.). Using the average mean response as a general indicator, respondents from the following countries have mean responses that exceed (or equal) the average mean for each of the 12 issue propositions: Germany and the People's Republic of China (7 of 12 each); the former Soviet Union (6 of 12); the United States and Yugoslavia (5 of 12 each); and Japan, Venezuela, and Chile (4 of 12 each). This corresponds to 18 of 36 (50 percent) for the respondents from the combined three collectivist countries, compared to 16 of 36 (44 percent) and 8 of 24 (33 percent) for those respondents from the three market-oriented and two Latin American countries, respectively.

In terms of the overall mean response, the respondents as a whole perceive that the United Nations is somewhat effective (3.10-proposition 1) and that it should be used more to resolve international disputes (3.74-proposition 2). As to the latter, the mean responses by respondents from the eight countries are very high, ranging from 3.47 (Japan) to 4.01 (Venezuela). While support for the United Nations is relatively high, there is less overall support for a world government type of institution (2.96-proposition 3), which would tend to dilute nationalistic priorities.

Propositions 4 and 5 deal with the effectiveness of multinational security organizations and economic alliances. As a whole, the combined respondents perceive these in a somewhat favorable way with average means of 3.19 and 3.17, respectively. While the perceived effectiveness of international legal/judicial systems (proposition 6) is not as favorable (2.88), the General Agreement on Tariffs and Trade (GATT) is perceived to be somewhat more effective (3.00).

Propositions 8 and 9 relate to the International Monetary Fund and the international monetary system. These are perceived to be less effective than the United Nations (2.99 and 2.65, respectively). Regarding the remaining three issues propositions, there is an overall perception that more international regulations are needed to safeguard the natural environment (4.12-proposition 10), and cultural exchanges between nations serve to reduce international stress/conflicts (3.93-proposition 11). Finally, except for the respondents from the former Soviet Union (1.98), respondents perceive that there are not too many restrictions on international travel.

Table 8.3 shows the overall perceived effectiveness of world governance/cooperative organizations by respondents from each country surveyed. This overall perception is the combined responses to the 12 issue propositions summarized previously. The chi square analysis indicates that there are some significant differences (.00 level) in the overall perception of the effectiveness of world governance/cooperative organizations according to the country of the respondents (.50 coefficient of contingency). The mean responses shown on Table 8.3 reflect a relatively high perceived effectiveness of world governance/cooperative organizations, with an average mean of 3.26. Moreover, the range of mean responses is 3.16 to 3.40, and this narrow range indicates a reasonably high congruency of perceived effectiveness.

The ANOVA Scheffe test results shown on Table 8.3 tend to confirm this congruency of perceived effectiveness, except for the respondents from Germany, whose mean response (3.40) is significantly higher than that of each of the other seven countries. This indicates that the German

Table 8.3
Overall Perceived Effectiveness of World Governance/Cooperative Organizations

A	Response Frequency (%) 1	2	3	4	5	N	X̄	Scheffe Test / B GER.	U.S.	JAPAN	YUG.	P.R.C.	F.S.U.	VEN.	CHILE
GER.	6.1	16.4	25.8	34.6	17.2	905	3.40		X	X	X	X	X	X	X
U.S.	7.0	16.5	30.0	34.3	12.1	1770	3.28				X				
JAPAN	5.9	17.8	35.7	29.6	11.0	302	3.22								
YUG.	10.1	20.3	26.7	29.7	13.2	736	3.16								
P.R.C.	4.9	23.3	18.3	45.7	7.7	990	3.28				X				
U.S.	10.3	22.1	17.6	32.1	17.8	1242	3.25				X				
VEN.	8.7	19.0	24.0	32.5	15.8	954	3.28				X				
CHILE	6.1	22.2	27.2	30.7	13.7	314	3.24								
TOTAL	7.5	19.3	25.0	34.6	13.6	7213	3.26								

* = Significantly greater perceived level for each pair of countries (.05 level)-A versus B

ANOVA F Ratio = 31.52 (.00 level)

Total mean = average of eight means
Chi Square (Pearson) = 2442.23 (.00 level)
Coefficient of Contingency = .50
1 = Strongly Disagree; 5 = Strongly Agree

respondents tend to perceive a higher level of effectiveness of world governance/cooperative organizations than do the other seven respondent groups.

EMPHASIS ON NATIONALISM

The emphasis on nationalism as an issue focuses on the responsibilities, prerogatives, and independence of a society in relation to world governance/cooperative institutions and initiatives. The perceived emphasis on nationalism is reflected in the following 17 issue propositions. These propositions are among those that are commonly used in assessing the overall strength or preference for national priorities.

1. National security is the first priority.

JAPAN	F.S.U.	U.S.	YUG.	A.M.	P.R.C.	VEN.	CHILE	GER.
4.11	3.79	3.63	3.62	**3.44**	3.26	3.26	2.95	2.91

2. All countries need the right of national self-determination.

F.S.U.	VEN.	P.R.C.	GER.	A.M.	CHILE	YUG.	U.S.	JAPAN
4.39	4.22	4.06	4.02	**3.96**	3.92	3.84	3.68	3.56

3. Change political ideology if needed to cope with international problems.

JAPAN	GER.	U.S.	CHILE	P.R.C.	A.M.	VEN.	YUG.	F.S.U.
3.02	2.55	2.53	2.52	2.48	**2.47**	2.28	2.18	2.17

4. Multinational corporations exert too much influence on domestic goals/priorities.

VEN.	YUG.	GER.	CHILE	A.M.	JAPAN	P.R.C	U.S.	F.S.U.
3.20	3.62	3.47	3.47	**3.30**	3.14	3.10	3.04	2.87

5. World foreign aid levels are too high.

F.S.U.	U.S.	A.M.	JAPAN	YUG.	VEN.	P.R.C.	CHILE	GER.
3.77	3.30	**2.77**	2.74	2.62	2.56	2.53	2.39	2.21

6. The level of foreign debt is too high.

VEN.	YUG.	U.S.	CHILE	A.M.	F.S.U.	P.R.C.	GER.	JAPAN
4.45	4.27	4.21	4.11	**3.75**	3.46	3.45	3.36	2.68

7. There is an economic overdependence on foreign countries.

VEN.	YUG.	CHILE	U.S.	A.M.	F.S.U.	JAPAN	P.R.C.	GER.
3.73	3.60	3.48	3.35	3.16	3.02	2.79	2.66	2.61

8. The level of foreign aid should relate directly to the level of domestic welfare programs.

F.S.U.	P.R.C.	VEN.	CHILE	A.M.	JAPAN	YUG.	U.S.	GER.
4.09	3.84	3.54	3.49	3.48	3.43	3.37	3.18	2.90

9. Reducing world hunger does not require extensive international cooperation.

P.R.C.	CHILE	F.S.U.	A.M.	U.S.	VEN.	JAPAN	YUG.	GER.
2.25	1.98	1.84	1.77	1.75	1.62	1.61	1.58	1.55

10. Reducing world hunger is not the highest international priority.

U.S.	P.R.C.	GER.	CHILE	A.M.	JAPAN	VEN.	YUG.	F.S.U.
2.94	2.29	2.21	2.20	2.17	2.11	1.98	1.93	1.73

11. Developing the oceans' resources should be the responsibility of individual nations.

F.S.U.	CHILE	VEN.	A.M.	JAPAN	U.S.	P.R.C.	YUG.	GER.
3.61	2.74	2.56	2.49	2.35	2.29	2.26	2.18	1.89

12. Exploring space should be the responsibility of individual nations.

U.S.	F.S.U.	CHILE	A.M.	VEN.	JAPAN	P.R.C.	YUG.	GER.
3.15	3.13	2.74	2.54	2.48	2.41	2.37	2.11	1.93

13. Reducing international terrorism does not require international cooperation.

P.R.C.	CHILE	JAPAN	A.M.	VEN.	U.S.	F.S.U.	GER.	YUG.
1.94	1.88	1.75	1.69	1.67	1.60	1.60	1.56	1.55

14. Individual nations, rather than international organizations, have the primary responsibility for safeguarding human rights.

F.S.U.	VEN.	CHILE	YUG.	U.S.	A.M.	JAPAN	P.R.C.	GER.
3.60	3.06	3.04	3.03	3.02	2.80	2.66	2.36	1.66

15. Immigration policies are ineffective.

VEN.	JAPAN	YUG.	F.S.U.	U.S.	A.M.	GER.	P.R.C.	CHILE
3.76	3.66	3.55	3.50	3.43	3.36	3.00	2.98	2.97

16. The threat of military conflicts is great.

YUG.	VEN.	CHILE	P.R.C.	A.M.	U.S.	JAPAN	F.S.U.	GER.
3.96	3.27	3.23	3.18	3.18	3.13	2.94	2.87	2.84

17. Disarmament is not the highest international priority.

U.S.	VEN.	CHILE	GER.	A.M.	P.R.C.	JAPAN	YUG.	F.S.U.
3.01	2.51	2.51	2.32	2.31	2.26	2.22	1.98	1.63

The combined group of 17 issue propositions reflects the overall perceived emphasis on nationalism by respondents from each country surveyed, and for the combined countries as measured by the average mean (A.M.). When the average mean is used as a general indicator, respondents from the following countries have mean responses that exceed (or equal) the average mean for each of the 17 issue propositions: Chile (13 of 17); the United States and Venezuela (10 of 17 each); the former Soviet Union (9 of 17); Yugoslavia and the People's Republic of China (7 of 17 each); Germany (5 of 17); and Japan (4 of 17). This corresponds to 23 of 34 (68 percent) for the combined respondents from the two Latin American countries, compared to 23 of 51 (45 percent) and 19 of 51 (37 percent) for the respondent groups from the three collectivist and three market-oriented countries, respectively.

The responses to the first three propositions in general reflect a strong national emphasis among respondents from almost all of the countries. The average mean for proposition 2 (3.96) pertaining to the right of national self-determination is very high, and the reluctance to change political ideology is evident in proposition 3 (2.47). Moreover, respondents believe that multinational corporations exert too much influence on domestic goals and priorities (3.30-proposition 4), immigration policies are ineffective (3.36-proposition 15), and the level of foreign aid should relate directly to the level of domestic welfare programs (3.48-proposition 8).

Except for the respondents from the former Soviet Union (3.77) and the United States (3.30), the respondent groups do not believe that foreign aid levels are too high, with mean responses below the average mean of 2.77. Moreover, all respondent groups, with the exception of those from Japan, believe that the level of foreign debt is too high (3.75-proposition 6) and there is an economic overdependence on foreign countries (3.16-proposition 7).

Yet on the other hand, respondents as a whole disagree with the proposition that the individual nations should be responsible for resolving some international problems. These include reducing world hunger (1.77-proposition 9), developing the oceans' resources (2.49-proposition 11), exploring space (2.54-proposition 12), reducing international terrorism (1.69-proposition 13), and safeguarding human rights (2.80 - proposition 14). The responses to these five propositions seem somewhat contrary to the general support for nationalism as discussed earlier. There are some exceptions to this view that support multinational initiatives, such as that of the respondents from the former Soviet Union regarding the oceans' resources (3.61-proposition 9), that of respondents from the United States and the former Soviet Union for space exploration (3.15 and 3.13, respectively-proposition 12), and those of respondents from the former Soviet Union (3.06), Venezuela (3.06), Chile (3.03), and the United States (3.02) regarding safeguarding human rights (propositions 14).

Table 8.4 shows the overall perceived emphasis on nationalism by respondents from each country surveyed as reflected in the combined responses to the 17 issue propositions summarized. The chi square analysis indicates that there are some significant differences (.00 level) in the overall perceived emphasis on nationalism according to the country of the respondents (.63 coefficient of contingency). The mean responses shown on Table 8.4 reflect a relatively lower perceived emphasis on nationalism by the countries as a whole (average mean of 2.85). Only the respondents from the United States have a mean response in excess of 3.00.

The ANOVA Scheffe test results reflect a somewhat mixed relative emphasis on nationalism. The mean responses of the respondents from the United States are significantly higher (5 of 7 paired comparisons), followed by those of respondents from the former Soviet Union and Venezuela (4 of 7 higher paired comparisons each). On the other hand, respondents from Germany (0 of 7), and those from Japan and the People's Republic of China (1 of 7 each), fall at the other extreme.

SUMMARY AND CONCLUSIONS

This chapter summarizes the overall international climate as perceived by respondents from the eight countries surveyed. This comparison focuses on four broad issues: (1) international economic climate for trade and development, (2) need to develop resources, (3) effectiveness of world governance/cooperative organizations, and (4) emphasis on

Table 8.4
Overall Perceived Emphasis on Nationalism

A — Response Frequency (%)

	1	2	3	4	5	N	$\overline{X}$
GER.	23.9	31.9	19.0	18.6	6.6	905	2.52
U.S.	13.7	24.3	21.9	27.4	12.6	1771	3.01
JAPAN	15.9	29.6	26.4	19.7	8.5	302	2.75
YUG.	20.4	24.3	17.2	25.0	13.2	742	2.86
P.R.C.	11.0	40.7	15.0	27.1	6.2	990	2.77
F.S.U.	17.1	25.2	14.5	29.7	13.5	1243	2.97
VEN.	17.3	26.7	13.5	26.4	16.1	955	2.97
CHILE	16.4	25.9	19.5	26.0	12.2	314	2.92
TOTAL	16.6	28.3	17.9	25.9	11.5	7222	2.85

B — Scheffe Test

A	GER.	U.S.	JAPAN	YUG.	P.R.C.	F.S.U.	VEN.	CHILE
GER.								
U.S.	X		X	X	X			X
JAPAN	X							
YUG.	X		X		X			
P.R.C.	X							
F.S.U.	X		X	X	X			
VEN.	X		X	X	X			
CHILE	X		X		X			

Total mean = average of eight means
Chi Square (Pearson) = 4655.56 (.00 level)
Coefficient of Contingency = .63
1 = Strongly Disagree; 5 = Strongly Agree

* = Significantly greater perceived level for each pair of countries (.05 level)-A versus B

ANOVA F Ratio = 258.35 (.00 level)

nationalism.

Using the Scheffe test results that compared the mean responses of respondents from each country with the mean responses of respondents from each of the other seven countries, Table 8.5 summarizes the perceived overall international climate as reflected in these four issues. The numerical data shown on Table 8.5 are taken from Tables 8.1 through 8.4, and they reflect the frequencies of significantly higher mean responses (.05 level). The focus of these comparisons is on the significant differences in the perceived international climate by respondent groups, rather than simply the level of perceptions as measured by a mean response score.

The first issue shown on Table 8.5 directly reflects the perceived favorable economic climate for trade and development, while issue 3 reflects the perceived effectiveness of international cooperative organizations that facilitate trade and development through more world governance initiatives. On the basis of the maximum frequency of 14 paired comparisons for these two issues combined, the respondents from Germany perceive a more favorable international climate (14 of 14-100 percent). Those respondents from the United States, Japan, and Chile (5 of 14 each-36 percent) tend to perceive the next higher favorable level of international climate, however, this perception is primarily due to the responses to the economic climate issue, and not the effectiveness of world governance/cooperative initiatives. At the other extreme, in terms of issues 1 and 3, respondents from the three collectivist countries and those from Venezuela perceive a much lower favorable international economic climate.

The respondents from Yugoslavia and the People's Republic of China perceive a higher need to develop resources as reflected in issue 2 (5 of 7 each, or 71 percent of paired comparisons). The emphasis on nationalism is higher for respondents from the United States (5 of 7, or 71 percent), followed by respondents from the former Soviet Union and Venezuela (4 of 7 each, or 57 percent), then Yugoslavia and Chile (3 of 7 each, or 43 percent).

Table 8.5
Summary of Perceived Overall International Climate

ISSUES	GER.	U.S.	JAPAN	YUG.	P.R.C.	F.S.U.	VEN.	CHILE
1. Economic Climate for Trade and Development	7	4	5	0	1	0	0	5
2. Need for Resource Development	0	1	2	5	5	2	2	2
3. Effectiveness of World Governance and Cooperative Organizations	7	1	0	0	1	1	1	0
4. Emphasis on Nationalism	0	5	1	3	1	4	4	3

Note: Numbers equal frequencies of significantly higher mean responses using ANOVA Scheff tests of paried comparisons (0 - 7 are the possible range of frequencies) for each of the four issues.

9

Profile of Issue Priorities

Chapters 6 through 8 analyzed a variety of perceived issues at the organizational, national, and international levels. The analysis of these issues highlighted the significant differences in mean responses between pairs of countries surveyed using chi square analysis and Anova Scheffe test procedures. Moreover, the analysis focused on mean responses to individual issue propositions within a number of issues for each of the three levels of analysis. This chapter continues with an analysis of the general congruence of respondents' perceptions within and between the three levels of issues, organizational, national, and international. Moreover, responses are analyzed to ascertain the significant differences that exist according to the country of the respondents. Then an analysis of the ranking of a set of issues by respondents in each country follows. Finally, a profile of issues as perceived by respondents from each of the eight countries is developed.

CONGRUENCE OF PERCEPTIONS OF ISSUES

The perceived issues by respondents from each country that were analyzed in Chapters 6 through 8 reflect three levels of issues. Table 9.1 compares the combined mean responses for each of these three levels of issues. The mean responses shown in Table 9.1 are the average of the mean responses pertaining to the issue propositions. For example, the organizational issue includes the five mean responses shown in Tables 6.1 through 6.5; the national issue reflects the mean responses in Tables 7.1 through 7.3; and the international issue those shown in Tables 8.1 through 8.2, for each respondent group. The higher the mean response, the higher perceived favorableness of the organizational, national, or international climate by each respondent group. The two issues regard-

Table 9.1
Summary of Favorable Organizational, National, and International Climates in Terms of Combined Mean Responses

COUNTRY	ORGANIZATIONAL	NATIONAL	INTERNATIONAL	COMBINED
Germany	**3.14**	**3.03**	**3.33**	**3.17**
United States	**3.37**	**2.93**	3.06	**3.12**
Japan	**3.13**	**2.93**	**3.11**	**3.06**
Yugoslavia	2.42	2.36	2.95	2.58
People's Republic of China	**2.94**	**2.88**	3.03	**2.95**
Former Soviet Union	2.77	2.40	3.01	2.73
Venezuela	**2.94**	2.32	3.05	2.77
Chile	2.85	**2.86**	**3.09**	**2.93**
Average Mean	2.87	2.71	3.07	2.88

Numbers in bold type indicate mean responses exceed the average mean.

ing the perceived need to develop resources (Table 8.3) and the perceived emphasis on nationalism (Table 8.4) are excluded from the following results, and will be discussed separately as ancillary issues.

The preceding mean response data indicate the perceived overall combined climate is higher for the respondents from each of the three market-oriented countries, plus those from the People's Republic of China and Chile, using the average mean (2.88) as a general indicator. Only the respondents from Germany and Japan perceive a more favorable climate (i.e., higher than the average mean) for all three levels of issues, organizational, national, and international. On the basis of the average mean, the respondents from the United States and the People's Republic of China perceive a slightly less favorable international climate, compared to the organizational and national climates within each of their respective countries. The respondents from Chile, on the other hand, perceive a less favorable organizational climate compared to the national and international climate.

The foregoing summary of the relative differences in the perceptions of the favorableness of organizational, national, and international climates by each respondent group uses the average mean as a basic benchmark. Table 9.2 summarizes the frequencies of significantly higher mean responses for each respondent group using the Scheffe test procedures for each of the three levels of issues. These mean responses reflect the overall perceptions of the favorableness of the organizational, national, and international climates by respondents from each country, and are taken from Tables 4.6, 7.4, and 8.5, respectively. Moreover, a perception of the climate combined for the three levels is shown for each respondent group.

For the perception of the combined climate, the mean responses of respondents from Germany and the United States are significantly higher, at 76 and 71 percent, respectively, of the paired comparisons of mean responses. This indicates a higher perceived favorable combined climate, when compared to the perceptions of the respondents from Japan (53 percent), the People's Republic of China (44 percent), and Chile (36 percent). The perceptions of the respondents from Yugoslavia (1 percent), the former Soviet Union (13 percent), and Venezuela (21 percent) are at the other extreme, indicating a less favorable perceived combined climate in these countries. The relatively more favorable combined climate perceived by respondents from Germany and the United States is due to a great extent to the respondents' higher perceptions of a favorable organizational climate. If this level were ex-

Table 9.2
Summary of Favorable Overall Organizational, National, and International Climates

COUNTRY	ORGANIZATIONAL	NATIONAL	INTERNATIONAL	COMBINED
Germany	23	16	14	53 (76%)
United States	33	12	5	50 (71%)
Japan	21	11	5	37 (53%)
Yugoslavia	0	1	0	1 (1%)
People's Republic of China	16	13	2	31 (44%)
Former Soviet Union	5	3	1	9 (13%)
Venezuela	14	0	1	15 (21%)
Chile	9	11	5	25 (36%)
Maximum Frequencies	35	21	14	70

Numbers are combined frequencies taken from Tables 6.6, 7.4, and 8.5.

cluded, the respondents from Germany would still perceive a more favorable national and international climate (30 of 35 higher paired comparisons of means). However, the respondents from the United States and the People's Republic of China (15 of 35 paired comparisons each) and those from Chile (16 of 35 paired comparisons) would be quite similar in their perceptions of the combined issues climate.

The perceptions of the respondent groups concerning the need to develop resources and the emphasis placed on nationalism (as shown in Tables 8.3 and 8.4, respectively) are summarized. These are ancillary factors which tend to influence the international climate by developing general competition for resources, or by restricting in a general way the initiatives to establish more formal world governance organizations. At least the perceptions about both of these issues will tend to influence the type and form of economic trade and development, as well as world governance, organizations.

The perceived need to develop resources tends to be high when compared to the average mean (3.37) for all respondents except those from Germany (2.80) and the United States (3.15). The range of mean responses for these other six respondent groups is 3.39 (Chile) to 3.61 (People's Republic of China). Thus, from an overall standpoint, the need to develop resources tends to be an important issue.

The perceived emphasis placed on nationalism as measured by the mean response of the combined respondents (2.85) is lower than the perceived need to develop resources (3.37). The respondents from the United States (3.01), the former Soviet Union and Venezuela (2.97 each), Chile (2.92), and Yugoslavia (2.86) tend to place higher emphasis on nationalism using the average mean as a benchmark. However, mean responses of all respondent groups for this issue tend to be lower, ranging from 2.52 (Germany) to 3.01 (the United States).

ISSUE PRIORITIES

The final segment of the survey of issues includes a ranking of 15 issues by the respondents from each of the eight countries. Respondents ranked these 15 issues as follows: "1" indicates the highest priority and "15" the lowest priority. The issues were selected jointly by members of the research group, and the rankings generally show the relative importance of each. These issues can be viewed as basic concerns of each group of respondents.

The mean ranks of respondents from each country, and the average mean rank (A.M.) of the eight means, are shown next for each of the 15 issues. The issues are listed in the rank order, or priority, based on the average mean rank: "Achieving world peace" is the highest priority (1), and "Developing nuclear energy" is the lowest priority (15) in terms of the average rank of each (4.12 and 10.64, respectively).

Of the five highest priority issues based on the average rank as a general indicator, only one, controlling inflation (4), is directly related to economic concerns. Reducing unemployment is the sixth priority. Three of the five highest priorities, world peace (1), the environment (2), and national security (5), in general include an international dimension.

1. Achieving world peace.

F.S.U.	GER.	YUG.	JAPAN	U.S.	A.M.	VEN.	CHILE	P.R.C.
2.91	3.34	3.39	3.76	3.90	4.12	4.14	4.90	6.59

2. Protecting the environment.

GER.	F.S.U.	YUG.	U.S.	JAPAN	A.M.	VEN.	CHILE	P.R.C.
3.03	3.58	3.98	4.12	4.26	4.28	4.82	4.85	5.59

3. Reducing the crime rate and corruption.

VEN.	F.S.U.	U.S.	CHILE	A.M.	GER.	YUG.	P.R.C.	JAPAN
4.21	4.71	4.84	5.41	5.56	6.07	6.21	6.21	6.78

4. Controlling inflation.

P.R.C.	VEN.	YUG.	A.M.	F.S.U.	CHILE	U.S.	JAPAN	GER.
3.78	4.21	5.54	6.15	6.23	6.30	6.47	8.28	8.41

5. Maintaining national security.

JAPAN	YUG.	F.S.U.	U.S.	A.M.	GER.	P.R.C.	VEN.	CHILE
5.13	5.20	5.87	5.88	6.27	6.55	6.78	7.29	7.49

6. Reducing unemployment.

YUG.	CHILE	GER.	VEN.	A.M.	U.S.	P.R.C.	JAPAN	F.S.U.
5.41	5.46	5.85	6.33	7.01	7.13	8.57	8.61	8.73

7. Reducing international terrorism.

GER.	CHILE	U.S.	YUG.	VEN.	A.M.	F.S.U.	JAPAN	P.R.C.
6.12	6.15	6.66	7.03	7.09	7.42	7.57	8.84	9.87

8. Improving cooperation between developed and developing countries.

VEN.	CHILE	GER.	JAPAN	A.M.	YUG.	U.S.	F.S.U.	P.R.C.
5.85	6.34	6.89	7.16	7.68	8.26	8.55	8.67	9.70

9. Population growth.

P.R.C.	JAPAN	CHILE	A.M.	U.S.	GER.	VEN.	YUG.	F.S.U.
2.87	6.65	7.78	7.78	7.86	8.17	8.75	9.38	10.78

10. Safeguarding the right to national self-determination.

F.S.U.	CHILE	P.R.C.	GER.	A.M.	VEN.	U.S.	YUG.	JAPAN
6.43	7.64	7.95	7.99	8.03	8.19	8.26	8.80	8.98

11. Maintaining existing social systems.

CHILE	GER.	VEN.	F.S.U.	JAPAN	A.M.	U.S.	P.R.C.	YUG.
6.92	7.49	7.88	8.25	8.41	8.81	9.49	9.88	12.13

12. Reducing government controls and regulation.

VEN.	F.S.U.	YUG.	GER.	CHILE	A.M.	JAPAN	P.R.C.	U.S.
8.16	8.98	9.00	9.15	9.16	9.19	9.41	9.62	10.02

13. Increasing the power/influence of the United Nations and world governance organizations.

GER.	CHILE	JAPAN	YUG.	F.S.U.	A.M.	VEN.	U.S.	P.R.C.
9.19	9.22	9.59	9.71	10.15	10.15	10.72	11.08	11.52

14. Expanding space exploration.

F.S.U.	YUG.	U.S.	JAPAN	A.M.	P.R.C.	GER.	CHILE	VEN.
8.93	9.66	9.87	10.12	10.24	10.62	10.67	10.68	11.33

15. Developing nuclear energy.

JAPAN	CHILE	P.R.C.	A.M.	U.S.	F.S.U.	VEN.	GER.	YUG.
9.39	9.41	9.98	10.64	10.67	10.72	10.95	11.68	12.35

Two of the lowest perceived priorities are developing nuclear energy (15) and expanding space exploration (14), followed by increasing the power/influence of the United Nations and world governance organizations (13), reducing government controls and regulations (12), and maintaining the existing social system (11).

The 15 issue ranks fall within three general, somewhat related groups. The first group pertains to perceived economic issues that include the following six issues: protecting the environment (2),   controlling inflation (4), reducing unemployment (6), population growth (9), expanding space exploration (14), and developing nuclear energy (15). Using the average mean as a general indicator, respondents from the following countries have mean ranks that are less than the average rank (higher priority) for this group of six issues: Japan and Yugoslavia (4 of 6 each), the People's Republic of China and Chile (3 of 6 each), and the remaining four countries (2 of 6 each). Thus, on the basis of the frequencies, the respondents from Japan and Yugoslavia tend to place a higher priority on the economic issues than the other six respondent groups, especially those from Germany, the United States, the former Soviet Union, and Venezuela.

Table 9.3 shows the overall ranks of the combined economic issues by respondents from each of the eight countries surveyed, as reflected by the combined responses to the six issues discussed (2, 4, 6, 9, 14, and 15). The frequency response data shown on Table 9.3 for the 15 ranks are condensed into five groups as follows: 1 - 3 = highest three ranks; 4 - 6 = next highest; 7 - 9 = middle ranks; 10 - 12 = next lowest; and 13-15 = lowest three ranks. The chi square analysis indicates that there are some significant differences (.00 level) in the overall rank of this combined set of six issues and according to the country of the respondents (.37 coefficient of contingency). The respondents from the People's Republic of China (6.90) have the lowest overall mean rank, and therefore they place a higher priority on this overall issue relative to the priorities of the other countries. This can be seen more clearly in the ANOVA Scheffe test results that indicate where differences in mean ranks are significant. Keep in mind that the lower mean ranks reflect higher priorities of issues. Respondents from the People's Republic of China have the greatest frequency of significantly higher ranks of issues (lower mean ranks) than all of the other seven countries. In terms of the analysis of significant differences in pairs of mean ranks, the respondents from Germany, Japan, and the former Soviet Union tend to place the lowest priority on the overall economic issue.

The second group of issues includes three issues dealing with perceived sociopolitical stability: reducing the crime rate and corruption (3), maintaining the existing social system (11), and reducing government controls and regulations (12). Respondents from the following countries have mean ranks that are lower (higher priority) than the average ranks for this group of three issues: the former Soviet Union, Venezuela, and Chile (3 of 3 each); Germany (2 of 3); and the United States, Japan, and Yugoslavia (1 of 3 each). These latter four countries tend to place a lower priority on issues dealing with sociopolitical stability.

Table 9.3
Overall Rank of the Combined Economic Issue

A	Response Frequency (%)					N	$\overline{X}$	Scheffe Test (B)							
	1-3	4-6	7-9	10-12	13-15			GER.	U.S.	JAPAN	YUG.	P.R.C.	F.S.U.	VEN.	CHILE
GER.	25.8	16.3	16.1	16.5	25.4	882	7.97								
U.S.	22.3	20.5	20.3	18.8	18.0	1757	7.69						X		
JAPAN	22.6	19.0	18.6	19.4	20.3	294	7.89								
YUG.	26.3	19.4	14.6	16.9	22.9	655	7.70						X		
P.R.C.	30.8	19.8	17.2	16.9	15.2	989	6.90	X	X	X	X		X	X	X
F.S.U.	22.8	16.7	16.2	20.4	23.9	1233	8.16								
VEN.	26.7	16.9	16.0	18.7	21.9	958	7.71						X		
CHILE	34.3	13.5	12.6	15.5	24.1	297	7.41	X					X		
TOTAL	25.5	18.2	17.1	18.2	20.9	7065	7.68								

Total mean = average of eight means
Chi Square (Pearson) = 1117.50 (.00 level)
Coefficient of Contingency = .37
1 = Strongly Disagree; 5 = Strongly Agree

* = Significantly greater priority for each pair of countries (.05 level)-A versus B

ANOVA F Ratio = 39.96 (.00 level)

The 15 response frequencies are condensed into five groups as shown.

Table 9.4 shows the overall ranks of the combined sociopolitical stability issue by respondents from each of the countries surveyed as reflected by the combined responses to the three issues considered (3, 11, and 12). Note that the 15 ranks are condensed into five groups of frequencies. The chi square analysis indicates that there are some significant differences (.00 level) in the overall rank of this set of three issues according to the country of the respondents (.41 coefficient of contingency). The mean ranks shown on Table 9.4 reflect a greater variability than those shown on Table 9.3 relating to the economic issue and the average rank of the eight ranks is higher (7.85), generally reflecting a lower priority for this issue.

The ANOVA Scheffe test results indicate where differences in mean ranks are significant. Keep in mind that lower mean ranks indicate higher priorities of issues. Respondents from Venezuela have the greatest frequency of significantly lower mean ranks in 6 of 7 paired comparisons of mean responses, followed by those respondents from Germany, the former Soviet Union, and Chile (4 of 7 paired comparisons each). Thus, these respondent groups place a higher priority on the sociopolitical stability issue. The respondents from Yugoslavia (0 of 7) and those from Japan and the People's Republic of China (1 of 7 each) are at the other extreme, indicating a lower priority for this issue relative to the other respondent groups.

The third group of issues pertains to a variety of concerns dealing with the relationships between societies as they relate to world problems and the general need for world governance and cooperative initiatives. The six issues included under this broad umbrella of world governance are world peace (1), national security (5), international terrorism (7), cooperation between developed and developing countries (8), national self-determination (10), and power/influence of United Nations/world governance organizations (13). Respondents from the following countries have mean ranks that are lower (higher priority) than the average ranks for this group of six issues: Germany (5 of 6); Japan, Yugoslavia, the former Soviet Union, and Chile (4 of 6 each); the United States (3 of 6); Venezuela (2 of 6); and the People's Republic of China (1 of 6). It is interesting to note the lower priority placed on these issues by the respondents from the United States and the People's Republic of China, in view of their large size and their influence on world affairs, albeit in different ways.

Table 9.5 shows the overall rank of the combined world governance issue by respondents from each of the countries surveyed, and reflects

Table 9.4
Overall Rank of the Sociopolitical Stability Issue

A	Response Frequency (%) 1-3	4-6	7-9	10-12	13-15	N	$\overline{X}$	Scheffe Test (B) GER.	U.S.	JAPAN	YUG.	P.R.C.	F.S.U.	VEN.	CHILE
GER.	18.2	25.6	21.6	21.3	13.3	880	7.56		X	X	X	X			
U.S.	20.1	19.7	17.7	20.7	21.8	1753	8.11				X	X			
JAPAN	17.2	19.7	22.4	21.9	18.9	277	8.23				X				
YUG.	13.0	18.3	20.2	18.4	30.1	650	9.11								
P.R.C	15.0	22.1	18.3	20.7	23.9	986	8.55				X				
F.S.U.	25.2	23.5	16.8	16.9	17.5	1229	7.31		X	X	X	X			
VEN.	27.5	25.9	16.3	17.7	12.6	958	6.75	X	X	X	X	X	X		
CHILE	31.0	18.4	14.5	17.0	19.1	293	7.15		X	X	X	X			
TOTAL	20.8	22.1	18.1	19.5	19.6	7026	7.85								

Total mean = average of eight means
Chi Square (Pearson) = 1414.86 (.00 level)
Coefficient of Contingency = .41
1 = Strongly Disagree; 5 = Strongly Agree

* = Significantly greater priority for each pair of countries (.05 level)-A versus B

ANOVA F Ratio = 79.06 (.00 level)

The 15 response frequencies are condensed into five groups as shown.

the combined responses to the six issues referred to above (1, 5, 7, 8, 10, and 13), using five groups of frequency responses. The chi square analysis indicates that there are some significant differences (.00 level) in the overall rank of this combined set of six issues according to the country of the respondents (.46 coefficient of contingency). The range of mean ranks of respondent groups shown on Table 9.4 is from 6.67 (Germany) to 8.75 (the People's Republic of China), with an average rank of 7.27. This tends to indicate a lower overall priority for this issue by all respondent groups.

The ANOVA Scheffe test results indicate where differences in mean ranks are significant for the respondent groups. Respondents from Germany have the greatest frequency of higher priority of this issue, as reflected in the lowest mean rank in 5 of 7 paired comparisons, followed by the respondents from Yugoslavia, the former Soviet Union, and Chile (2 of 7 paired comparisons each). The respondents from the People's Republic of China (0 of 7) place the lowest priority on this issue, followed by those from the United States, Japan, and Venezuela (1 of 7 each).

SUMMARY AND CONCLUSIONS

This chapter develops a profile of issue priorities for respondents from each of the eight countries surveyed. These priorities are based on the results of the analysis of three levels of issues, organizational (Chapter 6), national (Chapter 7), and international (Chapter 8), plus the ranking of the 15 issues by respondents as discussed earlier. On the basis of the foregoing analysis of issues priorities, a general profile of issues for respondents from each of the eight countries is summarized in the discussion that follows. These profiles reflect the perceptions by each respondent group that have at least four of seven frequencies of significantly higher mean responses using the Scheffe test of paired comparison of means. The following profiles show the general priorities of issues and/or the general perceptions of greater favorableness of organizational, national, and international climates.

Germany: More favorable organizational communications, motivation, job security/standard of living, and productivity; more favorable national economic climate and standard of living; and more favorable international trade/development climate and world governance

Table 9.5
Overall Rank of the Combined World Governance Issue

A	Response Frequency (%)					N	X̄	Scheffe Test (B)							
	1-3	4-6	7-9	10-12	13-15			GER.	U.S.	JAPAN	YUG.	P.R.C.	F.S.U.	VEN.	CHILE
GER.	28.4	24.5	18.5	17.9	10.6	879	6.67		X	X	X	X		X	
U.S.	25.0	20.5	18.8	19.3	16.5	1754	7.39					X			
JAPAN	24.7	20.9	20.9	19.0	14.4	277	7.24					X			
YUG.	26.5	18.7	22.4	21.2	11.4	652	7.05		X			X			
P.R.C.	12.1	19.6	23.4	23.1	21.7	987	8.75								
F.S.U.	28.4	20.4	19.9	17.5	13.9	1233	6.93		X			X			
VEN.	27.3	20.4	17.9	17.1	17.3	957	7.21					X			
CHILE	35.5	17.4	12.3	12.8	22.0	293	6.95		X			X			
TOTAL	25.1	20.5	19.6	19.0	15.8	7032	7.27								

Total rank = average of eight means
Chi Square (Pearson) = 1842.49 (.00 level)
Coefficient of Contingency = .46
1 = Strongly Disagree; 5 = Strongly Agree

* = Significantly greater priority for each pair of countries (.05 level)-A versus B

ANOVA F Ratio = 120.30

The 15 response frequencies are condensed into five groups as shown.

organizations.

United States: More favorable organizational participation, communications, motivation, job security/standard of living, and productivity; more favorable national economic climate and standard of living; and more favorable international trade/development climate. Also, more emphasis on nationalism.

Japan: More favorable organizational participation, communications, job security/standard of living, and productivity; more favorable national standard of living; and more favorable international trade/development climate.

Yugoslavia: Need to develop resources.

People's Republic of China: More favorable organizational participation and communications; and more favorable national sociopolitical climate. Also, more need to develop resources.

Former Soviet Union: No frequencies greater than 4.

Venezuela: More favorable organizational participation. Also, more emphasis on nationalism.

Chile: More favorable organizational productivity; more favorable national economic climate; and more favorable international trade/development climate.

On the other hand, let us summarize the issues priorities reflected in the respondents' ranks of 15 issues. The frequencies of significantly lower mean ranks (higher priorities) of issues are shown in the following categories relating to economic, sociopolitical, and world governance concerns. These data are taken from the Scheffe test results shown on Tables 9.3 through 9.5, respectively.

	Economic	Sociopolitical	World Governance
Germany	0	4	5
United States	1	2	1
Japan	0	1	1
Yugoslavia	1	0	2
People's Republic of China	7	1	0
Former Soviet Union	0	4	2
Venezuela	1	6	1
Chile	2	4	2

The preceding data reflect the following relative perceived concerns of the respondents based on at least four of seven paired comparisons with significantly lower mean ranks (higher priority or concern) using the Scheffe test procedures.

Germany: Greater concern for sociopolitical issues and world governance issues.
United States: Nominal relative concerns.
Japan: Nominal relative concerns.
Yugoslavia: Nominal relative concerns.
People's Republic of China: Greater concern for economic issues.
Former Soviet Union: Greater concern for sociopolitical issues.
Venezuela: Greater concern for sociopolitical issues.
Chile: Greater concern for sociopolitical issues.

Keep in mind that the summary of issues ranks reflects relative perceptions, not the level or depth of a specific concern.

10

Socioeconomic and Political Tenets

The discussion of people's perceptions of values and issues continues in this chapter by focusing on a number of basic socioeconomic and political tenets. These tenets broadly relate to views about capitalism and socialism, the need to change political ideologies, and the effectiveness of government. The perceptions about these tenets by respondents from the eight countries surveyed are compared.

EMPHASIS ON CAPITALISM

The perceived emphasis on capitalism by respondents is reflected in the four general propositions summarized next. These propositions include some basic views and some related requisites related to more capitalistic societies. The mean response of respondents from each country surveyed, and the average mean (A.M.) of the eight means, are shown for each proportion.

1. Capitalism usually reduces unemployment/poverty.

U.S.	YUG.	JAPAN	A.M.	GER.	F.S.U.	P.R.C.	CHILE	VEN.
3.16	3.10	2.93	2.89	2.88	2.83	2.79	2.75	2.71

2. Capitalism usually results in high levels of innovation and motivation to work.

YUG.	U.S.	JAPAN	GER.	F.S.U.	P.R.C.	A.M.	VEN.	CHILE
3.78	3.72	3.65	3.63	3.60	3.53	3.53	3.21	3.14

3. Economic development requires political democracy.

YUG.	F.S.U.	P.R.C.	GER.	A.M.	VEN.	JAPAN	CHILE	U.S.
4.28	4.19	3.97	3.93	3.93	3.91	3.83	3.72	3.62

4. A business career is preferable to a career in government.

VEN.	U.S.	CHILE	GER.	A.M.	YUG.	F.S.U.	P.R.C.	JAPAN
4.19	3.82	3.78	3.77	**3.50**	3.24	3.23	3.06	2.91

The combined group of these four general propositions reflects the overall favorable perception of capitalism by respondents from each country, and for the combined countries as measured by the average mean. Respondents from the following countries have mean responses that exceed the average mean for each of the four propositions: Germany, the United States, and Yugoslavia (3 of 4 each); Japan, the People's Republic of China, and the former Soviet Union (2 of 4 each), and Venezuela and Chile (1 of 4 each). This corresponds to 8 of 12 (67 percent) for the three market-oriented countries, compared to 7 of 12 (58 percent) and 2 of 8 (25 percent) for the three collectivist and two Latin American countries, respectively. Of the three groups of respondents who have an overall favorable perception of capitalism, Germany, the United States, and Yugoslavia, it is interesting to note that the respondents from Yugoslavia are included since this country has been historically viewed as a collectivist country.

The first two propositions deal with direct economic benefits of capitalism. Only the respondents from the United States, Japan, and Yugoslavia perceive that capitalism reduces unemployment/poverty and results in high levels of innovation and motivation, as indicated by mean responses that exceed the average means. In terms of the average mean, the respondents as a whole more strongly perceive that capitalism results in innovation and motivation (3.53), compared to its ability to reduce unemployment/poverty (2.89). Respondents from all of the eight countries have mean responses greater than 3.00 for proposition 2 (innovation and motivation), a result which is somewhat higher than expected.

The average mean for proposition 3 (3.93), relating to the need for political democracy for economic development, is the highest of the four propositions (ranging from 3.62 for the respondents from the United States to 4.28 for those from Yugoslavia). Of the eight countries surveyed, only the respondents from Yugoslavia have mean responses higher than the average means for each of the first three propositions. Although all of the mean responses are very high for proposition 3, it is interesting to note that the respondents from the United States have the lowest mean response (3.62) of the eight respondent groups. On the other hand, the mean responses of those from the three collectivist countries indicate that they perceive more strongly the importance of political democracy for economic development.

The last proposition relates to the relative preference of respondents for a career in business versus one in government. You would expect that those respondents who tend to perceive more benefits from capitalism would also prefer a career in business rather that in government. The average mean for the respondents as a whole is quite high (3.50), and respondents from each country have a mean response higher than 3.00, except those from Japan (2.91). The lower relative preference for careers in business by the respondents from Japan is somewhat surprising.

Table 10.1 shows the overall perceived emphasis placed on capitalism by respondents from each of the countries surveyed. This overall perception is the combined responses to the four general propositions summarized. The chi square analysis indicates that there are some significant differences (.00 level) in the overall perception of capitalism according to the country of the respondents (.27 coefficient of contingency). The respondents from Yugoslavia have the highest mean response (3.72), those from Chile have the lowest (3.22), and all mean responses tend to be high.

The ANOVA Scheffe test results included on Table 10.1 show where there are significant differences in these high mean responses of respondents from each country. The mean responses of respondents from Yugoslavia are significantly higher in 7 of 7 paired comparisons, compared to 3 of 7 for respondents from the former Soviet Union, and 2 of 7 each for the respondents from Germany, the United States, Japan, and the People's Republic of China. Therefore, on the basis of the frequency of significantly higher mean responses, the respondents from the three collectivist countries tend to emphasize these tenets of capitalism more strongly in twice as many paired comparisons (12 of 21, or 57 percent) than those from the three market-oriented countries (6 of 21, or 29 percent). However, the respondents from Yugoslavia account for 7 of these 12 higher mean comparisons, therefore, excluding the Yugoslav respondents, these five countries tend to place similar emphases on capitalism. The respondents from Venezuela and Chile place the lowest emphasis on capitalism relative to the other six respondent groups.

Table 10.1
Overall Perceived Emphasis on Capitalism

A	Response Frequency (%)					N	X̄	Scheffe Test (B)							
	1	2	3	4	5			GER.	U.S.	JAPAN	YUG.	P.R.C.	F.S.U.	VEN.	CHILE
GER.	7.1	14.2	20.5	39.6	18.6	899	3.49							X	X
U.S.	4.9	12.9	26.1	39.4	16.7	1758	3.50							X	X
JAPAN	2.6	11.8	32.9	40.4	12.2	288	3.48							X	X
YUG.	5.4	8.9	21.2	37.2	27.3	739	3.72	X	X	X		X	X	X	X
P.R.C.	5.4	18.7	17.1	42.8	16.1	986	3.46		X					X	X
F.S.U.	4.2	13.2	21.9	40.8	19.8	1206	3.59					X		X	X
VEN.	10.2	18.5	20.6	34.4	16.2	955	3.28								
CHILE	10.0	18.8	24.7	32.6	13.9	311	3.22								
TOTAL	6.0	14.4	22.5	38.9	18.1	714	3.47								

Total mean = average of eight means
Chi Square (Pearson) = 573.56 (.00 level)
Coefficient of Contingency = .27
1 = Strongly Disagree; 5 = Strongly Agree

* = Significantly greater emphasis for each pair of countries (.05 level)-A versus B

ANOVA F Ratio = 36.76 (.00 level)

EMPHASIS ON SOCIALISM

The perceived emphasis on socialism by respondents is reflected in the four general propositions summarized in the following. These propositions closely parallel those discussed under capitalism. The mean response of respondents from each country surveyed and the average mean (A.M.) of the eight means, are show for each proposition.

1 Socialism usually provides more equal distribution of income.

VEN.	JAPAN	P.R.C.	U.S.	GER.	A.M.	CHILE	F.S.U.	YUG.
3.40	3.36	3.29	2.91	2.88	2.88	2.87	2.20	2.13

2. Socialism usually results in low levels of innovation and motivation to work.

GER.	YUG.	JAPAN	U.S.	A.M.	CHILE	P.R.C.	F.S.U.	VEN.
3.83	3.61	3.57	3.53	3.34	3.18	3.12	3.08	2.81

3. Economic development requires government wage and price controls.

P.R.C.	F.S.U.	JAPAN	YUG.	CHILE	A.M.	VEN.	U.S.	GER.
3.57	3.43	3.16	3.16	2.95	2.94	2.65	2.46	2.12

4. State-owned industries are efficient.

YUG.	P.R.C.	VEN.	JAPAN	F.S.U.	A.M.	U.S.	GER.	CHILE
3.77	3.64	3.61	3.47	3.43	3.41	3.27	3.20	2.87

The combined group of these four general propositions reflects the overall favorable perception of socialism by respondents from each country, and for the combined countries as measured by the average mean. Respondents from the following countries have mean responses that exceed the average mean for each of the four propositions: Japan (4 of 4); Yugoslavia and the People's Republic of China (3 of 4 each); Germany, the United States, the former Soviet Union, and Venezuela (2 of 4 each); and Chile (1 of 4). This corresponds to 8 of 12 (67 percent) each for the three market-oriented and three collectivist countries, compared to 3 of 8 (38 percent) for the two Latin American countries. Compared to the perceptions of capitalism, the perceptions of the respondents from Yugoslavia are similar to those they hold for capitalism, using the average mean as a general benchmark.

The respondents as a whole do not strongly support the view that socialism usually provides more equal income distribution (2.88-proposition 1). However, those respondents from Venezuela (3.40),

Japan (3.36), and the People's Republic of China tend to support this view compared to the other five countries.

The respondents from Germany (3.83), Yugoslavia (3.61), Japan (3.57), and the United States (3.53) perceive that socialism results in low levels of innovation and motivation to work (proposition 2), and this response is consistent with their responses regarding capitalism's enhancing innovation and motivation. Except for the respondents from Venezuela (2.81), all mean responses tend to be high (with an average mean of 3.34).

Regarding the view that economic development requires wage and price controls (proposition 3), respondents from five of the eight countries tend to support this proposition with mean responses above the average mean (2.94). Of the four propositions relating to socialism, this proposition had the largest range of mean responses (2.12 for Germany to 3.57 for the People's Republic of China). The responses to the view that state-owned industries are efficient (proposition 4) is somewhat surprising. For respondents from all of the eight countries except Chile who have a mean response of 2.87, the lowest mean response is 3.20 for the respondents from Germany, with an average mean of 3.41.

Table 10.2 shows the overall perceived emphasis on socialism by respondents from each of the countries surveyed as reflected in the combined responses to the four general propositions. The chi square analysis indicates that there are some significant differences (.00 level) in the overall perception of socialism according to the country of the respondents (.41 coefficient of contingency). The respondents from Japan (3.39), Yugoslavia (3.21), and the People's Republic of China (3.41) have higher mean responses relative to the average mean (3.15). Again, as in the case of perceptions of capitalism, all mean responses tend to be high.

The ANOVA Scheffe test results included on Table 10.2 show where there are significant differences in these high mean responses of respondents from each country. The respondents from Japan and the People's Republic of China each have significantly similarly higher mean responses in 6 of 7 paired comparisons, followed by those from Yugoslavia (4 of 7) and Venezuela (6 of 7). All of these respondent groups tend to place a greater emphasis on socialism than do the respondents from Germany, the United States, the former Soviet Union, and Chile, who are at the other extreme, each with 0 of 7 significantly higher means.

Table 10.2
Overall Perceived Emphasis on Socialism

A

	Response Frequency (%)					N	X̄
	1	2	3	4	5		
GER.	16.2	21.6	19.7	30.1	12.3	904	3.01
U.S.	11.5	22.7	28.0	26.2	11.6	1758	3.04
JAPAN	5.0	14.0	29.6	40.3	11.1	294	3.39
YUG.	14.2	16.3	21.6	29.8	18.1	733	3.21
P.R.C.	5.7	18.9	15.3	48.6	11.4	987	3.41
F.S.U.	12.0	23.6	24.4	31.1	8.9	1238	3.01
VEN.	16.1	22.8	12.6	29.3	19.2	958	3.13
CHILE	11.5	26.5	23.6	30.4	7.9	314	2.97
TOTAL	12.0	21.4	21.7	32.3	12.7	7186	3.15

Total mean = average of eight means
Chi Square (Pearson) = 1439.97 (.00 level)
Coefficient of Contingency = .41
1 = Strongly Disagree; 5 = Strongly Agree

B

	Scheffe Test							
	GER.	U.S.	JAPAN	YUG.	P.R.C.	F.S.U.	VEN.	CHILE
GER.								
U.S.								
JAPAN	X	X		X		X	X	X
YUG.	X	X				X	X	X
P.R.C.	X	X		X		X	X	X
F.S.U.								
VEN.	X					X		X
CHILE								

* = Significantly greater emphasis for each pair of countries
(.05 level)-A versus B

ANOVA F Ratio = 55.03 (.00 level)

NEED TO CHANGE POLITICAL IDEOLOGY

The perceived need to change a political ideology is reflected in the two general propositions summarized next. These propositions focus on two types of situations that may support the need for change: increase economic development and increase social welfare programs. The mean response from each country, and the average mean (A.M.) of the eight means, are shown for each proposition.

1. Change political ideology to increase economic development.

YUG.	F.S.U.	VEN.	P.R.C.	A.M.	CHILE	U.S.	JAPAN	GER.
4.23	3.99	3.75	3.74	3.55	3.46	3.36	3.01	2.86

2. Change political ideology to increase social welfare programs.

F.S.U.	VEN.	YUG.	CHILE	A.M.	P.R.C.	JAPAN	GER.	U.S.
4.09	3.97	3.86	3.67	3.57	3.53	3.24	3.15	3.02

The respondents from Yugoslavia, the former Soviet Union, and Venezuela support the view that political ideologies should be changed for both economic development and social welfare reasons. This is based on their mean responses being higher than the average mean for both of these two propositions. As a whole, the mean responses by all respondent groups to these two propositions are very high, with mean responses above 3.00 for all respondents, except those from Germany regarding economic development (2.86-proposition 1). On the basis of lower mean responses relative to the average means, the respondents from Germany, the United States, and Japan do not support the changing of political ideologies for either of the two reasons. On the other hand, the respondents from the three collectivist countries have higher mean responses than the average means in 5 of 6 cases (83 percent) followed by 3 of 4 (75 percent) for the two Latin American countries. In terms of these data, the respondents from these five countries tend to have a greater inclination to change political ideologies compared to those of the other three countries.

Table 10.3 shows the overall perceived need to change a political ideology by respondents from each of the countries surveyed. This overall perception is the combined responses to the two general propositions summarized. The chi square analysis indicates that there are some significant differences (.00 level) in the overall perception of the need to change ideologies according to the country of the respondents

Table 10.3
Overall Perceived Need to Change Political Ideology

A	Response Frequency (%)					N	X̄	Scheffe Test (B)							
	1	2	3	4	5			GER.	U.S.	JAPAN	YUG.	P.R.C.	F.S.U.	VEN.	CHILE
GER.	13.1	19.7	28.4	31.2	7.7	884	3.01								
U.S.	8.7	15.8	33.0	33.2	9.4	1720	3.19	X							
JAPAN	4.5	19.8	42.2	25.4	8.1	240	3.13	X	X						
YUG.	2.6	5.0	14.3	41.2	36.9	721	4.05	X	X	X		X		X	X
P.R.C.	2.6	14.6	13.9	54.4	14.6	965	3.64	X	X	X					
F.S.U.	2.5	5.7	11.7	45.4	34.7	1191	4.04	X	X	X		X		X	X
VEN.	5.9	7.2	12.6	44.4	30.0	941	3.85	X	X	X		X			X
CHILE	5.5	14.7	17.5	42.8	19.6	302	3.56	X	X	X					
TOTAL	6.1	12.2	21.1	40.4	20.2	6964	3.56								

Total mean = average of eight means
Chi Square (Pearson) = 2322.71 (.00 level)
Coefficient of Contingency = .50
1 = Strongly Disagree; 5 = Strongly Agree

* = Significantly greater need for each pair of countries (.05 level)-A versus B

ANOVA F Ratio = 270.88 (.00 level)

(.50 coefficient of contingency). The average mean (3.56) of the eight countries is quite high, with the respondents from Yugoslavia (4.05) and the former Soviet Union (4.04) having the highest mean responses.

The ANOVA Scheffe test results included on Table 10.3 show where there are significant differences in these high mean responses for each country's respondents. The respondents from Yugoslavia and the former Soviet Union each have significantly higher mean responses in 6 of 7 paired comparisons, followed by those from Venezuela (5 of 7) and the People's Republic of China and Chile, each with 3 of 7 higher mean responses. The respondents from Germany and the United States (0 of 7) and Japan (1 of 7) are at the other extreme regarding the need to change political ideologies. In a general way, these perceptions may be influenced by the relative economic status of each country: respondents from those countries with more favorable economic circumstances tend to perceive less of a need for change.

EFFECTIVENESS OF GOVERNMENT

The final two socioeconomic and political tenets relate to the perceived importance of communications and a general limit to the level of government expenditures as two major propositions that reflect more effective government. These two propositions are shown as general ingredients for effective government. The mean responses of respondents from each country, and the average mean rank (A.M.) of the eight means are shown for each of the two tenets.

1. Effective government requires extensive communications with the people governed.

VEN.	GER.	JAPAN	U.S.	P.R.C.	CHILE	A.M.	YUG.	F.S.U.
4.21	4.18	4.18	4.11	4.00	3.87	**3.79**	3.35	2.43

2. Level of government expenditures should relate directly to level of gross national product (GNP) or gross domestic product (GDP).

YUG.	F.S.U.	P.R.C.	VEN.	A.M.	CHILE	U.S.	GER.	JAPAN
3.87	3.86	3.83	3.64	**3.60**	3.48	3.40	3.37	3.31

Concerning the need for extensive communications as a requirement for effective government (proposition 1), except for the former Soviet Union (2.43), all mean responses are relatively high, as is the average mean (3.79). The ANOVA Scheffe test results shown below for tenets 1 and 2 are formatted differently than in tables previously shown since only one proposition is involved for each of the two tenets. In terms of the ANOVA Scheffe test results shown next for only proposition 1, the respondents from Germany and Venezuela each have significantly higher (.05 level) mean responses in 4 of 7 paired comparisons, followed by those from the United States (3 of 7). Thus, these respondent groups tend to perceive a greater association between extensive communications and effective government than do the respondents from the other countries.

	GER.	U.S.	JAPAN	YUG.	P.R.C.	F.S.U.	VEN.	CHILE
GER.				X	X	X		X
U.S.				X		X		X
JAPAN				X		X		
YUG.								
P.R.C.						X		
F.S.U.				X		X		
VEN.				X	X	X		X
CHILE				X		X		

ANOVA F Ratio = 411.28 (.00 level)

Chi Square = 2356.71 (.00 level), .52 coefficient of contingency

Turning to the view that government expenditures should be directly related to the level of gross national product or gross domestic product (proposition 2), all mean responses are relatively high as well, as is the average mean (3.60). As in the case of the tenet dealing with communications, only one proposition applies to level of government expenditures. The ANOVA Scheffe test results for proposition 2 are as follows. The respondents from the three collectivist countries, Yugoslavia, the People's Republic of China, and the former Soviet Union, each have significantly higher (.05 level) mean responses in 5 of 7 paired comparisons, thus indicating a greater inclination to place limits on government expenditures. At the other extreme are the respondents from the three market-oriented countries and Venezuela (0 of 7 each), with those respondents from Chile somewhere in the middle (3 of 7).

	GER.	U.S.	JAPAN	YUG.	P.R.C.	F.S.U.	VEN.	CHILE
GER.								
U.S.								
JAPAN								
YUG.	X	X	X				X	X
P.R.C.	X	X	X				X	X
F.S.U.	X	X	X				X	X
VEN.								
CHILE	X	X	X					

ANOVA F Ratio = 46.08 (.00 level)

Chi Square = 791.51 (.00 level), .33 coefficient of contingency

SUMMARY AND CONCLUSIONS

This chapter compares the relative perceptions of respondents about a number of socioeconomic and political tenets. This comparison focuses on the relative significant differences in mean responses to a number of general propositions relating to five areas: (1) capitalism, (2) socialism, (3) the need to change political ideology, (4) the importance of communication for effective government, and (5) the need to limit government expenditures.

On the basis of the ANOVA Scheffe test of paired comparisons of mean responses, Table 10.4 summarizes the perceptions of the socioeconomic and political climate within the five areas. The numerical data shown on Table 10.4 are taken from Tables 10.1 through 10.3, plus subsequent summaries relating to government effectiveness. The focus in this comparative analysis is on the relative significant differences in mean responses, rather than simply on the level of perception as measured by a mean response score.

For the data included on Table 10.4, the frequencies of significantly higher mean responses in at least four of seven paired comparisons for each of the five areas are shown in bold type in Table 10.4. In terms of these frequencies (at least 4 of 7), profiles of mean responses for respondents from each country surveyed can be summarized as follows:

Germany: Higher emphasis on the tenet supporting communications

Table 10.4
Summary of Socioeconomic and Political Tenets

TENETS	GER.	U.S.	JAPAN	YUG.	P.R.C.	F.S.U.	VEN.	CHILE
10.1 Emphasis on Capitalism	2	2	2	7	2	3	0	0
10.2 Emphasis on Socialism	0	0	6	4	6	0	3	0
10.3 Change Political Ideology	0	1	0	**6**	3	**6**	**5**	3
Communications Needed for Effective Government	4	3	2	1	2	0	4	2
Relate Government Expenditures to GNP/GDP	0	0	0	**5**	**5**	**5**	0	3

Numbers indicate the frequencies of significantly higher mean responses (.05 level) based on ANOVA Scheffe tests. Numbers in bold type indicate at least four frequencies.

for effective government.

United States: Nominal relative emphasis.

Japan: Higher emphasis on tenets related to socialism.

Yugoslavia: Higher emphasis on tenets related to capitalism, tenets related to socialism, tenet supporting changing a political ideology if needed, and tenet that advocates the need to relate government expenditures to GNP/GDP.

People's Republic of China: Higher emphasis on the tenets related to socialism and the tenet that advocates the need to relate government expenditures to GNP/GDP.

Former Soviet Union: Higher emphasis on the tenet supporting changing a political ideology if needed, and the tenet that advocates the need to relate government expenditures to GNP/GDP.

Venezuela: Higher emphasis on the tenet supporting changing a political ideology if needed, and the tenet supporting the need for communications for effective government.

Chile: Nominal relative emphasis.

Keep in mind that the profiles reflect relative differences in the perceptions based on significantly higher mean responses in 4 of 7 paired comparisons. They do not mean to imply that the strength of emphasis of any respondent group for any particular tenet is or is not meaningful, but only that it is different, as shown in the data on Table 10.4.

11

Relationships Between Values and Perceptions of Issues

Our focus thus far has been on analyzing significant differences in various cultural, family, and workplace values according to the country of the respondents. Two broad sets of values were developed, one reflecting a tendency toward individualism and the other toward collectivism. Moreover, our research analyzed perceptions of various socioeconomic and political issues at the organizational, national, and international levels according to the country of the respondents. The results of this research discussed in previous chapters indicate that there are some significant differences in people's values and their perceptions of issues according to the country of the respondents.

The discussion in this chapter searches for significant relationships between people's values and their perception of political economy issues that may exist according to the country of the respondents. Our analysis uses the values presented in Chapters 3 through 5, grouped into two broad sets. The first set, individualism, consists of the following five values, plus one individualism rank, that are directly related to the overall tendency toward individualism.

Work Ethic
Personal Individualism
Masculinity
Family Individualism
Family Economic Orientation
Individualism Value Rank

Those three values discussed in Chapter 3 that are inversely related to overall individualism are analyzed separately: leisure ethic, uncertainty avoidance, and power distance.

The second set of values, collectivism, includes five values, plus two value ranks relating to collectivism:

Organizational Beliefs
Humanistic Beliefs
Marxist Beliefs
Paternalism
Family Social Cohesion/Status
Family Leisure Value Rank
Social/Salesfaction Value Rank

These 16 values reflect the independent variables that may influence people's perceptions of political economy issues (the dependent variables).

The political economy issues presented in Chapters 6 through 8 are grouped into three sets that relate to perceptions of the organizational, national, and international climates as follows:

Organizational Climate
Opportunity for participation
Adequacy of communications
Level of motivation
Adequacy of standard of living/job security
Level of productivity

National Climate
Favorable economic climate
Adequacy of standard of living
Favorable sociopolitical climate

International Climate
Favorable economic climate
Effectiveness of world governance/cooperation

In addition to the perceptions of issues contained in each of the preceding issues, there are two other issues presented in Chapter 8 that influence the perceptions of the overall international climate: the need to develop resources and the emphasis on nationalism. Moreover, there are three issue ranks presented in Chapter 9 that reflect the priorities of respondents regarding their perceptions of the organizational, national, and international climates: economic/resource development, sociopolitical stability, and world governance/cooperation. Finally, there are four tenets that were analyzed in Chapter 10 relating to characteristics of socioeconomic and political systems. These tenets are also analyzed in relation to the 16 values.

To summarize, from an overall standpoint, this chapter searches for relationships between 16 values and 19 issues/tenets by using simple regression analysis. The focus of this analysis is on whether there are significant differences in the general influence of values on the perceptions of issues according to the country of the respondents, rather than on the strength of these differences in terms of a particular regression coefficient.

INDIVIDUALISM VALUE RELATED TO ISSUES/TENETS

Chapter 3 analyzed five values that directly reflect individualism as an overall value tendency: work ethic, individualism, masculinity, family individualism, and family economic orientation. Moreover, Chapter 5 analyzed the ranking of 10 values within three groups of ranks. One of these groups focuses on the individualism value rank. These five values and one individualism value rank are analyzed in relation to people's perceptions of 19 issues/tenets in terms of the country of the respondents. The results of the simple regression analysis are shown in Appendix 11A (Tables 11A.1 through 11A.6). The data shown in Appendix 11A are the significance levels for the T-ratios generated.

Table 11.1 summarizes the significance levels shown in Tables 11A.1 through 11A.6 of Appendix 11A, treating the six individualism values as a single overall individualism value tendency. The tendency toward individualism is analyzed in relation to respondents' perceptions of organizational, national, and international climates, plus two other issues related to the international environment, three issue ranks, and four socioeconomic and political tenets. The results of this analysis are shown on Table 11.1. Moreover, the data shown in Table 11.1 are the frequencies of significance levels that are at the .05 level or less as shown on Tables 11A.1 through 11A.6 in Appendix 11A. The numbers in the parentheses reflect how many of the total reported frequencies shown on Table 11.1 have inverse relationships to the overall individualism value.

Table 11.1

Frequency of Significance Levels (.05 or Less) Relating Perceptions of Organizational, National, and International Climates, Plus Other Issues/Tenets to the Overall Individualism Value (Six Values)

CLIMATES/ISSUES/TENETS	GER.	U.S.	JAPAN	YUG.	P.R.C.	F.S.U.	VEN.	CHILE
1. Organizational Climate	10(1)	25(13)	3(3)	9(5)	6(5)	11(2)	11(5)	7(1)
2. National Climate	5(1)	12(5)	1	8(7)	6(5)	5(2)	12(4)	6(1)
3. International Climate	6(1)	6(4)	4(2)	4(2)	7(4)	7(4)	7(3)	2
4. Need for Resource Development	4(1)	3(1)	1	1	4(1)	0	4(2)	2(1)
5. Emphasis on Nationalism	3(1)	4(2)	5(2)	2(1)	2(2)	1	4(2)	1
6. Issue Ranks								
a. Economic/Resource Development	2(1)	4(1)	2(1)	2(1)	0	4(1)	2(1)	4(2)
b. Sociopolitical Stability	3(3)	3(2)	2(1)	3(1)	1(1)	1	4(2)	4(2)
c. World Governance/Cooperation	2	3	2(1)	4(1)	1	2	5(2)	4(2)
7. Tenets								
a. Capitalism	3	3(1)	2(1)	2	4(1)	3(3)	3	3(2)
b. Socialism	3	2	2(1)	1	4	2(1)	2(1)	2(1)
c. Change Political Ideology	3(1)	4(2)	3(2)	2	5	0	4(1)	2
d. Requisites of Government	2	3(2)	3(1)	4	3	1	3	3(1)

Numbers in parentheses reflect the inverse relationships of the totals shown.

The first item shown on Table 11.1 reflects the respondents' perceptions of the overall organizational climate in relation to overall individualism. This includes five related issues concerning a favorable organizational climate: opportunity for participation, adequacy of communications, level of motivation, adequacy of standard of living/job security, and level of productivity. Keep in mind that the respondents' perceptions of favorableness generally are based on their particular experiences and environments, and therefore there is no fixed scale that indicates a higher or lower level of favorableness that applies uniformly to all of the countries surveyed. Instead, their perceptions reflect their views, which are based on their personal values and needs as conditioned by their individual experiences.

The frequencies of significance levels at the .05 level or less shown on Table 11.1 are based on a maximum of 30 for each country (5 organizational climate issues times 6 values/ranks relating to individualism). The responses from the respondents from the United States appear to reflect a strong relationship between the overall individualism value and a perception of a favorable organizational climate (25 of 30 frequencies of significance levels at the .05 level or less). However, about half of these frequencies (13) are inversely related. Thus, the overall individualism value does not appear to be related to respondents' perceptions of the favorableness of organizational climate, with the partial exception of the perceptions of the respondents from the United States.

The favorableness of the overall national climate is the second item shown on Table 11.1. It includes three related issues: favorable economic climate, adequate standard of living, and favorable sociopolitical climate. For this set of issues, the maximum frequency of significance levels at the .05 level or less is 18 (3 national issues times 6 values/ranks). Only the respondents from the United States and Venezuela (12 of 18 each) have frequencies of significance levels for at least half of the maximum 18 cases. About two-thirds of these frequencies (7 and 8, respectively) reflect a direct relationship between the individualism value and a perception of a favorable overall national climate.

The third item on Table 11.1 reflects the favorableness of the overall international climate, and it includes two issues: favorable economic climate and effectiveness of world governance/cooperative organizations. The maximum possible frequencies of significance levels is 12 (2 issues times 6 values/ranks). The respondents from Germany, the United

States, the People's Republic of China, the former Soviet Union, and Venezuela have frequencies of significance levels at the .05 level or less for at least half of the 12 cases (6 or 7 frequencies each). Note that about half (3 or 4) of these frequencies reflect an inverse relationship between the individualism value and the perceived favorableness of the overall international climate, except for the respondents from Germany (only 1 of 6 are inversely related). The relationships between the overall individualism value and the organizational, national, and international climates seem only tentative for the eight countries surveyed. Where strong relationships exist, the direction of these relationships tends to be mixed.

There are two other perceptions of issues that do not directly indicate the favorableness of the overall international climate, but are perceptions of important developments within the international environment. These are shown on Table 11.1 as items 4 and 5, and they refer to the need to develop resources and the emphasis on nationalism, respectively. Each of these two perceptions of issues has a maximum frequency of six significant levels at the .05 level or less (reflecting the 6 values).

Pertaining to the need to develop resources relative to the overall individualism value, the respondents from Germany, the People's Republic of China, and Venezuela each have a frequency of 4 of 6, and at least half of the relationships are directly related. In a general way, this indicates a moderate relationship between the overall individualism value and the need to develop resources for respondents from these countries. The respondents from Japan (5 of 6), and those from the United States and Venezuela (4 of 6 each), also tend to show a moderate relationship between nationalism and overall individualism, however, with some (2) inverse relationships.

Turning to the three issue ranks on Table 11.1 (6 a - c), there appears to be only a moderate relationship between the overall individualism value and the rank of issues relating to economic/resource development (6a), sociopolitical stability (6b), and world governance/cooperation (6c). The respondents from the United States, the former Soviet Union, and Chile show 4 of 6 frequencies of significance levels directly relating individualism to a need for economic/resource development. The respondents from the two Latin American countries show 4 of 6 frequencies of significance levels relating individualism to sociopolitical concerns, however, half of these are inversely related. Finally, the respondents from Venezuela (5 of 6) and Yugoslavia (4 of 6), with a higher emphasis on individualism, tend moderately to emphasize more of a need for world governance and cooperation.

The four socioeconomic and political tenets shown on Table 11.1 (7 a - d) similarly do not show strong relationships between individualism and these tenets. There is only a moderate relationship between individual and the premises presented regarding capitalism (7a) or socialism (7b), except perhaps for the respondents from the People's Republic of China (4 of 6 significant cases). Similarly, the need to change political ideologies (7c) is not strongly related to the individualism value, with the possible exception of the respondents from the United States and Venezuela (4 of 6 cases each). Again, the direction of the relationship is mixed, as is the case for the relationship discussed previously. Except for the respondents from Yugoslavia (4 of 6), the relationship between individualism and the requisites for effective government is weak as well.

In addition to the composite five individualism values and one individualism rank that are directly related to the overall individualism value, there are three values that are inversely related to individualism. These three values were discussed in Chapter 3; they are leisure ethic, uncertainty avoidance (the need for formal rules, regulations, and procedures), and power distance (the separation of management's responsibilities from workers' responsibilities through centralization of authority). Thus, those respondents reflecting high individualism as measured by the above overall individualism value are expected to reflect a low preference for these latter three values.

The results of the simple regression analysis to determine the relationships of each of these three values to the 15 issues and four socioeconomic and political tenets are shown in Appendix 11A (Tables 11A.7 through 11A.9). The data in these tables are the significance levels for the T-ratios generated. Table 11.2 summarizes these significance levels, treating the three values referred to as a single composite individualism value. Moreover, the data shown on Table 11.2 are the frequencies of significance levels that are .05 level or less taken from the Tables 11A.7 through 11A.9. A high frequency of significance levels on Table 11.2 indicates a strong relationship between an issue/tenet and this composite individualism value. The numbers in the parentheses reflect how many of the total reported frequencies reflect inverse relationships between the overall composite value and each issue/tenet shown on Table 11.2.

The frequencies of significance levels at the .05 level or less for the perceptions of the favorableness of the organizational climate shown on

Table 11.2

Frequency of Significance Levels (.05 or Less) Relating Perceptions of Organizational, National, and International Climates, Plus Other Issues/Tenets to the Overall Individualism Value (Three Values)

CLIMATES/ISSUES/TENETS		GER.	U.S.	JAPAN	YUG.	P.R.C.	F.S.U.	VEN.	CHILE
1.	Organizational Climate	6(6)	8(8)	0	8(1)	8(4)	6	7(3)	5(2)
2.	National Climate	3(2)	5(1)	1	8(3)	6(3)	8	9(3)	3(1)
3.	International Climate	1(1)	5(2)	3(2)	2(1)	3(1)	5	6	2(1)
4.	Need for Resource Development	2(1)	2(1)	1(1)	1	2(1)	2(2)	3(2)	1(1)
5.	Emphasis on Nationalism	1	3(1)	3(1)	2	2	2	3(1)	1
6.	Issue Ranks								
	a. Economic/Resource Development	1	0	1(1)	1(1)	2(1)	1	1(1)	0
	b. Sociopolitical Stability	1(1)	1(1)	1(1)	0	1(1)	1	1(1)	0
	c. World Governance/Cooperation	1	1	0	1(1)	2	1	0	0
7.	Tenets								
	a. Capitalism	0	0	1(1)	2(1)	2(1)	0	2	2
	b. Socialism	2	2	1	1	3	3	3(1)	2(1)
	c. Change Political Ideology	2	2(1)	3(1)	2(1)	3(2)	2(2)	3(2)	1
	d. Requisites of Government	2(1)	2(1)	1	0	0	2	1(1)	1(1)

Numbers in parentheses reflect the inverse relationships of the totals shown.

Table 11.2 are based on a maximum of 15 for each country (5 issues times 3 values). The respondents from the United States, Yugoslavia, and the People's Republic of China each have slightly more than half of the maximum frequencies (8 of 15 each). All of the frequencies pertaining to the respondents from the United States are inversely related to the overall perception of a favorable organizational climate, while only one of those from Yugoslavia is inversely related (the frequencies pertaining to the People's Republic of China are evenly split between direct and inverse relationships). As indicated earlier, we would expect an inverse relationship for these frequencies shown in Table 11.2 if the relationship between overall individualism and organizational climate shown earlier in Table 11.1 was direct. For the respondents from the United States this is only partially true in that about half (12 of 25) of the frequencies shown in Table 11.1 reflect a direct relationship. Moreover, neither frequencies for the respondents from Yugoslavia, or those from the People's Republic of China are consistent when comparing the data in Tables 11.1 and 11.2.

Turning to the overall perceptions of the favorableness of the national climate, the maximum frequency is 9 for each country (3 issues times 3 values). The respondents from the three collectivist countries and Venezuela have higher frequencies for at least two-thirds of the maximum (ranging from 6 to 9). However, except for the respondents from the former Soviet Union, when analyzing these results, the frequencies of significance levels become diffused because of multiple signs and a general inconsistency of results with those shown earlier on Table 11.1.

From an overall standpoint, the frequencies of significance levels at the .05 level or less shown on Table 11.2 for the overall perceptions of the international climate reflect a similar inconclusiveness about the relationship of this composite value to this issue. Moreover, this is true for the issue ranks and the tenets shown on Table 11.2. From an overall perspective based on the frequencies shown on both Tables 11.1 and 11.2, there appears to be a nominal general relationship between the individualism related values of respondents as measured in this research and the perceptions of these respondents of the overall favorableness of the organizational, national, and international climates, or of issue ranks and selected socioeconomic political tenets.

COLLECTIVISM VALUE RELATED TO ISSUES/TENETS

Five values related to collectivism were analyzed in Chapter 4: organizational, humanistic, Marxist, paternalism, and family social cohesion/status. Moreover, Chapter 5 analyzed the ranking of 10 values within three groups of ranks, two of which pertained to collectivism: family/leisure and family social/satisfaction. These seven collectivism values are analyzed using simple regression analysis to ascertain their relationships to people's perceptions of 15 issues and four socioeconomic and political tenets. The results of the simple regression analysis are shown in Appendix 11A (Tables 11A.10 through 11A.16). These data show the significance levels for the T-ratios generated.

Table 11.3 summarizes these significance levels shown in Tables 11A.10 through 11A.16, treating the seven collectivism values as a single overall value tendency. Moreover, the data shown in Table 11.3 are the frequencies of significance levels that are at the .05 level or less as shown on the tables in Appendix 11A. The numbers in the parentheses reflect how many of the total reported frequencies have inverse relationships to the overall collectivism value.

The first three items shown on Table 11.3 reflect the perceptions of respondents regarding the favorableness of the overall organizational, national, and international climates in relation to the overall collectivism value. For organizational climate, the maximum frequency of significance levels at the .05 level or less is 35 for each country (5 issues times 7 values). Only the respondents from the United States and Venezuela have high frequencies of significance levels (26 and 25, respectively). However, about half of Venezuela's have a negative sign, while 17 of 26 of those relating to the respondents from the United States are positive. This reflects the fact that a stronger relationship exists between the overall collectivism value and perceptions of a favorable organizational climate by respondents from the United States.

On the basis of a maximum frequency of 21 for the perceptions of the favorableness of the national climate (3 issues times 7 values), none of the respondent groups has a high frequency of significance levels, with the exception of those from Venezuela (18 of 21). However, 14 of these 18 frequencies have a negative sign. Moreover, the relationship between the overall collectivism value and the favorableness of the international climate is diffused. While respondents from the United States and Venezuela have higher frequencies of significance levels (11 of 14 each), they are about evenly split between positive and negative signs.

Table 11.3

Frequency of Significance Levels (.05 or Less) Relating Perceptions of Organizational, National, and International Climates, Plus Other Issues/Tenets to the Overall Collectivism Value

CLIMATES/ISSUES/TENETS	GER.	U.S.	JAPAN	YUG.	P.R.C.	F.S.U.	VEN.	CHILE
1. Organizational Climate	19(11)	26(9)	8(2)	15(10)	11(8)	13(5)	25(13)	18(13)
2. National Climate	11(6)	9(8)	4(4)	7(5)	7(5)	12(3)	18(14)	6(4)
3. International Climate	8(3)	11(6)	2	7(3)	7(2)	9	11(6)	8(3)
4. Need for Resource Development	3(2)	3	5(1)	4(1)	5	3(3)	3	5(1)
5. Emphasis on Nationalism	2(2)	1(1)	1(1)	2	4(4)	4	4(3)	1(1)
6. Issue Ranks								
a. Economic/Resource Development	2	4(1)	3(1)	2	1(1)	3	4(2)	7(5)
b. Sociopolitical Stability	3(1)	5(3)	1(1)	3(1)	1(1)	4	3	7(5)
c. World Governance/Cooperation	3(1)	3(1)	3(2)	6(3)	2(1)	2	4(1)	7(5)
7. Tenets								
a. Capitalism	3(1)	6(2)	2	4(1)	6	2	6(2)	5(1)
b. Socialism	5	5	6(2)	3	6	2	4(1)	5
c. Change Political Ideology	0	5	0	3	5	2(2)	5(1)	6(1)
d. Requisites of Government	5	5	5(1)	5(1)	6	5	4	7(2)

Numbers in parentheses reflect the inverse relationships of the totals shown.

For the remaining two issues relating to the international environment, plus the three issue ranks and the four socioeconomic and political tenets, the respondents from the following countries reflect some relationship between the overall collectivism value and the issues/tenets shown: need for resource development (the People's Republic of China, 5 of 7 frequencies; Japan and Chile, 5 of 7 frequencies each with 4 positive); emphasis on nationalism (former Soviet Union, 4 of 7 frequencies); sociopolitical stability issue rank (former Soviet Union, 4 of 7); perceptions of capitalism (the People's Republic of China, 6 of 7; the United States, Venezuela, and Chile, 4 of 7 positive frequencies each); perceptions of socialism (the People's Republic of China, 6 of 7; Germany, the United States, and Chile, 5 of 7 each); and the need to change political ideology (Chile, 5 of 7 positive frequencies; the United States and the People's Republic of China, 5 of 7 each). All of the respondents have high positive frequencies of significance levels for the last tenet, requisites for effective government, each having at least 4 of 7 positive frequencies.

Similarly to the results relating to the overall individualism value discussed earlier in this chapter, the relationship between the overall collectivism value is only moderately related to political economy issues and tenets. While some frequencies of significance levels at the .05 level or less appear to indicate some relationships exist, often they have conflicting signs or appear counter to expectations.

SUMMARY AND CONCLUSIONS

Table 11.4 summarizes the relationship between the perceptions of the favorableness of the organizational, national, international, and total climate and the overall individualism value as presented in Table 11.1. This overall value reflects the composite values that are directly related to individualism.

The maximum frequency of significance levels at the .05 level or less for the combined organizational, national, and international issues (i.e., total climate) is 60 for the overall individualism value. The respondents from the United States have the highest frequency of significance levels at the .05 level or less for the individualism value (43); however, the positive and negative relationships are about equal. The respondents from the United States have at least half of the maximum frequencies for each of the three levels: organizational (25 of 30), national (12 of 18), and international (6 of 12). However, as in the case of the total climate, the mix signs diffuse the results.

Table 11.4
Summary of Relationships Between Organizational Climate (OC), National Climate (NC), International Climate (IC), and Total Climate (TC) and the Overall Individualism Value

COUNTRY	OC	NC	IC	TC
Country Maximum	30	18	12	60
Germany	10(1)	5(1)	**6**(1)	**21**(3)
United States	**25**(13)	**12**(5)	**6**(4)	**43**(22)
Japan	3(3)	1	4(2)	8(5)
Yugoslavia	9(5)	8(7)	4(2)	21(14)
People's Republic of China	6(5)	6(5)	**7**(4)	19(14)
Former Soviet Union	11(2)	5(2)	**7**(4)	23(8)
Venezuela	11(5)	**12**(4)	**7**(3)	**30**(12)
Chile	7(1)	6(1)	2	15(2)
Total Countries	82(35)	55(25)	43(20)	180(80)
Total Maximum	240	144	96	480

Bold numbers indicate at least half of the maximum frequencies.

The respondents from Venezuela also have at least half of the maximum frequencies of significance levels at the .05 level or less for the perceptions of the total climate in relation to the overall individualism value (30 of 60, with mixed signs). Moreover, these respondents also have at least half of the maximum frequencies for perceptions of a favorable national climate (12 of 18) and international climate (7 of 12). Again, mixed signs diffuse these results as well. Of the remaining respondents, frequencies of at least half of the maximum are shown on Table 11.4 relating the favorableness of the international climate to the overall individualism value for the respondents from Germany (6 of 12), and those from the People's Republic of China and the former Soviet Union (7 of 12 each). However, except in Germany's case, the mixed signs are confusing. All of the other respondent groups do not have frequencies totaling more than half of the maximum frequency of 60, and all have mixed signs.

As to the perceptions of the total climate related to overall individualism, there are 180 of a total maximum 480 (33 percent) of significant frequencies at the .05 level or less for the total respondents. If we only consider those frequencies with positive signs, only 100 of 480 (21 percent) show a significant relationship between the perceived total climate and individualism.

Table 11.5 summarizes the relationship between the perceptions of the favorableness of the organizational, national, international, and total climates and the overall collectivism value as presented in Table 11.3. The maximum frequency of significance levels at the .05 level or less is 70 for the overall collectivism value. The respondents from the following countries have frequencies of significance levels at the .05 level or less as they relate the total climate to overall collectivism: Venezuela (54), the United States (46), and Germany (38). In all cases, these results are diffused because of the mixed signs.

The respondents from Venezuela are the only ones with at least half of the frequencies in excess of half of the maximum for each of the three levels of climate: organizational (25 of 35), national (18 of 21), and international (11 of 14). However, there are mixed signs in all of these three cases, and usually more inverse relationships prevail. Respondents from Germany (organizational and national), the United States (organizational and international), and Chile (organizational and international) reflect that some relationship exists between the collectivism value and the levels indicated, notwithstanding the mixed signs. Respondents from the former Soviet Union reflect a similar relationship between collectivism and the favorableness of the national climate.

Turning to the frequencies of significance levels at the .05 level or less for the total respondents, there are 272 of a total maximum of 560 (49 percent) significant frequencies relating overall collectivism to the total perceived climate. If we only consider the positive signs, only 129 of 560 (23 percent) show a direct relationship between collectivism and total climate.

Table 11.5
Summary of Relationships Between Organizational Climate (OC), National Climate (NC), International Climate (IC), and Total Climate (TC) and the Overall Collectivism Value

COUNTRY	OC	NC	IC	TC
Country Maximum	35	21	14	70
Germany	**19**(1)	**11**(6)	8(3)	**38**(20)
United States	**26**(9)	9(8)	**11**(6)	**46**(23)
Japan	8(2)	4(4)	2	14(6)
Yugoslavia	15(10)	7(5)	7(3)	29(18)
People's Republic of China	11(8)	7(5)	7(2)	25(15)
Former Soviet Union	13(5)	**12**(3)	9	34(8)
Venezuela	**25**(13)	**18**(14)	**11**(6)	**54**(33)
Chile	**18**(13)	6(4)	8(3)	32(24)
Total Countries	135(71)	74(49)	63(23)	272(143)
Total Maximum	280	168	112	560

Bold numbers indicate at least half of the maximum frequencies.

In conclusion, the search for possible relationships between people's values and their perceptions of political economy issues/tenets does not produce significant results from an overall standpoint, even though there are some differences according to the country of the respondents. For example, when you consider the perceptions of the total climate shown on Table 11.4 and 11.5 in relation to the individualism and collectivism values, respectively, the respondents from Japan have the lowest frequencies of significance levels at the .05 or less level, 8 or 60 (individualism) and 14 of 70 (collectivism). These results are somewhat unexpected in view of Japan's success in growth and development. At the other extreme, the respondents from the United States have the highest frequency for individualism (43 of 60), while respondents from Venezuela have the highest for collectivism (54 of 60).

In reference to the perceptions of the favorableness of the total climate as they are related to the individualism and collectivism values, there appears to be a somewhat greater perception of favorableness by those respondents with a greater emphasis on collectivism. This is reflected in the higher percentage of the maximum frequency of significance levels at the .05 level or less for collectivism (49 percent) versus that for individualism (33 percent). However, excluding the negative signs, these frequencies are about equal (23 and 21 percent, respectively).

Some of the diffusion in results from the regression analysis can be attributed no doubt to the structure and language of the survey instrument pertaining to values and perceptions of issues. Also, the respondents' perceptions of issues are naturally influenced by their own specific circumstances within their socioeconomic and political environment. Moreover, the period of data collection (1990 - 1992) was generally turbulent throughout the world in terms of changes in socioeconomic and political systems and initiatives.

Notwithstanding the inconclusive relationships between values and issues as discussed in this chapter, there are some differences in the frequency of significance levels at the .05 level or less according to the country of the respondents. In other words, some relationships between people's values and their perceptions of political economy issues exist for some of the respondent groups as shown on Tables 11.4 and 11.5.

APPENDIX 11A

SIGNIFICANCE LEVELS FOR T-RATIOS

Table 11A-1
Relationship Between Issues and the Work Ethic Value
(Significance Levels for T-Ratios)

ISSUES CATEGORIES	GER.	U.S.	JAPAN	YUG.	P.R.C.	F.S.U.	VEN.	CHILE
Organizational								
Participation	.95-	.00-	.21	.30	.89	.21	.20-	.86
Communications	.00	.00-	.38	.77-	.85	.00	.11	.17
Motivation	.25	.00-	.10	.67-	.52	.00	.10-	.16
Jobs/Standard of Living	.01	.00-	.17	.75-	.24	.00-	.96	.89
Productivity	.06	.00-	.31	.31	.55	.00	.00	.01
National								
Economic Climate	.85-	.26-	.27-	.61-	.15	.13	.00	.36
Standard of Living	.18	.00-	.65	.84-	.43	.44-	.04	.26
Sociopolitical Climate	.19-	.00	.08	.71	.52	.00	.02	.95-
International								
Economic Climate	.02-	.01	.77	.17-	.94-	.09	.44	.71-
World Governance	.44-	.00-	.50-	.19	.00	.00	.07	.00
Resource Development	.00	.03	.08	.12	.00	.22-	.13	.28
Nationalism	.01	.00	.00	.00	.03-	.43	.02	.20-
Issue Ranks								
Economic/Resource Development	.36-	.01-	.54-	.58-	.29-	.32	.85	.00-
Sociopolitical Stability	.00-	.00-	.00-	.63	.05-	.90	.00-	.00-
World Governance/ Cooperation	.22	.57	.09-	.65-	.12	.03	.01-	.00-
Tenets								
Capitalism	.00	.00-	.28	.07	.00	.08	.00	.62
Socialism	.00	.15	.70	.13	.02	.00	.00	.08
Change Political Ideology	.00	.23	.00	.86	.00	.37-	.08	.00
Requisites of Government	.00	.00-	.03	.02	.00	.07	.22-	.80-

Bold numbers indicate significance at .05 level or less. Negative signs indicate inverse relationships.

Table 11A-2
Relationship Between Issues and the Individualism Value
(Significance Levels for T-Ratios)

ISSUES CATEGORIES	GER.	U.S.	JAPAN	YUG.	P.R.C.	F.S.U.	VEN.	CHILE
Organizational								
Participation	.24	.24	.01-	.00-	.00-	.56-	.60	**.03**
Communications	**.01**	**.04**	.03-	.01-	.00-	.12-	**.04-**	.82
Motivation	**.02**	**.05**	.04-	.01-	.67-	**.00-**	.44-	.33
Jobs/Standard of Living	.10	**.00**	.09-	.83-	.01-	.25	.34-	.09
Productivity	.83	**.00**	.72	.00-	.03-	.49	.93	.77-
National								
Economic Climate	.24	**.01-**	.57-	.00-	.33-	**.00-**	.19-	.90-
Standard of Living	**.00**	.26-	.21-	.00-	.56-	.65	.44	**.01**
Sociopolitical Climate	.25	**.00-**	.86-	.00-	.00-	**.00-**	**.00-**	.81
International								
Economic Climate	**.00**	.11-	**.01**	.10-	.34	**.00-**	.06-	.97
World Governance	.08	**.02-**	.26-	.73-	**.00-**	**.00-**	.60	.14-
Resource Development	.09-	**.00-**	.34-	.97-	.86	.24	**.00**	**.05-**
Nationalism	**.04-**	**.02-**	**.00-**	**.00-**	.21-	.22-	.24	.16-
Issue Ranks								
Economic/Resource Development	.72	**.02**	.47	.73	.44-	**.05-**	.42-	**.00**
Sociopolitical Stability	.77-	.14	.35	.73	.36	.21-	.55	**.05**
World Governance/ Cooperation	.46	.31-	.34	**.00**	.87	.20-	.82-	**.00**
Tenets								
Capitalism	.67	.33	.09-	.09	.43	**.01-**	**.00**	.98
Socialism	.06-	.39-	.45-	.77	.06-	**.00-**	**.00-**	.14-
Change Political Ideology	.33	.25	**.00-**	.04	**.00**	.13	**.01**	.71
Requisites of Government	.33-	.34	.31	**.02**	.36	.63-	.31	**.02**

Bold numbers indicate significance at .05 level or less. Negative signs indicate inverse relationships.

Table 11A-3
Relationship Between Issues and the Masculinity Value
(Significance Levels for T-Ratios)

ISSUES CATEGORIES	GER.	U.S.	JAPAN	YUG.	P.R.C.	F.S.U.	VEN.	CHILE
Organizational								
Participation	.00	.38-	.73	.00	.75-	.26-	.04-	.00
Communications	.91	.02-	.24	.00	.08-	.03	.00	.17
Motivation	.94-	.22-	.16	.09	.51	.47	.00	.00
Jobs/Standard of Living	.57-	.04-	.46-	.81	.81-	.32	.00	.03
Productivity	.54	.00-	.69-	.05	.43	.02	.70-	.89
National								
Economic Climate	.05	.00	.76	.24	.09-	.65	.00	.02
Standard of Living	.00	.00	.74	.00	.01-	.26	.00	.00
Sociopolitical Climate	.00	.00	.12	.16	.00-	.17	.00	.04
International								
Economic Climate	.40-	.22	.77-	.15	.61-	.68-	.00	.43
World Governance	.04	.00-	.01-	.03	.44-	.00-	.00	.19-
Resource Development	.05	.08	.82	.32-	.00	.78-	.00-	.52-
Nationalism	.00	.00	.00	.16	.07-	.22	.15	.01
Issue Ranks								
Economic/Resource Development	.00-	.30-	.01-	.10-	.64	.73	.40-	.12
Sociopolitical Stability	.00-	.00-	.06-	.02-	.80	.49	.94-	.25
World Governance/ Cooperation	.11	.00	.62	.44	.82	.49-	.01	.37
Tenets								
Capitalism	.01	.40	.56-	.29	.00	.67-	.52	.08
Socialism	.01	.02	.06	.38-	.01	.86-	.26	.25
Change Political Ideology	.00	.00-	.08	.94-	.00	.26	.00-	.41
Requisites of Government	.16	.00-	.80-	.38	.00	.41-	.11-	.68-

Bold numbers indicate significance at .05 level or less. Negative signs indicate inverse relationships.

Table 11A-4
Relationship Between Issues and the Family Individualism Value
(Significance Levels for T-Ratios)

ISSUES CATEGORIES	GER.	U.S.	JAPAN	YUG.	P.R.C.	F.S.U.	VEN.	CHILE
Organizational								
Participation	.13	**.04**	.07	.07-	.44-	.50-	.40-	**.00-**
Communications	.34	**.01**	.10	.16-	.47	.48	.50	.51-
Motivation	**.00**	**.00**	.10	.33-	.99	.91	.88	.09-
Jobs/Standard of Living	**.00**	**.00**	.12	**.02-**	.08	.86-	.59	.70-
Productivity	.95	**.00**	.59	.06-	.14	**.02**	**.04**	**.04**
National								
Economic Climate	.07	.07	.23	**.00-**	.12-	.77-	**.01-**	.42-
Standard of Living	.07	**.00**	.84	**.00-**	.06-	.84	.67-	.33-
Sociopolitical Climate	.09-	**.01-**	.09-	.06-	.36-	.13	.97-	.93
International								
Economic Climate	**.04**	.95	.26	**.00-**	**.05-**	.20	**.00**	.54-
World Governance	**.00**	**.00**	**.00**	**.00**	**.00**	**.02**	**.00**	**.01**
Resource Development	**.01**	**.02**	**.00**	**.00**	**.00**	.41	**.00**	**.05**
Nationalism	.95	.68	**.03-**	.99-	**.00-**	.19-	**.00**	.42
Issue Ranks								
Economic/Resource Development	.23-	**.00**	.76	.95	.99-	**.00**	.07	**.00-**
Sociopolitical Stability	**.03-**	.45-	.37	**.05**	.78	.41	**.00**	**.00-**
World Governance/ Cooperation	.41-	.55-	**.00-**	**.05-**	.74-	.27	**.02**	.00-
Tenets								
Capitalism	**.00**	**.00**	**.00**	**.00**	**.00**	**.02-**	.45	**.00**
Socialism	**.01**	**.00**	**.00**	**.00**	**.02**	.90-	.61-	**.01**
Change Political Ideology	.90	**.00**	.24-	**.00**	**.00**	.27-	**.02**	**.00**
Requisites of Government	**.02**	**.00**	**.00**	**.00**	**.00**	.10-	**.00**	**.00**

Bold numbers indicate significance at .05 level or less. Negative signs indicate inverse relationships.

Table 11A-5
Relationship Between Issues and the Family Economic Orientation
(Significance Levels for T-Ratios)

ISSUES CATEGORIES	GER.	U.S.	JAPAN	YUG.	P.R.C.	F.S.U.	VEN.	CHILE
Organizational								
Participation	.00	.00-	.84-	.40-	.91	.47	.00-	.25
Communications	.08-	.00-	.12	.77	.13-	.05	.72	.37
Motivation	.11-	.00-	.14	.15-	.13-	.04	.37-	.44
Jobs/Standard of Living	.51-	.03-	.67	.77-	.61	.69	.01-	.62-
Productivity	.00-	.00-	.20	.80-	.99	.00	.03-	.83-
National								
Economic Climate	.00-	.77-	.11	.00-	.00-	.06	.00-	.58-
Standard of Living	.11	.08-	.88-	.03-	.45-	.90-	.00-	.12-
Sociopolitical Climate	.07-	.00-	.06	.10-	.00-	.02	.00-	.03-
International								
Economic Climate	.22	.40	.53	.75	.13-	.00	.00-	.81-
World Governance	.13-	.05-	.83-	.17-	.01-	.13-	.01-	.39-
Resource Development	.43	.12-	.86-	.65	.00-	.38	.00-	.13
Nationalism	.09	.00-	.00	.46	.46	.01	.00-	.18
Issue Ranks								
Economic/Resource Development	.56-	.95	.09-	.03-	.34	.01	.03-	.65
Sociopolitical Stability	.97	.06-	.94-	.54-	.24-	.12-	.00-	.12
World Governance/ Cooperation	.00	.00	.50	.00	.52	.15	.00-	.06
Tenets								
Capitalism	.30	.12-	.62-	.00	.54-	.01-	.00	.00-
Socialism	.69	.12-	.35	.37	.17	.09	.09	.02-
Change Political Ideology	.88	.00	.37-	.06	.95-	.39-	.00	.91
Requisites of Government	.71-	.30-	.16-	.86	.11-	.01	.00	.71-

Bold numbers indicate significance at .05 level or less. Negative signs indicate inverse relationships.

Table 11A-6
Relationship Between Issues and Individualism/Economic Values Rank
(Significance Levels for T-Ratios)

ISSUES CATEGORIES	GER.	U.S.	JAPAN	YUG.	P.R.C.	F.S.U.	VEN.	CHILE
<u>Organizational</u>								
Participation	.67	.06	.37-	.65	.33	.96	.07	.20
Communications	.40	.17	.99-	**.05**	**.01**	.53	**.00**	.43
Motivation	.67-	**.00**	.85	.32	**.03-**	.52	.34	.98
Jobs/Standard of Living	.06-	**.00**	.14	.38	.50-	.18-	.53	.94
Productivity	**.00**	**.01**	.96	.69	.14-	.08	.07	.52-
<u>National</u>								
Economic Climate	.17	**.00**	.42	.94-	.90	.09	**.01**	.52
Standard of Living	.95	**.01**	.88	.90-	.37-	.97	.46	.44
Sociopolitical Climate	.53	.06	**.01**	.17	**.00**	**.03**	.30	.02
<u>International</u>								
Economic Climate	.00	.32-	.80	**.02-**	**.03-**	**.00-**	.81-	.45
World Governance	.44	.13	**.05-**	.22-	**.01**	.29-	**.01-**	.08-
Resource Development	**.00-**	.79-	**.06-**	.09	.15-	.91-	.71	.06-
Nationalism	.89-	.07-	.07-	.08-	.39	.40-	**.00-**	.69-
<u>Issue Ranks</u>								
Economic/Resource Development	**.00**	**.00**	**.00**	**.00**	.44-	**.00**	**.00**	**.00**
Sociopolitical Stability	**.00**	**.00**	**.03**	**.00**	.09	**.00**	**.00**	**.00**
World Governance/ Cooperation	**.00**	**.00**	**.00**	**.00**	**.03**	**.03**	**.00**	**.00**
<u>Tenets</u>								
Capitalism	**.95**	**.00**	**.00-**	.08-	**.01-**	.21-	.73	**.01-**
Socialism	.87-	.16	**.00-**	.72-	**.02**	.78	.07-	.37-
Change Political Ideology	**.05-**	**.00-**	**.00-**	.72	**.00-**	.06-	.21	**.01-**
Requisites of Government	.45	.76-	**.01-**	**.00**	.42-	.29-	**.02**	**.02-**

Bold numbers indicate significance at .05 level or less. Negative signs indicate inverse relationships.

Table 11A-7
Relationship Between Issues and the Leisure Ethic Value
(Significance Levels for T-Ratios)

ISSUES CATEGORIES	GER.	U.S.	JAPAN	YUG.	P.R.C.	F.S.U.	VEN.	CHILE
Organizational								
Participation	.00-	.00-	.76-	.90-	**.05-**	.43-	**.00-**	.42-
Communications	.00-	.01-	.81-	.44	.00-	.00	**.00-**	**.04-**
Motivation	.00-	.00-	.31-	.02-	.00-	.00-	**.04-**	.35-
Jobs/Standard of Living	.00-	.44-	.77	.50-	.00-	.11-	.38	.72
Productivity	.01-	.06-	.99-	.71	.11-	.00	.30-	**.03-**
National								
Economic Climate	.00-	.02-	.58	.00-	.00-	.01	.00	.60-
Standard of Living	.00-	.00	.95-	.00-	.00-	.48-	.00	.26-
Sociopolitical Climate	.16-	.14-	.50	.02-	.00-	.00	.00	**.02-**
International								
Economic Climate	.30	.03-	.05	.00-	.02-	.91-	.00	.73
World Governance	.26-	.00	.80-	.82-	.80-	.00	.00	.31-
Resource Development	.00-	.00	.13	**.04**	.00	.76	.00	**.05-**
Nationalism	.30-	.00-	.02-	.61-	.58	.54	.00	.00
Issue Ranks								
Economic/Resource Development	.00	.36-	**.05-**	**.01-**	**.01-**	.31	.10-	.26
Sociopolitical Stability	.66	.27	.58	.75	.23-	.18	.20	.76
World Governance/ Cooperation	.57-	**.01**	.82-	.19	**.01**	.06	.26	.19
Tenets								
Capitalism	.55	.83-	.13	.00	.00	.63-	.00	.67-
Socialism	.21	.02	.00	.00	.00	.00	**.00-**	**.05-**
Change Political Ideology	.00	.00	**.03-**	.00	.00	.01-	**.00-**	.36-
Requisites of Government	.00	.02	.00	.21	.20	.58	.97	**.04-**

Bold numbers indicate significance at .05 level or less. Negative signs indicate inverse relationships.

Table 11A-8
Relationship Between Issues and the Uncertainty Avoidance Value
(Significance Levels for T-Ratios)

ISSUES CATEGORIES	GER.	U.S.	JAPAN	YUG.	P.R.C.	F.S.U.	VEN.	CHILE
Organizational								
Participation	.36	.63-	.31	**.02**	**.02**	.81-	.18	.13-
Communications	.07	.17	.14	**.01**	**.00**	.47-	**.00**	.44
Motivation	.82	.24	.57	**.04**	**.87-**	**.00**	.54-	.81-
Jobs/Standard of Living	**.00-**	.78	.10	.18	.34	.84	.26-	.79
Productivity	.11-	.32	.75	**.04**	.16	.28-	**.01**	.75-
National								
Economic Climate	.12-	.06	.65-	**.00**	**.01**	**.00**	**.01-**	.99
Standard of Living	.96-	.17-	.77	**.01**	.12	**.00**	**.01-**	.59
Sociopolitical Climate	.67	.25-	.92-	**.00**	**.00**	**.01**	**.00-**	.82
International								
Economic Climate	**.02-**	.43	**.00-**	.17	.96-	**.00**	**.00-**	**.00-**
World Governance	.14-	**.00**	.45-	.17	**.00**	**.00**	**.00**	**.04**
Resource Development	**.01**	**.00-**	.94-	.84	.98-	**.00-**	**.00-**	.68-
Nationalism	**.00**	**.03**	**.05**	**.04**	**.01**	**.00**	**.00-**	.99-
Issue Ranks								
Economic/Resource Development	.92-	.53-	.07-	.76-	**.05**	.99	.24	.84
Sociopolitical Stability	.91-	**.00-**	.22-	.84-	.23-	.13	.25	.29-
World Governance/ Cooperation	.37	.64	.89	**.00-**	.64	.48-	.42	.49-
Tenets								
Capitalism	.21-	.80-	.54	**.01-**	**.03-**	.14	**.00**	.64-
Socialism	**.00**	**.05**	.08-	.52	**.00**	**.00**	**.00**	**.00**
Change Political Ideology	**.00**	.82	**.00**	**.01-**	**.00-**	**.02-**	**.00**	**.01**
Requisites of Government	**.04-**	.09	.11	.52	.61	**.00**	.64	.15

Bold numbers indicate significance at .05 level or less. Negative signs indicate inverse relationships.

Table 11A-9
Relationship Between Issues and the Power Distance Values
(Significance Levels for T-Ratios)

ISSUES CATEGORIES	GER.	U.S.	JAPAN	YUG.	P.R.C.	F.S.U.	VEN.	CHILE
Organizational								
Participation	.54	.02-	.99-	.00	.01	.34-	.54-	.00
Communications	.23	.00-	.19	.01	.00	.28	.02	.00
Motivation	.23	.04-	.07	.02	.73-	.03	.00	.00
Jobs/Standard of Living	.33-	.00-	.43	.57	.10	.22-	.00	.53
Productivity	.09-	.00-	.47	.27	.90-	.01	.12	.22
National								
Economic Climate	.14	.00	.28	.06	.08-	.00	.00	.00
Standard of Living	.00	.00	.94	.00	.48	.93	.00	.00
Sociopolitical Climate	.59	.00	.03	.00	.00	.02	.00	.07
International								
Economic Climate	.19-	.00	.44-	.00	.94-	.00	.00	.94-
World Governance	.07-	.00-	.03-	.21-	.01	.00	.00	.25-
Resource Development	.12	.24	.02-	.57-	.03-	.01-	.01-	.84-
Nationalism	.18	.00	.00	.00	.00	.00	.00	.38-
Issue Ranks								
Economic/Resource Development	.72-	.36-	.73-	.30-	.64-	.01	.02-	.16
Sociopolitical Stability	.00-	.08-	.01-	.38-	.04-	.03	.00-	.09
World Governance/ Cooperation	.01	.32	.63	.86	.03	.01	.08-	.22
Tenets								
Capitalism	.90-	.17	.00-	.13	.61	.44	.12-	.34
Socialism	.01	.13	.25-	.75-	.00	.00	.04	.68
Change Political Ideology	.25	.03-	.00	.82-	.00-	.31-	.00-	.90-
Requisites of Government	.25-	.00-	.44-	.93	.31	.00	.00-	.51-

Bold numbers indicate significance at .05 level or less. Negative signs indicate inverse relationships.

Table 11A-10
Relationship Between Issues and the Organizational Belief Systems Value
(Significance Levels for T-Ratios)

ISSUES CATEGORIES	GER.	U.S.	JAPAN	YUG.	P.R.C.	F.S.U.	VEN.	CHILE
Organizational								
Participation	.25	**.00**	**.00**	**.02**	**.00**	**.05-**	.62	**.00-**
Communications	.52	**.00**	**.00**	**.00**	**.00**	.24-	**.02-**	.47
Motivation	.37-	.17	**.00**	**.00**	.84	**.00**	**.05-**	**.08-**
Jobs/Standard of Living	.14-	.24	**.05**	.40	.38	**.00-**	.61	.38
Productivity	.19	**.00**	**.03**	**.00**	.12	.39	.07-	**.00**
National								
Economic Climate	**.02-**	.36	.35	**.03**	**.03**	**.00**	**.00-**	.13-
Standard of Living	**.00-**	.22-	.90-	.11	.90	**.01-**	.14-	**.00-**
Sociopolitical Climate	.88-	.58-	.75-	**.02**	**.00**	**.00**	**.00-**	.14
International								
Economic Climate	.09-	**.00-**	.19	.67-	.47	**.00**	**.00-**	.09-
World Governance	.21	**.00**	**.01**	**.00**	**.00**	**.00**	**.01**	**.00**
Resource Development	**.00**	**.00**	**.00**	**.02**	**.00**	.09-	**.00**	**.00**
Nationalism	.48	.06	.84-	**.02**	**.04-**	**.00**	**.00-**	.70
Issue Ranks								
Economic/Resource Development	.89	.72-	.38-	.23	.87	.39	.85-	**.00-**
Sociopolitical Stability	.94-	**.01-**	.19-	.53	.47-	.78	**.05**	**.00-**
World Governance/ Cooperation	.65	.54	**.00-**	**.00**	.52	.29	**.02**	**.00-**
Tenets								
Capitalism	.08	**.00**	**.00**	.60-	.46	.79	.19-	**.01**
Socialism	**.00**	**.00**	**.01**	.06	**.00**	.07	**.00**	**.00**
Change Political Ideology	.19	**.00**	.65	.56-	.28-	**.00-**	**.00**	**.00**
Requisites of Government	**.01**	**.00**	**.00**	**.01**	**.00**	**.00**	**.00**	**.00**

Bold numbers indicate significance at .05 level or less. Negative signs indicate inverse relationships.

Table 11A-11
Relationship Between Issues and the Humanist Belief System Value
(Significance Levels for T-Ratios)

ISSUES CATEGORIES	GER.	U.S.	JAPAN	YUG.	P.R.C.	F.S.U.	VEN.	CHILE
Organizational								
Participation	.02	.00	.12	.02-	.60	.46-	.19	.02-
Communications	.00	.00	.18	.10-	.62-	.39	.00-	.39
Motivation	.00	.00	.69-	.00-	.48	.01	.00-	.11-
Jobs/Standard of Living	.00	.00	.03	.00-	.75	.10-	.00-	.21-
Productivity	.02	.00	.10	.00-	.71-	.03-	.01-	.00
National								
Economic Climate	.00	.19-	.99-	.00-	.69-	.00	.00-	.14-
Standard of Living	.04	.44	.62	.00-	.56-	.02-	.00-	.03-
Sociopolitical Climate	.78-	.00-	.03-	.00-	.86-	.13	.00-	.27
International								
Economic Climate	.00	.00-	.08	.00-	.39-	.02	.00-	.20-
World Governance	.00	.00	.00	.00	.00	.00	.98	.00
Resource Development	.80-	.49-	.00	.00	.00	.00-	.00	.00
Nationalism	.00-	.93	.00	.19-	.00-	.00	.00-	.85
Issue Ranks								
Economic/Resource Development	.88-	.01	.61	.08	.48-	.33-	.97-	.00-
Sociopolitical Stability	.68	.69-	.62	.01	.98	.92-	.33-	.00-
World Governance/ Cooperation	.10-	.94	.01-	.32-	.59	.50	.36-	.00-
Tenets								
Capitalism	.00	.00	.00	.00	.00	.00	.00	.00
Socialism	.00	.00	.01	.00	.00	.47	.03	.00
Change Political Ideology	.25	.00	.16-	.00	.00	.74-	.00	.00
Requisites of Government	.00	.00	.00	.00	.00	.00	.00	.00

Bold numbers indicate significance at .05 level or less. Negative signs indicate inverse relationships.

Table 11A-12
Relationship Between Issues and the Marxist Belief Value
(Significance Levels for T-Ratios)

ISSUES CATEGORIES	GER.	U.S.	JAPAN	YUG.	P.R.C.	F.S.U.	VEN.	CHILE
Organizational								
Participation	.00-	.00-	.07-	.38-	.00-	.17	.00-	.00-
Communications	.01-	.00-	.01-	.65-	.00-	.04	.00-	.02-
Motivation	.00-	.00-	.23-	.03-	.00-	.01	.00-	.00-
Jobs/Standard of Living	.00-	.00-	.15-	.00-	.00-	.04-	.00-	.00-
Productivity	.00-	.00-	.01-	.50	.00-	.01	.00-	.55
National								
Economic Climate	.00-	.00-	.01-	.46	.00-	.00	.00-	.00-
Standard of Living	.00-	.00-	.05-	.20-	.00-	.16-	.00	.00-
Sociopolitical Climate	.00-	.00-	.00-	.47-	.00-	.00	.02-	.72-
International								
Economic Climate	.00-	.00-	.22-	.00-	.00-	.01	.00-	.00-
World Governance	.00-	.57-	.06-	.19-	.00	.00	.29-	.00
Resource Development	.01-	.02	.18	.86-	.00	.67-	.12	.00
Nationalism	.77	.27-	.83-	.12	.27-	.53	.00	.22
Issue Ranks								
Economic/Resource Development	.07	.00-	.09-	.12	.01-	.61-	.02-	.00-
Sociopolitical Stability	.07	.01-	.71	.21	.60-	.91	.40	.00-
World Governance/ Cooperation	.48	.61-	.17-	.00-	.01	.44	.00-	.00-
Tenets								
Capitalism	.00-	.00-	.66-	.00-	.00	.00	.00-	.11
Socialism	.01	.02	.21	.29	.00	.00	.00	.00
Change Political Ideology	.39	.00	.79-	.14-	.00	.29-	.06	.00
Requisites of Government	.02	.00	.05	.88-	.00	.02	.55-	.00

Bold numbers indicate significance at .05 level or less. Negative signs indicate inverse relationships.

Table 11A-13
Relationship Between Issues and the Paternalism Value
(Significance Levels for T-Ratios)

ISSUES CATEGORIES	GER.	U.S.	JAPAN	YUG.	P.R.C.	F.S.U.	VEN.	CHILE
Organizational								
Participation	.11-	.03	.15	.48	.90-	.16	.66	.03-
Communications	.93-	.00	.72-	.34-	.44	.06	.57	.14
Motivation	.09	.02	.23-	.13-	.52-	.00	.11	.02-
Jobs/Standard of Living	.00	.00	.09	.04-	.44	.59-	.00	.03-
Productivity	.91-	.00	.38-	.11-	.68	.73	.89	.00
National								
Economic Climate	.14	.71-	.20-	.50-	.43	.00	.01-	.08-
Standard of Living	.50-	.01-	.48-	.03-	.22-	.23-	.01-	.12-
Sociopolitical Climate	.02-	.33	.42-	.05-	.15	.00	.01-	.14
International								
Economic Climate	.01	.00-	.89	.00-	.19-	.00	.04-	.90-
World Governance	.00	.00	.65	.00	.00	.00	.00	.00
Resource Development	.18-	.10	.04	.01	.00	.00-	.00	.00
Nationalism	.00	.79-	.09-	.87	.01-	.00	.11	.59-
Issue Ranks								
Economic/Resource Development	.72	.85-	.07-	.59-	.84	.06	.27-	.00-
Sociopolitical Stability	.06	.82	.27-	.06	.66-	.02	.07	.00-
World Governance/ Cooperation	.00-	.80	.12-	.00-	.41	.01	.53	.00-
Tenets								
Capitalism	.00	.00	.10	.00	.01	.85-	.00-	.00
Socialism	.00	.01	.01	.00	.00	.00	.58	.00
Change Political Ideology	.38-	.00	.06-	.00	.09	.00-	.00	.00
Requisites of Government	.00	.00	.00	.01	.00	.00	.00	.00

Bold numbers indicate significance at .05 level or less. Negative signs indicate inverse relationships.

Table 11A-14
Relationship Between Issues and the Family Social Cohesion/Status Value
(Significance Levels for T-Ratios)

ISSUES CATEGORIES	GER.	U.S.	JAPAN	YUG.	P.R.C.	F.S.U.	VEN.	CHILE
Organizational								
Participation	.01	.00	.73	.61	.98	.03-	.09-	.03-
Communications	.19	.00	.98-	.04	.31-	.51-	.00-	.00
Motivation	.02-	.00	.14-	.25	.05-	.00	.42	.22-
Jobs/Standard of Living	.03	.02	.88	.72-	.43-	.08-	.00	.00-
Productivity	.93-	.00	.08	.65-	.56-	.27-	.00-	.00
National								
Economic Climate	.02	.23	.34	.91-	.86	.00	.00-	.59-
Standard of Living	.00	.60	.93	.23-	.64-	.08-	.01	.16-
Sociopolitical Climate	.00	.67	.62	.43-	.83	.67	.02-	.04
International								
Economic Climate	.33	.01	.10	.00-	.48-	.00	.01	.42-
World Governance	.00	.00	.26	.00	.00	.23	.00	.00
Resource Development	.40	.05	.01	.00	.00	.01-	.37	.06
Nationalism	.06	.19	.19	.00	.04-	.00	.16	.06
Issue Ranks								
Economic/Resource Development	.11-	.44	.02	.45-	.39-	.00	.00-	.00-
Sociopolitical Stability	.01-	.01-	.03-	.14	.44-	.00	.06-	.00-
World Governance/ Cooperation	.10-	.03-	.07-	.00-	.21	.06	.10-	.00-
Tenets								
Capitalism	.00	.00	.94	.01	.00	.29-	.04	.00
Socialism	.05	.00	.01	.01	.00	.20	.30	.01
Change Political Ideology	.43	.01	.74	.03	.00	.06-	.03-	.00
Requisites of Government	.04	.00	.42	.04	.00	.00	.00	.00

Bold numbers indicate significance at .05 level or less. Negative signs indicate
inverse relationships.

Table 11A-15
Relationship Between Issues and Family/Leisure Values Rank
(Significance Levels for T-Ratios)

ISSUES CATEGORIES	GER.	U.S.	JAPAN	YUG.	P.R.C.	F.S.U.	VEN.	CHILE
Organizational								
Participation	.28-	.25-	.49-	**.04-**	.84-	.21	**.00**	.74
Communications	.26	.21-	.37-	**.00-**	.28-	.38	**.00**	.27-
Motivation	.94	.42-	.67-	.26-	**.02**	.25-	**.01**	.92-
Jobs/Standard of Living	.38-	.34-	.22-	.91-	.17	.08-	**.00**	.89
Productivity	.25-	**.00-**	.10-	**.01-**	.74	**.00**	**.01**	**.03-**
National								
Economic Climate	.72	.07	.13-	.10-	.43	.09	00	.14
Standard of Living	.63	**.01**	.93-	.63-	.46	.87	**.00**	.17
Sociopolitical Climate	.18	.85	.83	.53-	**.02-**	**.00**	**.00**	**.04**
International								
Economic Climate	.51-	.62-	.53	.97-	.38	.46-	**.01**	**.09-**
World Governance	.15-	**.00-**	.95-	.94-	.37-	.49	.21	**.00-**
Resource Development	.80	.16	.10-	.52	.24	.89-	.71-	.28-
Nationalism	.50-	.55-	.06	.63	.09-	.99	.25-	**.02-**
Issue Ranks								
Economic/Resource Development	**.00**	**.00**	**.00**	**.00**	.07	**.00**	**.00**	**.00**
Sociopolitical Stability	**.00**	**.00**	.80-	**.01-**	.99	**.00**	**.00**	**.00**
World Governance/ Cooperation	**.00**	**.00**	.31	**.00**	**.05-**	**.00**	**.00**	**.00**
Tenets								
Capitalism	.43	.72	.43	.93	.17	.20-	**.03**	**.02-**
Socialism	.74	.15-	**.01-**	.85-	**.04**	.22	**.00-**	.57-
Change Political Ideology	.76	.44	.12	.30-	**.00**	.23-	.15-	.31-
Requisites of Government	.67-	.23	.06-	**.01-**	**.04**	.25-	.75-	**.00-**

Bold numbers indicate significance at .05 level or less. Negative signs indicate inverse relationships.

Table 11A-16
Relationship Between Issues and Social/Satisfaction Values Rank
(Significance Levels for T-Ratios)

ISSUES CATEGORIES	GER.	U.S.	JAPAN	YUG.	P.R.C.	F.S.U.	VEN.	CHILE
Organizational								
Participation	.02-	.00-	.86	.87	.02-	.94-	**.00**	.07
Communications	**.00-**	**.04-**	.96-	.76	**.00-**	.66-	**.00**	**.01-**
Motivation	**.01-**	**.00-**	.76	.95-	.32-	.40-	**.05**	.59
Jobs/Standard of Living	**.00-**	.22	.68-	.34	.11-	.98	**.04**	.72
Productivity	**.03-**	.22-	.06-	.47-	.29-	.96-	**.00**	.22-
National								
Economic Climate	.12-	**.00-**	.07-	.68	.13-	**.00-**	**.04**	.70
Standard of Living	.77	**.00-**	.16-	.70	.77	.86	.09	.36
Sociopolitical Climate	.34	**.04-**	.11	.57	**.00-**	.34-	.76	.27
International								
Economic Climate	.67-	.55-	.12-	.99-	.29	.18-	**.00-**	.88
World Governance	**.00-**	**.00-**	.19-	.31	**.00-**	.22-	**.00-**	**.00-**
Resource Development	**.02-**	.28	**.02-**	.14	.53	.19	.31	**.04-**
Nationalism	.06	**.02-**	.53	.95	.15	.10-	**.05-**	.27
Issue Ranks								
Economic/Resource Development	**.00**	**.00**	**.01**	**.00**	.07	**.00**	**.00**	**.00**
Sociopolitical Stability	**.00**	**.00**	.73-	**.00**	**.01-**	**.04**	**.00**	**.00**
World Governance/ Cooperation	**.00**	**.00**	**.02**	**.00**	.37	.45-	**.00**	**.00**
Tenets								
Capitalism	.99-	**.01-**	.80	.35	**.02**	.63	**.00**	.25-
Socialism	.19-	.55	**.00-**	.88-	.93	.61	.27-	.77-
Change Political Ideology	.31-	.29	.57-	.93-	**.00**	.19	**.04**	**.04-**
Requisites of Government	.78	.38-	**.00-**	.25	.15-	.79-	.84-	**.00-**

Bold numbers indicate significance at .05 level or less. Negative signs indicate inverse relationships.

12

Summary, Conclusions, and Future Directions for Research

OVERVIEW OF RESEARCH

This research focuses on differences in people's values and their perceptions of political economy issues, which are based on eight different socioeconomic and political systems. These eight systems are grouped into three categories: (1) market-oriented systems (Germany, the United States, and Japan); (2) collectivist systems (Yugoslavia, the People's Republic of China, and the former Soviet Union); and hybrid systems or Latin American countries (Venezuela and Chile).

Figure 12.1 summarizes the structure of this research project. While this report discusses some of the major results within this overall research structure, there are numerous other possible analyses that can be conducted, as well as other analytical techniques that can be used. It is important, however, in this first report to provide an extensive overview of the entire scope and structure of the research, especially the responses to all of the 250 propositions relating to values and issues/tenets.

The 16 values researched as part of this study are based on 94 value propositions that respondents reacted to using a Likert-type scale. Moreover, the 16 values are grouped into two broad value sets: (1) those that reflect a tendency toward individualism (9 values based on 49 propositions) and (2) those that reflect a tendency toward collectivism (7 values based on 45 propositions). The responses pertaining to the individualism values are discussed in Chapter 3, while those pertaining to collectivism are the focus of Chapter 4. In Chapter 5, an analysis of value priorities and a comparison of responses relating to the two broad value tendencies are presented.

The 19 political economy issues and tenets researched as part of this

Figure 12.1
Overview of Research

ANALYSIS OF VALUES (Chapters 3 - 5)			SEARCH FOR RELATIONSHIPS (Chapter 11)	ANALYSIS OF ISSUES/TENETS (Chapters 6 - 10)		
Propositions	Values	Values Sets		Issues/Tenets Sets	Issues/Tenets	Propositions
49	Work Ethic Individualism Masculinity Family Individualism Family Economic Orientation Individualism/Economic Leisure Ethic Uncertainty Power Distance	Individualism Tendency		Favorable Organizational Climate	Participation Communications Motivation Standard of Living/Job Security Productivity	40
				Favorable National Climate	Economic Climate Standard of Living Sociopolitical Climate	39
45	Organizational Beliefs Humanistic Beliefs Marxist Beliefs Paternalism Family Social Cohesion/Status Family/Leisure Social Satisfaction	Collectivism Tendency		Favorable International Climate	Economic Climate World Governance/Cooperation Need to Develop Resources Emphasis on Nationalism	50
				Overall Issues Priorities	Economic/Resource Development Sociopolitical Stability World Governance/Cooperation	15
				General Tenets	Capitalism Premises Socialism Premises Need to Change Political Ideology Requisites of Government	12
94	16	2	(Chapter 12: Summary, Conclusions, and Future Decisions)	5	19	156

study are based on 156 issue/tenet propositions that respondents reacted to using a Likert-type scale. Similarly to the values research, the 19 issues/tenets are grouped into five broad sets: (1) those relating to perceptions of the favorableness of the overall organizational climate (5 issues based on 40 propositions), (2) those relating to perceptions of the favorableness of the overall national climate (3 issues based on 39 propositions), (3) those relating to perceptions of the favorableness of the overall international climate (4 issues based on 50 propositions), (4) those reflecting overall issue priorities (3 issues priorities based on 15 propositions), and (5) those relating to agreement concerning general premises about socioeconomic and political tenets (4 tenets based on 12 propositions). Chapters 6 through 8 focused on the results pertaining to the favorableness of the overall organizational, national, and international climates, respectively. The analysis of overall issue priorities and responses to the premises relating to the general socioeconomic and political tenets is discussed in Chapters 9 and 10, respectively.

The focus of the research framework is primarily on the analysis of significant differences in values and in the perceptions of issues/tenets according to the country of the respondents. This research does not attempt to define the strength of the value preference or concern for an issue/tenet in terms of a numerical score, such as a mean response for a particular group of respondents. Instead, it searches for significant differences (at the .05 level or less) in mean responses according to the country of the respondents using chi square analyses and ANOVA Scheffe test procedures. This is the focus of Chapters 3 through 10.

In Chapter 11, the focus is on the relationships between values and issues/tenets. Each of the 16 values is analyzed in relation to each of the 19 issues/tenets using simple regression analysis. These results are shown in Appendix 11A. The discussion in Chapter 11 summarizes these results, focusing on the two broad value sets (individualism and collectivism) and their relationships to the five broad sets of issues/tenets (organizational, national, and international climates, plus the issues priorities and general tenets), using the data from Appendix 11A. Again as in the analysis of differences in values and issues/tenets covered in Chapters 3 through 10, the focus of analysis in Chapter 11 is on determining the differences according to the country of respondents, rather than showing the strength of the relationship between a value set and an issue/tenet set.

RECAP OF DIFFERENCES IN VALUES

The following indicates which of the 16 values shown on Figure 12.1 receive significantly greater emphasis from respondents in each country surveyed using the ANOVA Scheffe test of paired comparisons. *Significantly greater* means that at least 4 of 7 comparisons have significantly higher mean responses (.05 level). These results are based on the analysis of values presented in Chapters 3 through 5.

Germany: Paternalism and social satisfaction/status.

United States: Individualism, family individualism, family economic orientation, uncertainty avoidance, humanistic beliefs, and family social cohesion/status.

Japan: Masculinity and leisure ethic.

Yugoslavia: Work ethic, family individualism, leisure ethic, humanistic beliefs, Marxist beliefs, and family social cohesion/status.

People's Republic of China: Work ethic, masculinity, uncertainty avoidance, power distance, organizational beliefs, Marxist beliefs, and social satisfaction/status.

Former Soviet Union: Work ethic, masculinity, leisure ethic, power distance, organizational beliefs, humanistic beliefs, Marxist beliefs, paternalism, and social satisfaction/status.

Venezuela: Individualism/economic, organizational beliefs, humanistic beliefs, paternalism, and family social cohesion/status.

Chile: Individualism/economic and family economic orientation.

Three of the 16 values shown on Figure 12.1 are based on combining the rankings of 10 value propositions that asked respondents to prioritize their needs into three ranks. These 10 priorities are reflected in the following three ranks: individualism/economic value (the People's Republic of China, Venezuela, and Chile), social satisfaction/status value (Germany and the former Soviet Union), and the family/leisure value (none).

To determine the differences in the values of each group of respondents in terms of their overall tendency toward individualism or collectivism, we first focused on the 13 values analyzed in Chapters 2 and 3, respectively (e.g., excluding the three values ranks analyzed in Chapter 5). On the basis of the total frequencies of mean responses that are significantly higher (.05 level) for each value set using the Scheffe test procedure, reinforced with a subjective analysis of responses to individual value preferences within each set, the following overall summary of value preferences is developed:

	Individualism	Collectivism
Germany	Lower	Lower
United States	Higher	Lower
Japan	Lower	Lower
Yugoslavia	Higher	Higher
People's Republic of China	Moderate	Moderate
former Soviet Union	Higher	Higher
Venezuela	Lower	Higher
Chile	Lower	Lower

Keep in mind that the preceding summary focuses on relative differences between groups of respondents. Thus a higher or lower tendency toward one value set or another should not be viewed as a measure of the strength of the tendency, but only of a relative difference that exists among the respondent groups.

RECAP OF DIFFERENCES IN PERCEPTIONS OF ISSUES

The discussion that follows focuses on the 19 issues/tenets shown on Figure 12.1. The first 12 issues reflect how respondents perceive the favorableness of the organizational, national, and international climates in each of their respective socioeconomic and political systems. The next three issues reflect each respondent group's priorities or ranks of issues. The final four items shown on Figure 12.1 reflect each respondent group's level of agreement about selected tenets of socioeconomic and political systems, each of which is based on a number of propositions.

The following indicates which of the 19 values/tenets receive significantly higher emphasis from respondents from each country surveyed using the ANOVA Scheffe test of paired comparisons. As in the case of values, *significantly higher* indicates that at least 4 of 7 comparisons have significantly higher mean responses (.05 level). These results are based on the analysis of issues/tenets presented in Chapters 6 through 10. Moreover, the term *higher* indicates more favorable perceptions of organizational, national, or international climate (first 12 issues); more important issue priorities (next 3 issues); or greater level of agreement about the propositions relating to the four tenets (last 4 items).

Germany: Organizational-communications, motivation, standard of living/job security, and productivity; National-economic climate and standard of living; International-economic climate and world governance/cooperation; and Issues Priorities-sociopolitical stability and world governance/cooperation.

United States: Organizational-participation, communications, motivation, standard of living/job security, and productivity; National-economic climate and standard of living; and International-economic climate and emphasis on nationalism.

Japan: Organizational-participation, communications, standard of living/job security, and productivity; National-standard of living; International-economic climate; and Tenets-socialism.

Yugoslavia: International-need to develop resources; and Tenets-capitalism, socialism, and change political ideology.

People's Republic of China: Organizational-participation; National-sociopolitical stability; International-need to develop resources; Issues Priorities-economic/resource development; and Tenets-socialism.

Former Soviet Union: International-emphasis on nationalism; Issues Priorities - sociopolitical stability; and Tenets-change political ideology.

Venezuela: Organizational-participation; International-emphasis on nationalism; Issues Priorities-sociopolitical stability; and Tenets-change political ideology.

Chile: Organizational-productivity; National-economic climate; International-economic climate; and Issues Priorities-sociopolitical stability.

To determine the differences in the perceptions of each group of respondents in terms of the overall favorableness of the organizational, national, and international climates, we focused on the first 12 issues shown in Figure 12.1, which were analyzed in Chapters 6 through 8 and constitute these three issue sets. On the basis of the total frequencies of mean responses that are significantly higher (.05 level) for each issue set, and through a subjective analysis of responses to individual issue perceptions within each set, Table 12.1 summarizes the perceptions of the overall favorableness of the three climates. Comments regarding the major issues priorities as they relate to these perceptions are also included in the table. The favorableness of the international climate shown in Table 12.1 is based only on the perceptions of the economic climate and the effectiveness of world governance/cooperation; it excludes perceptions about the need to develop resources and the emphasis placed on nationalism since they are only indirectly related to this issue set.

Some comments are in order regarding the above perceptions about the overall favorableness of the organizational, national, and international climates and how these perceptions relate to the three issues priorities of each group of respondents as shown in the last column of the summary in Table 12.1.

Table 12.1
Summary of Perceptions of Favorableness of Organizational (OC), National (NC), and International (IC) Climates Plus Summary of Issue Priorities (IP)

	OC	NC	IC	IP
Germany	Higher	Higher	Higher	Sociopolitical Stability; World Governance or Cooperation
United States	Higher	Higher	Moderate	Nominal
Japan	Higher	Higher	Moderate	Nominal
Yugoslavia	Lower	Lower	Lower	Nominal
People's Republic of China	Moderate	Higher	Lower	Economic or Resource Development
Former Soviet Union	Lower	Lower	Lower	Sociopolitical Stability
Venezuela	Moderate	Lower	Lower	Sociopolitical Stability
Chile	Lower	Higher	Moderate	Sociopolitical Stability

For example, the respondents from Germany perceive higher favorable climates at all three levels, yet they have some concerns about sociopolitical stability and the effectiveness of world governance/cooperation. The perceptions of the favorableness of the three climates are similar, as are the issues priorities, for the respondents from the United States and Japan. The perceptions of the respondents from the three collectivist countries tend to reflect less optimism, with the exception of those from the People's Republic of China and especially relative to the respondents from the other two collectivist countries. The respondents from Chile seem to be more optimistic about the three levels of environmental climate than those from Venezuela, except for the organizational level. Keep in mind that the preceding summary focuses only on the relative difference between groups of respondents as discussed in the recap of values preferences.

RECAP OF RELATIONSHIPS BETWEEN VALUES AND PERCEPTIONS OF ISSUES

This section summarizes the relationships between perceptions of favorable organizational, national, and international climates and the two broad value sets-tendency toward individualism and tendency toward collectivism. Using simple regression analysis, significance levels for T-ratios are computed as shown in Appendix 11A. Those respondent groups with significance levels for the T-ratio at the .05 level or less indicate whether the value tendency (individualism or collectivism) is significantly related to a specific issue. The individualism value set includes a composite of six values (work ethic, individualism, masculinity, family individualism, and family economic orientation values plus the individualism value rank), while the collectivism value set includes a composite of seven values (organizational, humanistic, Marxist, paternalism, and family social cohesion/status values plus family/leisure and social/satisfaction values). Those respondent groups with significance levels at the .05 level or less for at least half of the maximum number of regressions for each of the two value sets are considered to have a higher perception of the favorableness of the organizational, national, or international climate. Moreover, these results reflect only the differences between individualism and collectivism for each country's respondents; they do not reflect the relative differences between the respondent groups according to country origin.

Tables 11.4 and 11.5 discussed in Chapter 11 provide a summary of the regression analysis relating perceptions of organizational, national, and international climates with the values of individualism and collectivism, respectively. These results are further summarized later. Concerning the favorableness of the organizational climate as related to individualism, only the respondents from the United States have a frequency of significance levels (.05 level or less) for at least half of the regressions (Table 11.4). However, about half of these have a negative sign. The frequencies of significance levels for the other respondent groups showed a wide range of values. Moreover, the signs for significance levels of all countries are mixed.

As to the favorableness of the organizational climate as related to collectivism (Table 11.5), the respondents from the United States, Venezuela, Germany, and Chile have frequencies of significance levels (.05 level or less) for at least half of the regression cases. Except for the respondents from Germany, all of these respondent groups have a large number of mixed signs for their significance levels, which dilute the relationships. For the respondents from Germany, 18 of the 19 significant cases were positive; this result tends to indicate a relationship between collectivism and perceptions of organizational climate.

Concerning the favorableness of the national climate as related to individualism, the respondents from the United States and Venezuela have frequencies of significance levels (.05 or less) for 12 of the 18 regressions (with about one-third of those with negative signs). Moreover, for most of the groups the signs were mixed, thus the overall relationship between individualism and favorableness of national climate is weak for respondents from all of the countries.

The same is true for the relationship between the favorableness of the national climate and collectivism. Although the frequencies of significance levels are higher, the signs are mixed, thus diffusing the results. The respondents from Germany, the former Soviet Union, and Venezuela are the only groups with frequencies of significance levels for at least half of the regressions; however, many of these have negative signs, therefore diluting the relationship.

In reference to the favorableness of the international climate in relation to individualism, the respondents from Germany, the United States, the People's Republic of China, the former Soviet Union, and Venezuela have frequencies of significant levels at the .05 level or less for at least half of the 12 regressions. Because of the low frequencies of significance levels at the .05 level or less, and because of the mixed signs, there does not seem to be a clear relationship between international climate and individualism for any of the respondent groups. Moreover, this is true in terms of the relationship between favorableness of international climate and collectivism.

Looking at the total climate that reflects the combined three levels of favorable climates (organizational, national, and international), the relationship between issues and values is diffused (as shown in Tables 11.4 and 11.5). These results are summarized in Table 12.2. The numbers for each country indicate the frequencies of T-test significance levels at the .05 level or less when the combined total climate issues are related as a single climate to the individualism and collectivism values. The numbers in the parentheses indicate the negative signs that are included in each total number. The summary reflects a weak overall relationship between values and issues. Even if you discount the negative signs, only a few respondent groups have frequencies of significance levels (.05 level or less) for at least half of the regressions: Germany (collectivism), the United States (both individualism and collectivism), and Venezuela (both individualism and collectivism).

There is also a weak relationship between the issues priorities and the individualism and collectivism values as shown in Tables 11.1 and 11.2 and discussed in Chapter 11. The frequencies of significance levels (.05 or less) for the regression T-tests tend to be diluted because of the mixed signs for these relationships. Concerning collectivism, the respondents from Chile have the maximum frequency of significance levels for each of the three issue priorities, however, most of the signs are negative.

The responses to the four tenets are also inconclusive as they relate to the individualism value. However, there appears to be a stronger relationship between collectivism and the tenets of some of the respondent groups. These relationships are summarized as follows:

Germany: Socialism and requisites for government.
United States: Socialism, need to change political ideology, and requisites for government.
People's Republic of China: Capitalism, socialism, need to change political ideology, and requisites for government.
Former Soviet Union: Requisites for government.
Chile: Socialism, need to change political ideology, and requisites for government.

Table 12.2
Frequencies of Significance Levels (.05 or Less) Relating the Total Climate Issues to the Individualism and Collectivism Values

COUNTRY	Individualism	Collectivism
Country Maximum	60	70
Germany	21(3)	**38(20)**
United States	**43(22)**	**46(23)**
Japan	8(5)	14(6)
Yugoslavia	21(14)	29(18)
People's Republic of China	19(14)	25(15)
former Soviet Union	23(8)	34(8)
Venezuela	**30(12)**	**54(23)**
Chile	15(2)	32(20)
	180(80)	272(133)
Total Maximum	480	560

Bold numbers indicate at least half of the maximum frequencies.

From an overall standpoint, there is considerable diffusion in the relationship between issues and values. Part of this is attributable, no doubt, to the structure, size, and language of the survey instrument pertaining to values and issues. The perceptions of issues by respondent groups are also naturally influenced by their own specific circumstances within different socioeconomic and political environments. Moreover, the data collection period (about 1990 - 1992) reflects a generally turbulent time throughout the world, when many changes in socioeconomic and political systems and initiatives were underway.

Notwithstanding the diffusion and inconclusiveness about the impact of values on issues, there are some differences between respondent groups. These differences are reflected in the varying frequency of the regression analysis significance levels at the .05 level or less according to the country of respondents. Thus, some relationships between values and issues exist to a greater or lesser extent for some of the respondent groups as shown in the preceding summary.

SOME LIMITATIONS AND PROBLEMS ENCOUNTERED

As in any large scale empirical research project, many ideas come to mind concerning what might have been done differently. This project is no different. Yet because of the comprehensiveness of the survey instrument and the communications distances it was not always possible to make adjustments in a timely manner. Some of the most important items that could have been adjusted are discussed in this section.

The first item pertains to the length and format of the survey instrument. It was very long and took considerable time to complete. This required an ongoing presence of someone associated with this research project to assist respondents by clarifying questions and terminologies used in the instrument. Using the Likert-type response scale simplified some of the problems associated with the time required to complete the instrument. However, using a number scale to reflect preferences or perceptions, even though convenient, loses some value in the transposition.

The second item relates to the translation of the survey instrument. As a whole, the translations followed one of two procedures. The translation-back translation method was used whereby the english version was translated into another language, then subsequently this language version was translated back into english by a different person. In addition, faculty reworded some of the translations at the data collection site. This was done for several of the eight countries. Moreover, the project personnel supervising the data collection helped to clarify parts of the translations within the survey instrument as needed.

A third item relates to the difficulty of achieving timely data collection on a uniform schedule. This is probably never possible in the strictest sense, yet some reasonable beginning or starting points should be established.

Coordination and communications among the project group are the fourth item of importance. Using hindsight, a meeting of the total group would have been very useful prior to starting the data collection. Some meetings were possible prior to data collection, but not with all of the project group members. However, the project group met regularly (annually) once the project began, and the meetings were very useful.

A fifth item relates to encoding the responses into a computerized format at a single location. This was done for six of the eight countries' data and proved to be very useful for minimizing data input errors. Once all the data were encoded into a standardized computer format, all project participants received a computer disk containing all of the data for all of the countries to begin their individual analyses. As the project group began to compare some initial results, it was decided that a preliminary analysis should be done by one group to serve as a draft for other project personnel to amend, add to, or refine as the case might be. These inputs would be fused into a final manuscript by one group for the entire project. This proved to be very effective.

A sixth item deals with the analysis of the data. In this initial book, a major goal is to present as much information about responses to each of the 250 questions relating to value or issue propositions as possible. This was accomplished. Moreover, because of the size limitations of the book, only basic descriptive statistical procedures were used, including chi square analysis, ANOVA Scheffe test procedures, and simple regression analysis. While these methodologies provide a good feel for the research and its results, certainly more sophisticated statistical procedures could be applied to some of the mass of data collected.

The preceding six items reflect some of the concerns that were encountered and some of the decisions that were made as the research project progressed. The distance and time dimensions were probably the more difficult hurdles to adjust to, but because of the excellent rapport and mutual support among the project members, the research was successfully completed in a reasonable length of time.

FUTURE DIRECTIONS FOR RESEARCH

This research project has produced two books. The first, *Cross-Cultural Analysis of Values and Political Economy Issues* (Voich and Stepina, eds., Praeger, 1994), is a volume of essays contributed by members of the project group. These essays present a survey of historical and current research on values and issues within the respective countries represented by the project group. This volume continues this stream of research on values and issues, but utilizes empirical data from the eight countries surveyed.

Our project group strongly believes that cross-cultural studies, especially empirical ones and those focusing on values and political economy issues, continue to be extremely important. Even though this type of research is more difficult and time consuming, the results generated are valuable. Moreover, the personal contacts and dialogues among peers from diverse cultures are invaluable. They enrich the results and contribute to better understanding of theory and practice from a multicultural and multidisciplinary perspective. This generates multidirectional learning, and enhances our ability to interpret world events and initiatives within each of our respective disciplines and within interactive socioeconomic and political systems.

One major research initiative that the research group believes is important, as well as manageable, is to conduct a survey of people's perceptions of major issues and some of their basic values every three to five years. This would be accomplished by using a predesigned standardized survey instrument, much shorter than the one used in this study. A more careful selection and stratification of the sample size and makeup would be specified. The focus would be on the younger population, 18 to 25 years of age, who tend to reflect emerging and future value changes and priorities. These values and issues of young people would serve as indicators of possible future developments in each of the countries surveyed, and generally throughout major regions of the world.

Bibliography

Adler, N. J. 1986. *International Dimensions of Organizational Behavior*. Boston: Kent Publishing.

Agüero, F. 1993. "Chile: South America's Success Story." *Current History*. 92: 575, pp. 130 - 135.

Ali, A. 1988. "A Cross-National Perspective of Managerial Work Value Systems." In R. N. Farmer and E. G. McGoun, eds., *Advances in International Comparative Management*. (Vol. 3, pp. 151 - 170). Greenwich, CT: JAI Press.

Allport, G. 1961. *Pattern and Growth in Personality*. New York: Holt, Rinehart and Winston.

Allport, G., Vernon, P. E., and Lindzey, G. 1931. *Study of Values*. Boston: Houghton Mifflin.

Andreenkova, N. V. 1971. "Socialization of the Individual at the Beginning of Work Activity," (in Russian). Ph.D. dissertation. University of Moscow.

____. 1988. *A Study of Labor Activity at the Contemporary Stage of the Socio-Economic Development of the USSR*. Moscow: Work and Society.

Aseyev, V. G. 1976. *The Motivation of Behavior and the Forming of the Individual* (in Russian). Moscow.

Baćević, Lj., et al. 1990. "Neposlusni medij" (Intractable media). Novi Sad, Yugoslavia: RTV.

____. 1991. "Jugoslavija na kriznoj prekretnici" (Yugoslavia at a turning point in crisis; summary in English). Belgrade, Yugoslavia: Institut drustvenih nauka.

Balakina, E. F. 1965. *Researchers Should Give Attention to the Problem of Values* (in Russian). Moscow: Voprosi Filosofii, 9.

Barton, A. 1963. *Measuring the Values of Individuals*. New York: Columbia University, BASR.

Barton, A., Denitch, B., and Kadushin, C. 1973. *Opinion-Making Elites in Yugoslavia*. New York: Praeger.

Beliayeva, J. F., and Y. G. Kopnin. 1989. *Attitude toward Work of Young Workers: Value-Motivational Aspect* (in Russian). Moscow: Scientific Research Institute of Work. Moscow (in Russian).

Bem, D. J. 1970. *Beliefs, Attitudes, and Human Affairs*. Belmont, CA: Brooks-Cole.

Bertch, G. 1976. *Values and Community in Multinational Yugoslavia*. New York: Columbia University Press.

Binyan, L. 1993. "The Long March from Mao: China's Decommunization." *Current History*. 92: 575, pp. 241 - 244.

Bojanović, R. 1989. "Authoritarianism and Youth," Belgrade (in Serbo-Croatian). Manuscript (Belgrade, Yugoslavia).

Buchholz, R. A. 1976. "Measurement of Beliefs." *Human Relations*. 29(12): 1177 - 1188.

____. 1977. "The Belief Structure of Managers Relative to Work Concepts Measured by a Factor Analytic Model." *Personnel Psychology*. 30: 567 - 587.

____. 1978. "An Empirical Study of Contemporary Beliefs about Work in American Society." *Journal of Applied Psychology*. 63(2): 219 - 227.

Buyeva, L. P. 1968. *The Social Environment and the Consciousness of the Individual* (in Russian). Moscow.

____. 1978. *Man: Activity and Association* (in Russian). Moscow.

Chavchavadze, N. Z. 1984. *Culture and Values* (in Russian). Tbilisi, Georgia.

Chernovolenko, V. F., Ossovsky, V. L., and Paniotto, V. J. 1979. *Prestige of Professions and Problems of the Social-Professional Orientation of Youth* (in Russian). Keyev.

Chinese Culture Connection. 1987. "Chinese Values and the Search for Culture-Free Dimensions of Culture." *Journal of Cross-Cultural Psychology*. 18: 143 - 164.

Chow, I. H. 1993. "Chinese Managerial Work." *Journal of General Management*. 17: 4, pp. 53 - 67.

Čulig, B., Fanuko, N., and Jerbić, V. 1982. "Values and Value-Orientation of Youth" (in Serbo-Croatian). Zagreb, Yugoslavia: CDD.

Dilić, E. 1971. *Social Structure and Orientation of the Rural Youth* (in Serbo-Croatian). Belgrade, Yugoslavia: Institute of Social Sciences.

Dilić, E. et al. 1977. *The Rural Youth Today* (in Serbo-Croatian). Zagreb, Yugoslavia: CDD.

Diligensky, G. T. 1976. *Problems of Human Needs Theory* (in

Russian). Moscow: Voprosi Filosofii.

____. 1986. *In Search of Sense and Purpose* (in Russian). Moscow.

Dorfman, P. W., and Howell, J. P. 1988. "Dimensions of National Culture and Effective Leadership Patterns: Hofstede Revisited." In R. N. Farmer and E.G. McGoun, eds., *Advances in International Comparative Management* (Vol. 8, pp. 127 - 150. Greenwich, CT: JAI Press.

Đurić, Đ. 1980. *The Psychological Structure of Ethnic Attitudes in Youth* (in Serbo-Croatian). Novi Sad, Yugoslavia: J. Vukanović.

____. 1987. *Socialization of the Young in a Multinational Society* (in Serbo-Croatian). Novi Sad, Yugoslavia: Pedagoški zavod Vojvodine.

Džinić, F. 1973. *Value-Orientations in Yugoslavia* (in Serbo-Croatian). Sarajevo, Yugoslavia: Pregled.

Džuverović, B. 1975. *Values and Rebellions in the Youth* (in Serbo-Croatian). Subotica, Yugoslavia: Radnički univerzitet.

England, G. W. 1975. *The Manager and His Values: An International Perspective.* Cambridge, MA: Ballinger Publishers.

Ewell, J. 1984. *Venezuela: A Century of Change.* Stanford, CA: Stanford University Press.

Flanagan, S. 1980. "Value Change and Partisan Change in Japan: The Silent Revolution Revisited" *Comparative Politics.* 11: 253 - 278.

Friedman, E. 1993. "China's North-South Split and the Forces of Disintegration." *Current History.* 92: 575, pp. 270 - 273.

Gibbins, J., ed. 1989. *Contemporary Political Culture.* London: Sage.

Goati, V., et al. 1989. *Jugosloveni o drustvenoj krizi* (What Yugoslavs think about the social crisis). Belgrade, Yugoslavia: Izdavacki centar "Komunist".

Gomez-Mejia, L. R., and McCann, J. D. 1986a. "Assessing an International 'Issues Climate': Policy and Methodology Implications." Gainesville, FL: INUBPRO Project unpublished report.

____. 1986b. "Caribbean/Latin America Issues Survey Results." Gainesville, FL: Unpublished report from the INUBPRO Project.

Hafner-Fink, M. 1989. "Ideology and Consciousness of Social Strata in Slovenia" (in Slovenian). Ljubljana, Yugoslavia.

Handy, R. 1970. *The Measurement of Values.* St. Louis, MO: Warren Green.

Harding, S., and Phillips, D. 1986. *Contrasting Values in Western Europe.* London: Macmillan.

Havelka, N. 1975. "Value Research in Yugoslavia" (in Serbo-Croatian, Summary in English) *Psihologija.* 3 - 4: 139-150.

Havelka, N., et al. 1990. *Educational and Developmental Achievements by Students at the End of Elementary Schooling.* Belgrade, Yugoslavia: Institute of Psychology, Faculty of Philosophy.

Herbig, P. A., and Miller, J. C. 1992. "Structural Components of an Enterprise Culture." *Multinational Business.* 2: 37.

Hofstede, G. 1980. *Culture's Consequences-International Differences in Work-Related Values.* Beverly Hills, CA: Sage.

____. 1983. "The Cultural Relativity of Organizational Practices and Theories." *Journal of International Business Studies* 14(2): 75 - 90.

____. 1985. "The Interaction Between National and Organizational Value Systems." *Journal of Management Studies* 22(4): 347 - 357.

Hofstede, G., and Bond, M. H. 1984. "Hofstede's Cultural Dimensions: An Independent Validation Using Rokeach's Value Survey." *Journal of Cross-Cultural Psychology* 15(4): 417 - 433.

Hrnjica, S. 1981. "Post-Materialism in an Environment of Insecurity." *American Political Science Review.* 75: 880 - 890.

____. 1985. "Aggregate Stability and Individual-Level Flux in Mass Belief Systems" *American Political Science Review* 78: 97 - 116.

____. 1990a. *Culture Shift in Advanced Industrial Society.* Princeton, NJ: Princeton University Press.

____. 1990b. *The Maturity of Personality* (in Serbo-Croatian, summary in English). Belgrade, Yugoslavia: Zavod za udžbenike.

Ikonnikova, S. N., and V. T. Lisovsky. 1969. *Youth on Themselves and Their Contemporaries* (in Russian). Leningrad.

Inglehart, R. 1977. *The Silent Revolution: Changing Values and Political Styles among Western Publics.* Princeton, NJ: Princeton University Press.

____. 1990. *Culture Shift in Advanced Industrial Society.* Princeton, NJ: Princeton University Press.

Inglehart, R., and Flanagan, S. 1987. Value Change in Industrial Societies *American Political Science Review.* 81: 1289 - 1319.

Inlow, G. 1972. *Values in Transition.* New York: Wiley.

Jacob, P. et al. 1971. *Values and Active Community: A Cross-Cultural Study of the Influence of Local Leaders.* New York: Free Press.

Janićijević, M. et al. 1966. *Yugoslav Students and Socialism* (in Serbo-Croatian, summary in English). Belgrade, Yugoslavia: Institute of Social Sciences.

Katunarić, V. 1987. "Authoritarianism-Ethnocentrism-Sexism" (in Serbo-Croatian, summary in English). *Sociologija* 3 - 4: 603 - 610.

Kelley, L., Whatley, A., and Worthley, R. 1987. "Assessing the

Effects of Culture on Managerial Attitudes: A Three Culture Test." *Journal of International Business Studies.* 18(3): 17 - 33.

Kelley, L., and Worthley, R. 1981. "The Role of Culture in Comparative Management: A Cross-Cultural Perspective." *Academy of Management Journal.* 24(1): 164 - 173.

Kharkov University. 1977. *The Communistic Ideals and the Formation of the Student's Personality* (in Russian). Kharkov, Ukrainian Republic.

Klineberg, O., et al. 1979. *Students, Values and Politics.* New York: Free Press.

Kluckhohn, C. 1952. "Values and Value Orientation in the Theory of Action." In T. Parsons, and E. Shils, eds., *Toward a General Theory of Action.* Cambridge, MA: Harvard University Press.

Kluckhohn, F. 1953. "Dominant and Variant Value Orientations." In C. Kluckhohn, H. Murray, and D. Schneider, eds., *Personality in Society, Nature and Culture* (pp. 342-357). New York: Knopf.

Kluckhohn, F., and Strodtbeck, F. 1961 *Variations in Value Orientations.* Evanston, IL: Row, Peterson.

Kroeber, A. L, and Kluckhohn, C. 1952. "Culture: A Critical Review of Concepts and Definitions." *Peabody Museum Papers.* 47. Cambridge, MA: Harvard University.

Kuzmanović, B. 1987. *The Problems of Motivational Foundations of Self-Management* (in Serbo-Croatian). Belgrade, Yugoslavia: Filozofski fakultet, Doctoral dissertation.

Lawson, D. 1993. "Humanism in China." *The Humanist.* May/June: pp. 16 - 19.

Leontiev, A. N. 1976. *Activity, Consciousness, Personality* (in Russian). Moscow.

Leung, K. and Bond, M. H. 1989. "On the Empirical Dimensions for Cross-Cultural Comparison." *Journal of Cross-Cultural Psychology.* 20: 133 - 151.

Lovejoy, A. O. 1950. "Terminal and Adjectival Values." *Journal of Philosophy.* 47: 593 - 608.

McCann, J. E. 1983. "Design Guidelines for Social Problem Solving Interventions." *Journal of Applied Behavioral Science.* 19: 177 - 189.

McClelland, David. 1961. *The Achieving Society.* New York: Van Nostrand Rinehold Company.

Marinović, D. 1988. "Youth and Religion" (in Serbo-Croatian, summary in English). In F. Radin, et al., eds., *The Fragments of*

Youth (pp. 153 - 198). Zagreb, Yugoslavia: IDIS.

Marx, K., and Engels, F. 1980. *Collected Works* (3). London: Lawrence Wishart, Ltd..

Maslow, A. H. 1954. *Motivation and Personality*. New York: Harper.

_____. 1960. *Toward a Psychology of Being*. New York: Van Nostrand.

_____. 1964. *Religions, Values and Peak Experiences*. New York, Viking Press.

Miočinović, Lj. 1988. *Cognitive and Affective Factors in Moral Development* (in Serbo-Croatian, summary in English). Belgrade, Yugoslavia: Institut za pedagoška istraživanja i Prosveta.

Mitchell, T. R., and James, L. R. 1989. "Situational Versus Dispositional Factors: Competing Explanations of Behavior." *Academy of Management Review.* 14(3): 330 - 331.

Momov, V. 1975. *Man, Morality, Education: Theoretical and Methodological Problems* (in Russian). Moscow.

Montero, M. 1987. *Ideologies, Alienacion e Identidad Nacional*. Caracas: Central University of Venezuela, Ediciones de la Biblioteca.

Morris, C. W. 1956. *Varieties in Human Values*. Chicago: University of Chicago Press.

Ničić, J., Bojanović, R., and Maksić, S. 1985. *Attitudes of Youth Toward Work*. Belgrade, Yugoslavia: IIC SSOS (mimeo, in Serbo-Croatian).

Noren, J. H. 1993. "The FSU Economies: First Year of Transition." *Post-Soviet Geography.* 34: 7, pp. 419 - 452.

Pantić, D. 1969. *The Values and Attitudes of Opinion-Makers* (in Serbo-Croatian). Mimeograph. Belgrade, Yugoslavia: Institute of Social Sciences.

_____. 1974. "Some Value Orientations of the Youth" (in Serbo-Croatian). In S. Joksimović, ed., *Attitudes and Beliefs of Yugoslav Youth* (pp. 25 - 53). Belgrade, Yugoslavia: Mladost.

_____. 1977. "Social Strata's Values and Ideological Orientations" (in Serbo-Croatian, summary in English). In M. Popović, ed., *Social Strata and Social Consciousness*. Belgrade, Yugoslavia: Institute of Social Sciences.

_____. 1981. "Value Orientations of the Youth in Serbia" (in Serbo-Croatian). Belgrade, Yugoslavia: Institute of Social Sciences

_____. 1990a. *Change in the Value-Orientations of the Young in Serbia* (in Serbo-Croatian, summary in English). Belgrade, Yugoslavia:

Institute of Social Sciences.

____. 1990b. "Political Culture of Youth in Serbia" (in Serbo-Croatian). In *The Young at the End of the Eighties*. Belgrade, Yugoslavia: IIC SSOS.

____. 1990c. "The Psychological Structure of Modernism as a Value Orientation and the Characteristics of Modern Personality" (in Serbo-Croatian, summaries in English and Russian). *Psihologija*. 3 - 4: 5 - 25.

____. 1990d. "Yugoslav Youth Values in the Age of Crisis: A Generation Characterized by Anomy and the Religiousness of the Yugoslav Youth: Cross-Cultural Diachronical and Social Coordinates" (in Serbo-Croatian, summary in English). In a S. Mihailović, ed., *The Children of the Crisis* (pp. 173 - 228). Belgrade, Yugoslavia: Institute of Social Sciences.

____. 1991. "Religiousness of Citizens of Yugoslavia" (in Serbo-Croatian). In Lj. Baćević, ed., *Yugoslavia at a Turning Point* (pp. 241 - 257). Belgrade, Yugoslavia: Institute of Social Sciences.

Parsons, T. 1957. *The Social System*. New York: Free Press.

Pettigrew, A. M. 1979. "On Studying Organizational Cultures." *Administrative Science Quarterly*. 24: 570 - 581.

Popadić, D. 1990. "Lifestyle Preferences of Students at the End of Elementary Schooling" (in Serbo-Croatian, summary in English). In N. Havelka, et al., eds., *Educational and Developmental Achievements by Students at the End of Elementary Schooling* (pp. 235 - 259). Belgrade, Yugoslavia: Belgrade: Institute of Psychology, Faculty of Philosophy.

Popović, B. 1973. *The Foundations of the Psychology of Morals* (in Serbo-Croatian, summary in English). Belgrade, Yugoslavia: Naučna knjiga.

Popović, B., Miočinović, Lj., and Ristić, Ž. 1981. *The Development of Moral Knowledge* (in Serbo-Croatian, summary in English). Belgrade, Yugoslavia: Institut za pedagoška istraživanja i Prosveta.

____. 1984. *Psychological Basis of Moral Thinking* (in Serbo-Croatian, summary in English). Belgrade, Yugoslavia: Institut za pedagoška istraživanja i Prosveta.

Powell, D. E. 1993. *Social Problems in Russia*. 92: 575, pp. 325 - 330.

Pugh, G. 1978. *Biological Origins of Human Values*. London: Routledge and Kegan Paul.

Radin, F. et al. 1988. *The Fragments of Youth* (in Serbo-Croatian, summary in English). Zagreb, Yugoslavia: IDIS.

Rankin, W. L. and Grube, J.W. 1980. "A Comparison of Ranking and Rating Procedures for Value System Measurement." *European Journal of Social Psychology*. 10: 233 - 246.

Rescher, N. 1969. *Introduction to Value Theory*. Englewood Cliffs, NJ: Prentice Hall.

Rokeach, M. 1968. *Beliefs, Attitudes, and Values*. San Francisco: Jossey-Bass.

____. 1973. *The Nature of Human Values*. New York: Free Press.

____. 1979. *Understanding Human Values: Individual and Social*. New York: Free Press.

Ronen, S., and Shenkar, O. 1985. "Clustering Countries on Attitudinal Dimensions: A Review and Synthesis." *Academy of Management Review*. 3: 435 - 454.

Roter, Z. 1986. *Religiousness and Irreligiousness in Slovenia*. Nis, Yugoslavia. Gradina, 1 - 2.

Rubinstein, S. L. 1957. *Being and Consciousness* (in Russian). Moscow.

Sapir, E. 1924. "Culture, Genuine and Spurious." *The American Journal of Sociology* 29(4): 401 - 429.

Scheibe, W. 1970. *Beliefs and Values*. New York: Holt, Rinehart and Winston.

Schwartz, Shalom H. 1992. "Universals in the Content and Structure of Values: Theoretical Advances and Empirical Tests in 20 Countries." In Mark P. Zanna, ed., *Advances in Experimental Social Psychology* (Vol. 25, pp. 1 - 64). San Diego, CA: Academic Press.

Segall, M. H., Dasen, P. R., Berry, J. W. and Poortinga, Y. H. 1990. *Human Behavior in Global Perspective: An Introduction to Cross-Cultural Psychology*. New York: Pergamon.

Šiber, I. 1974. *Social Structure and Political Attitudes* (in Serbo-Croatian). Zagreb, Yugoslavia: Narodno sveučilište.

Smirnov, V. Y. 1929. *The Psychology of Youth and Age* (in Russian). Moscow-Leningrad.

Smith, M. B. 1969. *Social Psychology and Human Values*. Chicago: Aldine.

Smolić-Krković, N. 1970. "On the Measuring of Interests" (in Serbo-Croatian). *Pedagoški rad*. 1 - 2: 37 - 46.

Sokolov, V. M. 1986. *Sociology of Moral Development of the Individual* (in Russian). Moscow.

Stepanov, D. 1993. "Russian Twenty-Somethings." *Current History*.

92: 575, pp. 32 - 35.

Thurston, A. 1993. "The Dragon Stirs." *China Quarterly.* Winter: pp. 10 - 37.

Toš, N. et al. 1987. *Public Opinion in Slovenia* (in Slovenian). Ljubljana, Yugoslavia: Delavska enotnost.

Uznadze, D.N. 1961. *The Basic Thesis of the Attitude Theory.* Tbilisi, Georgia.

____. 1969. *The Psychological Problems of the Motivation of the Individual Behavior* (in Russian). Moscow.

Vasović, M. 1988. "Values of the Members of Informal Groups in Youth." In S. Joksimović, et al., *Youth and Informal Groups* (pp. 174 - 216). Belgrade, Yugoslavia: IIC SSOS.

____. 1991. "Value Priorities of the Yugoslav Public" (in Serbo-Croatian, summary in English). In Lj. Baćević, ed., *Yugoslavia at a Turning Point in Crisis* (pp. 197 - 233). Belgrade, Yugoslavia: Institute of Social Sciences.

Vinokurova, S. P. 1988. *The Individual in the System of Moral Relations* (in Russian). Minsk.

Voich, D., and Stepina, L. P., eds., 1994. *Cross-Cultural Analysis of Values and Political Economy Issues.* Westport, CT: Praeger.

Vrcan, S., et al. 1986. *Social Position, Consciousness and Political Behavior of Youth* (in Serbo-Croatian). Zagreb, Yugoslavia: CIDID.

Vušković, B. et al. 1987. *Some Characteristics of the Political Profile of Youth.* Split, Yugoslavia: Pogledi.

Wright W. 1990. *Cafe con Leche: Race, Class, and National Image in Venezuela.* Austin, TX: University of Austin Press.

Yadov, V. A. 1983. *Attitude to Work: Conceptual Model and Real Tendencies* (in Russian). Sociological Researches, no. 3.

Yaroshevsky, M. S. 1966. *The History of Psychology* (in Russian). Moscow.

Yaroshevsky, T. M. 1973. *Individual and Society* (in Russian). Moscow.

Zdravomyslov, A. S. 1986. *Needs, Interests, Values* (in Russian). Moscow.

Zhi-Gang, W. 1990. *Value Structures in China: Within and Cross-Cultural Comparisons.* Nara, Japan: Paper presented at the 10th International Association of Cross-Cultural Psychology Congress.

Županov, J. 1970. "Egalitarianism and Industrialism" (in Serbo-Croatian). *Sociologija.* 1: 5 - 45.

Index

About the Author

DAN VOICH, JR., Director of the International Consortium for Management Studies and Professor of Management at Florida State University, Tallahassee, has served as the Associate Dean of the College of Business from 1979–1991. He is the co-author of seven books in management and comparative systems and the co-author of *Cross-Cultural Analysis of Values and Political Economy Issues* (Praeger, 1994).

ISBN 0-275-95169-3

9 780275 951696

HARDCOVER BAR CODE